Transnational German Film at the End of Neoliberalism

Screen Cultures: German Film and the Visual

Series Editors

Gerd Gemünden (*Dartmouth College*)
Johannes von Moltke (*University of Michigan*)

Also in this series

A New History of German Cinema, edited by
Jennifer M. Kapczynski and Michael D. Richardson (2012)

The Counter-Cinema of the Berlin School, by Marco Abel (2013)

Generic Histories of German Cinema,
edited by Jaimey Fisher (2013)

*The Autobiographical Turn in Germanophone
Documentary and Experimental Film*, edited by
Robin Curtis and Angelica Fenner (2014)

DEFA after East Germany, edited by
Brigitta B. Wagner (2014)

Last Features, by Reinhild Steingröver (2014)

The Nazi Past in Contemporary German Film,
by Axel Bangert (2014)

Continuity and Crisis in German Cinema, 1928–1936, edited by
Barbara Hales, Mihaela Petrescu, and Valerie Weinstein (2016)

Forgotten Dreams, by Laurie Ruth Johnson (2016)

Montage as Perceptual Experience, by Mario Slugan (2017)

Gender and Sexuality in East German Film, edited by
Kyle Frackman and Faye Stewart (2018)

Film and Fashion amidst the Ruins of Berlin,
by Mila Ganeva (2018)

Austria Made in Hollywood, by Jacqueline Vansant (2019)

Celluloid Revolt: German Screen Cultures and the Long 1968,
edited by Christina Gerhardt and Marco Abel (2019)

*Moving Images on the Margins: Experimental Film in
Late Socialist East Germany*, by Seth Howes (2019)

The Films of Konrad Wolf, by Larson Powell (2020)

*Film History for the Anthropocene: The Ecological Archive
of German Cinema*, by Seth Peabody (2023)

Transnational German Film at the End of Neoliberalism

Radical Aesthetics, Radical Politics

Edited by
Claudia Breger and Olivia Landry

Rochester, New York

Copyright © 2024 by the Editors and Contributors

All Rights Reserved. Except as permitted under current legislation, no part of this work may be photocopied, stored in a retrieval system, published, performed in public, adapted, broadcast, transmitted, recorded, or reproduced in any form or by any means, without the prior permission of the copyright owner.

First published 2024
by Camden House

Camden House is an imprint of Boydell & Brewer Inc.
668 Mt. Hope Avenue, Rochester, NY 14620, USA
and of Boydell & Brewer Limited
PO Box 9, Woodbridge, Suffolk IP12 3DF, UK
www.boydellandbrewer.com

ISBN-13: 978-1-64014-152-0

Library of Congress Cataloging-in-Publication Data

CIP data is available from the Library of Congress.

The publisher has no responsibility for the continued existence or accuracy of URLs for external or third-party internet websites referred to in this book, and does not guarantee that any content on such websites is, or will remain, accurate or appropriate.

Contents

Acknowledgments	vii
Introduction *Claudia Breger and Olivia Landry*	1

Part I.
Radical Pessimism as a Form of Resistance: Political Drama in the Age of Surplus Humanity and New Fascism

1:	*Transit* (2018) and Postfascism *Angelos Koutsourakis*	15
2:	"Her mit dem schönen Leben": Happiness and Access in *Berlin Alexanderplatz* (2020) *Priscilla Layne*	32
3:	Negative Futurability and the Politics of Pessimism in Fatih Akın's *Aus dem Nichts* (2017) *Gozde Naiboglu*	50

Part II.
Rethinking the Evidence: New Documentary Forms

4:	Forensic Fallacies *Lutz Koepnick*	69
5:	The Border as Abjecting Apparatus: *Shipwreck at the Threshold of Europe, Lesvos, Aegean Sea* (2020) and *Purple Sea* (2019) *Randall Halle*	83
6:	The Politics of the Machinic Voice in Gerd Kroske's Documentary *SPK Komplex* (2018) *Olivia Landry*	102

vi ♦ CONTENTS

Part III.
Reassembling the Archives
of Radical Filmmaking

7: Marking Time after Utopia 121
Richard Langston

8: Remediations of Cinefeminism in Contemporary
German Film 142
Hester Baer

9: A Few Takes toward Reassembling (the Dream of)
the People: Julian Radlmaier's *Selbstkritik eines
bürgerlichen Hundes* (2017) 162
Claudia Breger

Part IV.
Intimate Connections: Aesthetics and
Politics of a Cinema of Relations

10: Choric Configurations and the Collective:
Ruth Beckermann's Films 183
Fatima Naqvi

11: Aerial Aesthetics, Queer Intimacy, and the Politics of
Repose in the Cinema of Nils Bökamp and Monika Treut 202
Ervin Malakaj

12: Between Observational Detachment and Affective
Attachment: The Posthumanist Pedagogy of *Herr
Bachmann und seine Klasse* (2021) 219
Angelica Fenner

Notes on the Contributors 237

Index 241

Acknowledgments

WE WOULD FIRST OF ALL like to thank Jim Walker at Camden House, without whose initial encouragement this volume would never have come to be. He ushered the project through its many steps to completion with unflagging enthusiasm, support, and attentiveness. We are also grateful to the series editors for Screen Cultures: German Film and the Visual at Camden House, Gerd Gemünden and Johannes von Moltke, for their very encouraging commitment to the project. It's thrilling to be able to contribute to this marvelous series. Finally, we express our gratitude to the contributors, who not only made this volume what it is through their brilliant chapters, but were also a delight to work with.

Introduction

Claudia Breger and Olivia Landry

JULIAN RADLMAIER'S 2021 political comedy, *Blutsauger* (*Bloodsuckers*), is set in the late summer of 1928 in an unnamed Baltic Sea coastal village in Germany. Communism, capitalism, and fascism are in the sultry sea air, and vampires occupy the upper echelons of society. Indeed, entry into capitalism, specifically through the purchasing of stocks, is predicated on sucking the blood of an unsuspecting proletarian. In this freighted historical setting, we already know how the tale of political parody will end. In the diegetic world of Radlmaier's film, a local Chinese man, known simply as "der Algensammler" (algae collector), becomes a scapegoat for hate against the capitalists: the proletarian crowd turns into a fascist lynch mob. The capitalists perceive the communists as a much greater threat than the fascists because, as Corinna Harfouch's character Tante Erkentrud unapologetically declares, "Mit denen kann man wenigstens reden" (One can at least talk to them).

We evoke Radlmaier's most recent feature to open our discussion about contemporary transnational German film and the futures it points to, because *Blutsauger*'s portrayal of capitalists not only as vampires but as facilitators of fascism in a historical setting also appears to speak to our era of neoliberal crises and the sweeping embrace of authoritarianism across the globe. Through the diegetic employment of an array of old and new objects and styles, the film's anachronistic portrait of the Weimar period indirectly locates it in contemporary Germany and foregrounds the link between past and present. Despite its comedic mode and playfulness, Radlmaier's potentially historical projection of neoliberalism's trajectory is unmistakably bleak: the film dramatically concludes with murder by a fascist lynch mob. Beginning with a reading circle of volume one of Marx's *Capital*, however, the film also reminds us of the collective possibilities that open up at any moment of political instability, including the present late neoliberal moment.

Already in the early 2000s, Lisa Duggan declared that "if the triumph of neoliberalism brings us into the twilight of equality, this is not an irreversible fate. This new world order was invented during the 1970s and 1980s, and dominated the 1990s, but it may now be unraveling—if we are prepared to seize the moment of its faltering, to promote and ensure its downfall."[1] The protracted moment of neoliberalism's faltering extends into the present, although it may have developed a new dynamic as the realities of accelerating climate catastrophe, the COVID-19 pandemic, war, and political violence have intensified neoliberalism's structural tendencies toward crisis. Across the world, authoritarian if not downright fascist regimes have accumulated political victories—or are continuing to threaten democracy. Widely replaced by new anti-liberal ideologies and forms of governance, is neoliberalism perhaps in fact over? Or, as Elizabeth Bernstein and Janet R. Jakobsen ask in *The Paradoxes of Neoliberalism*, would it be more correct to assert that neoliberalism itself has taken a nationalist turn?[2] In its dismantling of democracy, equality, culture, and society, neoliberal rationality has, in Wendy Brown's words, "prepared the ground for the mobilization and legitimacy of ferocious antidemocratic forces in the second decade of the twenty-first century."[3] That is not to say that neoliberalism on its own has directly prompted the rise of the right in places like Europe and the United States or triggered the myriad worldwide catastrophes of the present. We do not mean to perpetuate the old claim of grand Marxist history that capitalism necessarily ends in fascism. But we do agree with Brown that "nothing is untouched by a neoliberal mode of reason and valuation"—and its undoing of egalitarian norms and democratic culture certainly hasn't helped.[4]

To speak of neoliberalism's end, as the title of this volume provocatively does, may seem impetuous in the midst of the current mess. Neoliberalism has not definitively come to an end. Perhaps it has really just shown itself to be a shapeshifting monstrosity, much like the capitalist vampires that populate both Marx's *Capital* and Radlmaier's film. But we cannot deny that there is something more in the air—and on the screen. While not simply over as a set of economic and political realities, neoliberalism is—ever more noticeably—at its end as an ideology or ensemble of norms that can offer an impression of stability. The norms that at one time possessed the power to effectively suture contemporary societies have become (for many) woefully impossible standards. The hegemony of neoliberalism as a seemingly self-understood basis for

---

1 Lisa Duggan, *The Twilight of Equality? Neoliberalism, Cultural Politics, and the Attack on Democracy* (Boston, MA: Beacon Press, 2003), xxii.

2 Elizabeth Bernstein and Janet R. Jakobson, "Introduction: Gender, justice, and the paradoxical persistence of neoliberal times," in *Paradoxes of Neoliberalism: Sex, Gender and Possibilities for Justice*, ed. Elizabeth Bernstein and Janet R. Jakobsen (New York: Routledge, 2022), 4, 9.

3 Wendy Brown, *In the Ruins of Neoliberalism: The Rise of Antidemocratic Politics in the West* (New York: Columbia University Press, 2019), 7–8.

4 Brown, *In the Ruins*, 8.

comprehending our world, what David Harvey refers to as "the common-sense way," has begun to teeter.[5] Ever louder challenges have been propelled and articulated not only by right-wing populisms and fascisms, but also by leftist, liberal, and radically democratic protest movements worldwide. To be sure, these political distinctions have at moments become blurry over the past few years, but we insist that this does not release us from the laborious task of articulating political difference.

Most importantly to the context of this volume, art and film have become crucial vehicles of probing, imagining, and modeling challenges to neoliberal reality. *Transnational German Film at the End of Neoliberalism* makes a bold claim for the emergence of a new, aesthetically and politically radical, transnational German cinema. With contributions from leading as well as emerging scholars of German and European cinema, the volume analyzes a number of key films produced since roughly 2015, ranging in genre and mode from dramas and comedies to documentaries and installations. In bringing these films together, the edited volume illuminates what we programmatically describe as a shift beyond neoliberal stasis to a renewed embrace of political filmmaking that confronts realities of the present. Through formal innovation as well as explicitly political storytelling, this cinema, the present volume argues, points beyond crisis standstill, social precarity, and the impasses of the present, sometimes with imagination and fantasy and often by embracing collectivity and resistance. Although such envisioning of collective action remains overshadowed by the specter of the fascist mob (as in Radlmaier's *Blutsauger*), we collectively argue, contemporary German film is also reimagining forms of (human and more-than-just-human) solidarity. This does not entail that our films—or the authors and editors of this volume—have necessarily worked out detailed drafts for a new society from a neo-Marxist, anarchist, radically feminist, queer, or decolonial angle. Most of these ideas circulate throughout the book, but we do not collectively advance a particular political solution. Like our films, many of us may still be "feeling out" where we *can* go from this current juncture, with either or both realism and radical imagination. The collection at hand does zoom in on this "feeling"—and thinking—"out." It partakes of contemporary films' probing of new aesthetic and digital possibilities in an effort to both sharpen our perception toward injustice and fashion new approaches of resistance. Keeping a close eye and ear to our films, we seek to learn from them through their observations in and responses to this political moment.

5   David Harvey, *A Brief History of Neoliberalism* (Oxford: Oxford University Press, 2007), 3.

Much recent scholarship on German cinema has focused on the Berlin School of the late 1990s and early 2000s. Frequently hailed as the first major film movement in Germany since New German Cinema, the Berlin School has been characterized as a new wave of art cinema known for its explorations of space, perspective, and everyday life in a society marked by increasing precarization. Emblematic of their time, the films of the Berlin School track fading fantasies of the so-called good life typified most prominently by the promulgation of economic prosperity, well-being, and stability. In her recent monograph, *German Cinema in the Age of Neoliberalism* (2021), Hester Baer compellingly argues that German film since the early 1980s, and culminating in the films of the Berlin School, has been paradigmatic in rendering visible and audible the neoliberal turn. "Whether by design or through analysis," she specifies, these films "can help us to see and respond to aspects of contemporary life that often remain obscured from our view, thereby making neoliberalism visible."[6] But while the films of the Berlin School at moments do gesture toward futural orientations beyond the crises and the contingency of the present, their politics remain ambiguous, abstractly utopian, and even specious.

The question of what has happened in German cinema since the height of the Berlin School, now over a decade ago, forms the starting point of the present study. Initial investigations of some of these new filmmaking departures have been undertaken by the 2019 special issue of *New German Critique*, "Contemporary German and Austrian Cinema: New Prospects," edited by Brad Prager and Eric Rentschler. The special issue makes a compelling argument for turning our attention to recent German-language features and documentaries other than the Berlin School, that are "equally worthy of critical attention,"[7] including films by Julian Radlmaier, Max Linz, Stephan Geene, Philip Scheffner, Nikolaus Geyrhalter, Ulrich Seidl, and Dominik Graf. A number of films by these directors are featured in the present volume as well. Expanding on the premise of Prager and Rentschler's special issue, our volume starts from the hypothesis that an ensemble of new cinematic projects, forms, and genres has moved contemporary German cinema beyond the films of the Berlin School: beyond the social-political impasses tracked by it, as well as its narrow range of genres and modes.

Transnational German film "after" the Berlin School—although in some cases also growing out of it—probes a range of new (stylized, comedic, dramatic, documentary, experimental) forms and thematic

---

6   Hester Baer, *German Cinema in the Age of Neoliberalism* (Amsterdam: Amsterdam University Press, 2021), 15.

7   Brad Prager and Eric Rentschler, "Introduction: New Prospects—After the Berlin School?," *New German Critique* 139 (2019): 5.

preoccupations, not least with more activist politics and modes of resistance. As indicated above, the volume at hand asks not only what these new politics might be, but especially what they look and sound like on screen. Film aesthetics thus forms a central part of the present project, albeit within a decidedly worldly approach. Taking *both* aesthetics and politics more seriously than usual, our investigations move beyond quick translations between formal elements and effects, on the one hand, and threadbare variations on the tired theme of global tensions between aesthetics and politics, on the other hand. In other words, we aim to do justice to both aesthetics and politics by entangling them ever more carefully and ever more forcefully.

With explorations of recent works by Fatih Akın, Irene von Alberti, Amel Alzakout and Khaled Abdulwahed, Forensic Architecture, Ruth Beckermann, Nils Bökamp, Susanne Heinrich, Gerd Kroske, Burhan Qurbani, Christian Petzold, Mario Pfeifer, Julian Radlmaier, Maria Speth, Tatjana Turanskyj, and Monika Treut, the contributions to our volume provide both a broad and an in-depth look at the contemporary moment in film. The results are aesthetically diverse: we present a range of film modes and genres, including the comedies dubbed "Neue deutsche Diskurskomödie" (New German Discourse Comedy), political dramas, observational documentaries, experimental essay films, and installation pieces. The politics that these films both track and contour are multifaceted but also indicate shared urgencies. Salient topics and debates include collectivity, migration, feminism, racism, queer identity, Marxism, and often militancy—also brought to bear on filmmaking itself. Across these concerns, our focus is on how the featured films grapple with this moment as one riddled with the turmoil of intensified crisis and right-wing threat, but also progressive activism. Methodologically, the aim of the volume is to refocus the study of film in this being-in-the-world-ness. This inquiry brings together longstanding approaches to political film form with insights from phenomenology, affect studies, and new materialisms that move beyond the established topoi of political film. Radical portrayals of intimate relations, grassroots activism, and resistance as well as violence and abjection display how film responds to and develops novel approaches to new worldly phenomena. At the same time, the new films under investigation also creatively rework "old" promises of film and filmmaking, for example film's early twentieth-century associations with assembling antifascist collectives.

Our book also draws on a number of other studies that have appeared in the last few years. In addition to Baer's aforementioned monograph, these recent works include the revised and expanded edition of *The German Cinema Book*, edited by Tim Bergfelder, Erica Carter, Deniz Göktürk, and Claudia Sandberg, Claudia Breger's *Making Worlds: Affect and Collectivity in Contemporary European Cinema*, and Maria

Stehle and Beverly Weber's *Precarious Intimacies: The Politics of Touch in Contemporary Western European Cinema.*[8] While largely focused on films released prior to 2015, these works resonate with and inform our methodological interests in cinematic politics of affect, intimacy, and care, as well as collectivity or community, resistance, and solidarity, in the face of neoliberal precarity and spreading politics of hate.

These recent studies furthermore share an emphasis on broader European and transnational film traditions, indexing, as the editors of *The German Cinema Book* indicate, "a general tendency in [German] cinema toward transnational and global interactions that destabilize the category of national cinema *tout court.*"[9] *Transnational German Film at the End of Neoliberalism* continues in this direction, even as we center on works at least co-produced in Germany or Austria. The scope of our inquiry and methodology exceeds such national categories in that many of the films are transnational in theme and form. They emphatically engage with a globalizing world through their emphasis on topics of migration or contemporary capitalism and through their applications of traveling forms and genres. Thus this book does not reduce the category of transnational film—certainly ever more prevalent—to international co-productions alone.[10] By calling film transnational, we seek to establish, as Steven Rawle words it (drawing on Aihwa Ong) "a way of talking about the movement of people, capital and culture across borders in an era of globalization."[11] At the same time, earlier scholarly declarations regarding the end of the nation and nationalism were evidently premature. The notion of transnationalism, as we understand it, acknowledges their continued significance along with the ways in which geopolitically materialized and imagined nations have always been made in transnational flows—of goods, power, people, and ideas.[12] Taking the German(-language) context as a local

---

8   Helga Druxes, Alexandar Mihailovic, and Patricia Anne Simpson's *Screening Solidarity: Neoliberalism and Transnational Cinema* (London: Bloomsbury, 2023) probes a more rigorous Marxist perspective.

9   Tim Bergfelder, Erica Carter, Deniz Göktürk, and Claudia Sandberg, "Introduction," in *The German Cinema Book* (London: British Film Institute, 2020), 5.

10   Nancy Mazdon, whose research looks at what she refers to as "French 'transnational' cinema," developed this argument in a roundtable discussion on transnational cinema. See Austin Fisher and Iain Robert Smith, "Transnational Cinemas: A Critical Roundtable," *Frames Cinema Journal* (2016): https://framescinemajournal.com/article/transnational-cinemas-a-critical-roundtable/.

11   Steven Rawle, *Transnational Cinema: An Introduction* (London: Bloomsbury, 2018), 2.

12   In addition to Rawle's work, see also Randall Halle, *German Film after Germany: Toward a Transnational Aesthetic* (Urbana-Champaign: University of Illinois Press, 2008).

and tangible focal point also permits a closer and more controlled look at new trends in film: the local configuration facilitates specificity and in-depth investigation within a larger framework. Combined, "transnational German" invites an examination of the national through its relationship to the transnational.

The volume is divided into four thematic sections, in part (but not exclusively) associated with new or newly revitalized genres. These sections map what we propose as key attributes of contemporary cinema aesthetics and politics. More specifically, each of them explores in distinct ways how film offers a powerful riposte to neoliberal capitalism. Part I, "Radical Pessimism as a Form of Resistance: Political Drama in the Age of Surplus Humanity and New Fascism," examines recent political dramas firmly embedded in the horrors of the arguably increasingly fascist present. Against the backdrop of ongoing refugee crises, the films foregrounded in these chapters take up themes of migration in ways that turn on new—or ever more prevalent—forms of authoritarianism, political violence, and human expendability. But as each contribution reveals, these films also practice resistance in variations of what Gozde Naiboglu refers to as "radical pessimism" in her contribution, for example through provocative anachronism or an embrace of violence that defies.

Angelos Koutsourakis's chapter opens this first section with a return to a more recent film by Christian Petzold, whose work has often been positioned as exemplary for the Berlin School, including its ambivalent turns to genre and storytelling in the 2010s. An adaptation of Anna Seghers's antifascist novel by the same name, Petzold's *Transit* (2018) draws parallels between Nazi Europe, rising neo-fascism in the present, and the refugee crisis in Europe. Engaging with postfascist thinkers, Koutsourakis analyzes the film's period anachronisms—with its 1944 story set in contemporary Marseille—as telltale signs of latter-day fascism. The film's adaptation of a historical antifascist work serves as a powerful, if indirect, reminder of what has been possible and still is. Also adapted from canonical German literature, Burhan Qurbani's *Berlin Alexanderplatz* (2020) is the focus of Priscilla Layne's chapter. Layne shows how Qurbani brings race, citizenship, and disability to his modern rendition of Alfred Döblin's Weimar. While Döblin's *Berlin Alexanderplatz* (1929) was about a working-class man unable to find his footing in a capitalist world, Qurbani's contemporary reimagining shows the cruel pursuit of the "good life" of the main protagonist, Francis, a Black, undocumented refugee from Bissau. With a voice-over narrator even more haunting than Petzold's as well as a forceful visual dramatization of contemporary city space, Qurbani's film powerfully exemplifies contemporary film's innovative explorations of a new political aesthetics. Gozde Naiboglu's chapter on Fatih Akın's *Aus dem Nichts* (*In the Fade*, 2017) concludes the book's first section. A film based on the hate murders of the National Socialist

Underground (2000–2011) that concludes in a violent act of revenge, *Aus dem Nichts*, Naiboglu argues, can be positioned as performing a "pessimistic" turn in the acclaimed director's oeuvre. This does not, however, mean that the film succumbs to nihilism; rather, Naiboglu proposes that it promotes pessimism as a politics of refusal, which she conceptualizes as "negative futurability."

Part II, "Rethinking the Evidence: New Documentary Forms," turns to documentary and other experimental modes of film. Documentaries have a tendency to reemerge during times of crises.[13] The mode itself has earned its value as a social-political instrument of evidentiary exploration and presentation concerned with the pursuit of "what really happened." Yet its reemergence in the last decade has been intensified by remarkable new technological possibilities that have dramatically reordered our audiovisual perceptions of events and narratives, including to the effect of ever more forcefully unsettling traditional promises of indexical truth-telling. The chapters that comprise this section tune in to the ways in which politically themed documentary films respond to this contemporary condition—and its explicit political exploitation in our so-called era of "post-truth"—not simply through the stories they tell but by way of their radical approaches to image and sound.

Lutz Koepnick's chapter, "Forensic Fallacies," transitions us from the earlier section on political dramas by returning to *Aus dem Nichts*, but bringing it into conversation with two documentary video installations: Forensic Architecture's *The Murder of Halit Yozgat* (2017) and Mario Pfeifer's *Again* (2018). This comparative reading across media forcefully turns our attention to how violent acts of hate go exonerated in the contemporary collapse of truth and forensic evidence. But it also asks how art might correct what the German legal system has failed to accomplish: namely, to bring about justice for wrongs committed against migrants. Randall Halle's contribution similarly extends attention to the forensic, and specifically the work of the London-based research collective Forensic Architecture, as he turns to Amel Alzakout and Khaled Abdulwahed's *Purple Sea* (2019) and Forensic Architecture's *Shipwreck at the Threshold of Europe, Lesvos, Aegean Sea* (2020), two highly experimental films about real-life shipwrecks in the European border zone. Through Julia Kristeva's theorization of the abject, Halle analyzes how the border takes shape as a brutal juridico-political apparatus of abjection in these

---

13   In her article, Carol Martin addresses documentary theater, but the same can be said of film. See Carol Martin, "Bodies of Evidence," *TDR: The Drama Review* 50, no. 3 (2006): 14. This sentiment has been echoed by other scholars, including more recently Ryan Watson in the context of film. See Ryan Watson, *Radical Documentary and Global Crisis: Militant Evidence in the Digital Age* (Bloomington: Indiana University Press, 2022), 4–5.

films. *Purple Sea* and *Shipwreck*, Halle demonstrates, develop two complementary, yet equally urgent, pieces to the puzzle of how to counter this regime of death: a methodologically innovative gathering of counterevidence and an autobiographical turn. In the final chapter of this section, Olivia Landry takes up the broader question of documentary's evidentiary effect and value in Gerd Kroske's *SPK Komplex* (2018). Focusing on the Marxist Sozialistisches Patientenkollektiv (Socialist Patients' Collective) of the early 1970s and the archive of objects it left behind, *SPK Komplex* also formally invites an exploration of the history of the voice-over in documentary. With attentiveness to the critical role of the voice and its mechanization in this film, Landry examines the ingredients of a political documentary—both authentic and representational—and the challenges of political filmmaking today.

In Part III, titled "Reassembling the Archives of Radical Filmmaking," three chapters discuss contributions to the "Neue deutsche Diskurskomödie" (New German Discourse Comedy). With its citational aesthetics, this group of films is the closest thing contemporary German cinema has to a new movement (after the Berlin School).[14] Consciously harking back to twentieth-century modes of aesthetic theatricality as well as a vast (filmic and theoretical) intertextual archive, these films present a new generation's forceful commitment to reimagining an avowedly political film aesthetics in a self-confident dialogue with generations of predecessors.

Richard Langston's chapter provides an introduction to this trend and its notable institutional association with the German Film and Television Academy in Berlin (DFFB) (also significant in the emergence of the earlier Berlin School) before homing in on an early example, Max Linz's *Ich will mich nicht künstlich aufregen* (*Asta Upset*, 2014). Langston treats the films of New German Discourse Comedy through their connection to the discourse theater of René Pollesch as well as to New German Cinema and an array of theoretical texts from an era preceding neoliberalism. If New German Cinema presented a utopian moment of political filmmaking in the 1970s, for Langston, Linz's aesthetics of the contemporary (defined with Paul Rabinow) intertwines old and new in order to hold open the possibility of looking forward in our challenging moment toward the prospect of a different future. Hester Baer brings the New German Discourse Comedy into conversation with contemporary feminist film. Analyzing *Das melancholische Mädchen* (*Aren't You Happy?*,

---

14 Volker Pantenburg, "Class Relations: Diagnoses of the Present in the Films of Julian Radlmaier and Max Linz," *New German Critique* 46, no. 3 (138) (2019): 56–57; Lars Meyer, Zu jedem Bett gehört ein Mann," *Die Zeit*, June 22, 2019, https://www.zeit.de/kultur/film/2019-06/das-melancholische-maedchen-film-susanne-heinrich.

2019) together with *Top Girl oder la déformation professionnelle* (*Top Girl*, 2014), and *Der lange Sommer der Theorie* (*The Long Summer of Theory*, 2017), she too detects a critical genealogy, in this case leading back to earlier feminist works by Helke Sander, Ula Stöckl, and Jutta Brückner, among others. The New German Discourse Comedy's audiovisual remediations of this legacy, Baer asserts, accompany and open up the more straightforward political endeavors of the concurrent Pro Quote Film initiative with renewed radical questions about representation, form, and possible feminist futures. Following a similar approach in its search for historical continuities, Claudia Breger's concluding chapter in this section tackles yet a different part of the New German Discourse Comedy's aesthetic and political ancestry. Starting from the explicit evocation of Gilles Deleuze in Julian Radlmaier's *Selbstkritik eines bürgerlichen Hundes* (*Self-Criticism of a Bourgeois Dog*, 2017), she reads the film as an exploration of how to aesthetically reassemble "the people"—as a political collective—that Deleuze declared to be missing in post-WWII European cinema. Tracing its intricate mixture of comedy, flamboyant fabulation, and (unexpected) moments of emphatic realism, Breger discusses how Radlmaier's film works through the totalitarian overshadowing of cinematic collectivity in the wake of Nazism and Stalinism. In the end, the film cautiously recuperates the possibility of, at least, dreaming of the revolution, without altogether abandoning political reality.

The chapters in the final section, Part IV, "Intimate Connections: Aesthetics and Politics of a Cinema of Relations" are not guided by a single mode or genre. Rather, they group different types of films together—experimental, narrative dramas, and documentary—through the themes of collectivity and relationality. With their focus on space and ephemerality, sound, affect, bodies, and intimacy, the contributions to this concluding section bring into view forms of politics that partly evade classical conceptions of political commitment. But the films they pursue present no less crucial building blocks to the project of reimagining cinematic politics. These chapters explore instances of spatiotemporal resonance, modes of breathing with each other, collectivity, and community in recent films.

Fatima Naqvi's contribution explores strikingly different renderings of the political collective in three recent documentary films by Ruth Beckermann, *Die Geträumten* (*The Dreamed Ones*, 2016), *Waldheims Walzer* (*The Waldheim Waltz*, 2018), and *Mutzenbacher* (2022), through what she conceptualizes as choric configurations. To set up her investigation, Naqvi turns to theater and the historical collective of the chorus as a force for both performing and disrupting hegemonic constellations of power. Voice, sound, and audition connect characters and audience across distances through Beckermann's aesthetically theatricalized films. They offer multifaceted reflections on the mediated collectivities of twentieth-century fascism, the possibilities of protesting its contemporary resurgences, and the patriarchal collective as an agent of sexual violence. On a less dramatic scale, Ervin Malakaj's contribution turns to the dimension of breath to think about intimacy and connectivity in two drama films associated with contemporary queer cinema, Nils Bökamp's *You & I* (2014) and Monika Treut's *Von Mädchen und Pferden* (*Of Girls and Horses*, 2014). In what at first glance may seem to constitute departures from the radical politics of earlier queer cinema, these films take us to the countryside, where breath, sounds of nature, and scent afford space and connection. But this focus on the senses, Malakaj demonstrates, offers crucial moments of (resistant) escape from neoliberal urbanism. Finally, this section—as well as our volume—comes to a close with Angelica Fenner's analysis of Maria Speth's observational documentary about a diverse primary school class, *Herr Bachmann und seine Klasse* (*Mr. Bachmann and His Class*, 2021). Fenner's close reading draws out the film's "posthuman pedagogy" in its impressive audiovisualization of a complex network of relations between people and between people, objects, and environments, or (in Bruno Latour's words) human and nonhuman actors. As developed in Speth's film, this experimentation with radically inclusive forms of collectivity affords attachments and relations divorced from—and aesthetically countering—neoliberal valorization.

Transnational German Film at the End of Neoliberalism thus explores a multifaceted ensemble of films that dramatize neoliberalism at its protracted end. Collectively, albeit in different ways, its chapters begin to imagine how the world might look and sound *on the other side*. Although no ready-made, or single, answer comes to surface, the individual films in focus are not altogether disconnected. Even across the volume's sections, we observe revealing aesthetic resonances. For example, we hear the (long-shunned) use of voice-over in the new dramas as well as the films of New German Discourse Comedy, albeit resounding in anything but the straightforwardly didactic ways of early documentary. We also view mise-en-scènes replete with bright, pop-cultural color schemes, and we note the incursion of documentary elements in both dramas and comedies. In sum, the experimental meets the traditional in many of these films through the application of new media formats as well as older techniques of storytelling and engagement. From this encounter, a richness of forms develops that radically challenges our audiovisual expectations. These new and revitalized forms do not directly cohere into a single new political aesthetics. Rather, in an affirmative and generative embrace of politics, the films gathered here herald new on-screen realities in the wreck of neoliberalism. This volume gives rise to manifold observations about contemporary German-language cinema and its aesthetic and political possibilities, as it foregrounds intersections of the two categories from a range of angles. We hope that it also offers new cinematic insights (and not simply platitudes) toward the ever-present question: where do we go from here?

Bibliography

Bergfelder, Tim, Erica Carter, Deniz Göktürk, and Claudia Sandberg, eds. *The German Cinema Book*. London: British Film Institute, 2020.

Bernstein, Elizabeth, and Janet R. Jakobson, eds. *Paradoxes of Neoliberalism: Sex, Gender and Possibilities for Justice*. New York: Routledge, 2022.

Breger, Claudia. *Making Worlds: Affect and Collectivity in Contemporary European Cinema*. New York: Columbia University Press, 2020.

Brown, Wendy. *In the Ruins of Neoliberalism: The Rise of Antidemocratic Politics in the West*. New York: Columbia University Press, 2019.

Druxes, Helga, Alexandar Mihailovic, and Patricia Anne Simpson. *Screening Solidarity: Neoliberalism and Transnational Cinemas*. London: Bloomsbury, 2023.

Duggan, Lisa. *The Twilight of Equality? Neoliberalism, Cultural Politics, and the Attack on Democracy*. Boston, MA: Beacon Press, 2003.

Fisher, Austin, and Iain Robert Smith. "Transnational Cinemas: A Critical Roundtable." *Frames Cinema Journal* (2016): https://framescinema-journal.com/article/transnational-cinemas-a-critical-roundtable/.

Halle, Randall. *German Film after Germany: Toward a Transnational Aesthetic*. Urbana-Champaign: University of Illinois Press, 2008.

Harvey, David. *A Brief History of Neoliberalism*. Oxford: Oxford University Press, 2007.

Martin, Carol. "Bodies of Evidence." *TDR: The Drama Review* 50, no. 3 (2006): 8–15.

Meyer, Lars. Zu jedem Bett gehört ein Mann," *Die Zeit*, June 22, 2019. https://www.zeit.de/kultur/film/2019-06/das-melancholische-maedchen-film-susanne-heinrich.

Pantenburg, Volker. "Class Relations: Diagnoses of the Present in the Films of Julian Radlmaier and Max Linz." *New German Critique* 46, no. 3 (138) (2019): 53–78.

Prager, Brad, and Eric Rentschler. "Introduction: New Prospects—After the Berlin School?" *New German Critique* 46, no. 3 (138) (2019): 1–9.

Rawle, Steven. *Transnational Cinema: An Introduction*. London: Bloomsbury, 2018.

Stehle, Maria, and Beverly Weber. *Precarious Intimacies: The Politics of Touch in Contemporary Western European Cinema*. Evanston, IL: Northwestern University, 2020.

Watson, Ryan. *Radical Documentary and Global Crisis: Militant Evidence in the Digital Age*. Bloomington: Indiana University Press, 2022.

Part I

Radical Pessimism as a Form of Resistance: Political Drama in the Age of Surplus Humanity and New Fascism

1: *Transit* (2018) and Postfascism

Angelos Koutsourakis

Introduction: Some Notes on Postfascism

CHRISTIAN PETZOLD'S *Transit* (2018) is an adaptation of Anna Seghers's homonymous antifascist novel that engages with the history of forced migration of European refugees in Marseille trying to flee fascism in the hope of getting asylum in North and South America. In Petzold's adaptation, Seghers's novel has been reworked to address contemporary political contradictions. The film's central anachronism is that although it is set in the past, it is filmed in the contemporary spaces of Marseille, thus foregrounding a dialectical tension between the history of fascism and the present reality of forced displacements, exile, and militarized border controls in Europe. Petzold justified this choice, explaining that the film seeks to identify the parallels between the past, rising neo-fascism, and the refugee crisis in Europe. As he states, "my aim was not Brechtian disruption, but to emphasize correspondences between then and now."[1] Indeed, scholars have been quick enough to recognize the film's references to the current refugee crisis, but nobody has paid attention to the issue of the rising fascism mentioned by the filmmaker.[2] In this chapter, I suggest that the film's anachronism points to the contemporary reality of postfascism, a term predominantly associated with the Hungarian philosopher Gáspár Miklós Tamás and secondarily with the Italian historian Enzo Traverso, both of whom argue that reactionary practices of exclusion that we identify with the history of European fascism have been embedded in mainstream politics. Postfascism, for these scholars, therefore refers to a

---

1   Christian Petzold, "Wartime out of Joint," trans. Becca Voelcker, *Film Comment* 55, no. 1 (2019): 6.

2   See Philipp Brunner, "Filmkritik: Transit," *Filmbulletin: Zeitschrift für Film und Kino* 3 (2018): 31–32; Olivia Landry, "The Beauty and Violence of *Horror Vacui*: Waiting in Christian Petzold's *Transit* (2018)," *German Quarterly* 93, no. 1 (2020): 90–105; Alice Bardan, "'Europe, Spectrality and 'Post-mortem Cinema': The Haunting of History in Christian Petzold's *Transit* (2018) and Aki Kaurismäki's *Le Havre* (2011)," *Northern Lights* 18, no. 1 (2020): 115–29; Max Nelson, "'Our Contemporary Winds': Christian Petzold's *Transit*," *Salmagundi* 204 (2019): 38–48.

historical period in which policies and ideas associated with the extreme right have become part of mainstream liberal politics. This leads also to the rise of neo-fascist movements precisely because their political narrative seems to have been vindicated by the (neo)liberal mainstream. Before analyzing the film, some further comments on postfascism are in order.

Introduced by Tamás in 2000, the term postfascism describes the present historical experience when contemporary fascism does not operate as a form of counter-revolution against international Socialism as it was the case with its twentieth-century precursor. Tamás suggests that contemporary liberal democracies are postfascist because they have undermined "the Enlightenment idea of universal citizenship," according to which every individual irrespective of race, class, origin, gender, and nationality should be part of the civic community. Socialist internationalism embodied this desire to complete the Enlightenment project that could not be realized in bourgeois societies. This project was based on the idea of liberating individuals through the eventual abolition of entrenched privilege. Contemporary societies function instead through the maintenance of privilege, domestically and internationally:

> Citizenship is today the very exceptional privilege of the inhabitants of flourishing capitalist nation-states, while the majority of the world's population cannot even begin to aspire to the civic condition, and has also lost the relative security of pre-state (tribe, kinship) protection. The scission of citizenship and sub-political humanity is now complete, the work of Enlightenment irretrievably lost. Postfascism does not need to put non-citizens into freight trains to take them into death; instead, it need only prevent the new non-citizens from boarding any trains that might take them into the happy world of overflowing rubbish bins that could feed them.[3]

A key precept of Tamás's argument is that contemporary liberal democracies operate on the basis of exclusion that is facilitated by the unlimited flow of capital across the globe and the restrictions on the movement of labor imposed by the core countries of the World-System. Exclusions aim to stabilize the division of the world into centers and peripheries, the global flow of capital, and the cheap cost of labor in the periphery as well as to prevent those who are considered "aliens" to achieve the status of universal citizenship. In these terms, postfascist movements are "protecting universal citizenship within the rich nation-state against the virtual-universal citizenship of all human beings, regardless of geography,

---

3 Gáspár Miklós Tamás "On Post-Fascism: The Degradation of Universal Citizenship," *Boston Review*, accessed August 3, 2022, http://bostonreview.net/world/g-m-tamas-post-fascism.

language, race, denomination, and habits."[4] Postfascism, therefore, refers to the reversibility of the Enlightenment project from within. It does not simply indicate the reemergence of extreme right movements across the globe—although it certainly includes that.

Tamás draws on George Bataille's well-known essay on the psychology of fascism and explains that postfascism abides by fascism's distinction between homogeneous and heterogeneous societies. For Bataille, a homogeneous society is a society of productive labor, exchange-value, "usefulness," and "sexual repression." Productivity is the central measure of social homogeneity. In these terms, the heterogeneous elements are those that cannot be assimilated to the productive system and/or pose a threat to its continuity. According to Bataille, fascism seeks to achieve social homogeneity by concentrating power—religious and military power—that can blend the social and class differences within the nation state. Fascist unification and homogeneity are achieved thanks to this concentration of power that makes political violence a fundamental part of the practice of power. For fascism, violence is the means to achieve social homogeneity because it enables the exclusion of all those who are considered to be unproductive and cannot be assimilated into the imaginary of the unitary nation-state.[5]

Taking a cue from Bataille's analysis, Tamás suggests that contemporary (neo)liberal democracies operate similarly and seek to exclude all those who threaten their homogeneity, which is also measured based on principles of productivity. Those who cannot integrate, such as the disabled, unemployed, refugees, and asylum seekers, are heterogeneous elements, who are deemed to be part of "passive populations" and thus "undeserving."[6] As Tamás suggests, it is ironic that presently the exclusion of the "unproductive" is not the outcome of an autocratic counterrevolutionary movement, but of policies formed in democratic societies that go hand in hand with the anti-welfare sentiment of neoliberal capitalism. When we add to this the fact that technological developments in postindustrial societies render many individuals doomed to a life of wagelessness and destitution, the amount of people deemed by the neoliberal consensus to be part of the passive populations is bound to increase. The implication is that more people are excluded from the civic condition, which is now turning into a privilege rather than a recognized right. As Tamás explains in a subsequent essay:

---

4   Tamás, "On Post-Fascism."

5   See Georges Bataille, "The Psychological Structure of Fascism," trans. Carl R. Lovitt, *New German Critique* 16 (1979): 64–87; Tamás, "On Post-Fascism."

6   Gáspár Miklós Tamás "A Postscript to 'Post-Fascism': Preliminary Theses to a System of Fear," *Details* (2011): 62.

The state of exception redefining friend and foe within national societies and nation-states remains the fundamental characteristic of post-fascism as I defined it in my essay a decade ago. Its model remains the rescinding of Jewish emancipation by the Third Reich. The transformation of the noncitizens into homines sacri is unchanged as well. Erecting tall dykes against migration, even at the price of slowing down capitalist fluxes, is still its main instrument. But the transformation of citizens into non-citizens on moralistic and biopolitical grounds—with such ferocity—is rather new. As long as there is no synthesis between the transcendental identity of the working and non-working, but mainly between the productive and nonproductive social groups as opposed to capital as such, something very like fascism will prevail . . . It is not only extremists and fools of the far right who are a threat. It is the widely accepted semblance of the unity between legitimate earners—capitalists and producers—united politically against the "passive" and the alien which is placing everyone in jeopardy.[7]

One conclusion to be drawn here is that the core features of postfascism are part and parcel of the neoliberal consensus and can be perpetuated and promoted not just by parties on the extreme right, but from the liberal center too. For example, the Fortress Europe policy that violently excludes non-European migrants from entering European shores or places those who manage to enter in overcrowded camps such as Moria, and the discrimination against the "unproductive" in core and peripheral economies have been so normalized and accepted that they are not even considered to be associated with the extreme right. The extreme right is also on the march, precisely because some of its key ideas have become part of the political mainstream making illiberalism a central feature of contemporary (neo)liberalism:

We are, then, faced with a new kind of extremism of the center. This new extremism, which I call post-fascism, does not threaten, unlike its predecessor, liberal and democratic rule within the core constituency of "homogeneous society." Within the community cut in two, freedom, security, prosperity are on the whole undisturbed, at least within the productive and procreative majority that in some rich countries encompasses nearly all white citizens. "Heterogeneous," usually racially alien, minorities are not persecuted, only neglected and marginalized, forced to live a life wholly foreign to the way of life of the majority.[8]

7   Tamás, "A Postscript to 'Post-Fascism,'" 62.
8   Tamás, "On Post-Fascism."

Given that his essay was written years before the present refugee crisis, one corrective that needs to be given here is that, at present, governments in the Global North do not just neglect but also actively persecute individuals (such as refugees) who are deemed unworthy of citizenship and risks to their societies' as well as to their imaginary social and national homogeneity, as per Bataille's essay, mentioned above. Overall, Tamás's comments resonate with recent critiques of contemporary liberal democracies whose contradictions can also be attributed to the lack of an emancipatory political alternative that could create competition in the public sphere and revitalize the political mainstream. This chimes neatly with Traverso's understanding of postfascism. For Traverso, postfascism is the consequence of the defeat of socialism. The "anti-politics" of the far-right poses the only alternative to the present system. Ironically, this "anti-politics" is the product of the anti-politics of contemporary neoliberalism that assumes that electoral changes should not be accompanied by changes in economic policies, to which no alternative should be envisioned. As he cogently explains, "the critics who denounce populist 'anti-politics' are often the same people responsible for these transformations: pyromaniacs disguised as firemen."[9] To put it simply, the challenge of the contemporary political landscape is that hostility to the Enlightenment project does not arise solely from the far right, but also from the liberal center itself.

From Antifascist Hope to Postfascist Deadlock: Petzold's Adaptation of Seghers's Novel

Anna Seghers's novel *Transit* is a paragon of antifascist literature. Seghers, an antifascist communist author of Jewish origin, owed a lot to Kafka and writers who were part of radical Jewish twentieth-century thought. Kafka's influence permeates other works of hers, such as *Reise ins elfte Reich* (*Journey into the Eleventh Realm,* 1939) and her 1953 collaboration with Bertolt Brecht for the Berliner Ensemble adaptation of her radio play *Der Prozess der Jeanne d' Arc zu Rouen 1431* (*The Trial of Jeanne d'Arc at Rouen, 1431,* 1937). In the latter work, Seghers and Brecht responded obliquely to the historical context of the Slánský trial in Czechoslovakia, and the play alludes to the forced confessions of the accused.[10] Kafkaesque themes also permeate *Transit,* and this is something that has been acknowledged by Petzold:

9   Enzo Traverso, *The New Faces of Fascism: Populism and the Far Right,* trans. David Broder (London: Verso, 2017), 28.
10   See Helen Fehervary, *Anna Seghers: The Mythic Dimension* (Ann Arbor: University of Michigan Press, 2001), 197–98.

> When you read "Transit" by Anna Seghers, she's using Kafka. Everybody who has used the word "Kafka" for "Transit," it's a trace Anna Seghers made by herself. . . . She uses Kafka because as she's sitting there in Marseille, the German literature surrounds her and the Jewish literature is totally destroyed. So, you have to take some of the literature with you. You never will forget it. It's a Kafkaesque situation. But in Kafka, there is no sun or wind. But there, you're surrounded by a fantastic Mediterranean sea, the blue sky, the fantastic food and coffee and pizza and Rosé, but it's also Kafka.[11]

The novel focuses on an apolitical, nameless German character, who has escaped a concentration camp in his homeland, and later a French camp in Rouen. Thanks to the support of a former girlfriend's husband, he assumes the identity of another missing refugee named Seidler. Paul Staubel, an acquaintance, asks the protagonist to deliver a letter to Weidel, a German Jewish author in Paris, but upon arriving at his hotel he realizes that Weidel has committed suicide. During his trip to Marseille, he opens Weidel's suitcase and finds a book manuscript, a letter from his wife who wants to leave him, another letter by her urging him to join her immediately to Marseille, and a note from the Mexican consulate informing him that his travel funds and visa are ready to be collected. Upon his arrival at the consulate, the authorities confuse Seidler for Weidel despite introducing himself as Seidler. The official disregards this attempt at being honest and asks him to submit a form that confirms that the person Seidler is the same as Weidel in order to receive his visa. The protagonist then assumes Weidel's identity and ends up, also by chance, befriending his wife, Marie, who left Paris with a doctor and is oblivious to her husband's death or to the fact that her new friend is impersonating him to the authorities. The novel focuses on the absurd bureaucratic situations experienced by the refugees, who need to be in possession of an exit visa that allows subjects to leave France as well as a transit visa "that gives you permission to travel through a country with the stipulation that you don't plan to stay."[12]

The story is based on Seghers's own family experiences as refugees in 1940–41 trying to leave Marseille for Mexico. According to Peter Conrad, "Seghers and countless others were like Kafka's Joseph K trying to get his credentials as a land surveyor recognized by the officials in the impenetrable castle."[13] The novel touches on issues of identity,

---

11 Cited in Vikram Murthi, "Christian Petzold on Transit, Kafka, His Love for Den of Thieves and More," accessed November 3, 2020, https://www.rogerebert.com/interviews/christian-petzold-on-transit-kafka-his-love-for-den-of-thieves-and-more.

12 Anna Seghers, *Transit*, trans. Margot Bettauer Dembo (New York: New York Review of Books, 2013), 40.

13 Peter Conrad, "Introduction," in Seghers, *Transit*, vii.

forced displacement, exile, and political prosecution, while it mourns the impending disappearance of a radical Jewish European culture committed to the project of universal emancipation. The latter point is confirmed by the fact that the figure of the dead author Weidel is modelled on the Jewish writer (and Kafka's friend) Ernst Weiss, while a certain passage in the novel also invokes Walter Benjamin's suicide.[14] Despite the text's historical dimensions, the emphasis is not on grand events; even the arrival of the Nazis is treated with restraint. Instead, much of the narrative focuses on mundane details, such as the monotony of waiting for documents, encountering unfriendly bureaucrats who typewrite every interview with the visa applicants, and repeated conversations in cafés and consulate corridors about documents needed to acquire transit and exit visas. The absurdity of the situation reaches its peak when we learn that people who had escaped from camps in France could not exit the country despite having valid visas from the future host countries, because they did not possess release certificates from the relevant camps. The text abounds with analogous stories of people who have managed to receive a visa from host nations only to be unable to leave because their transit or exit visa has expired. Typical in this respect is the main character's encounter with a Jewish man born in a small town that used to be part of Russia before the First World War, only to become Polish territory later. From his encounters with the Mexican consuls, he gets to learn that his Polish identity card is now invalid, because his hometown is currently part of Lithuania. As such, his visas are considered unacceptable and he is asked to provide new birth and citizenship certificates from Lithuania, a challenging task given that the town is under Nazi occupation. To the main character's astonishment, he declares that he has decided to go back to his town. In a characteristic passage, evocative of Kafka's "Before the Law" parable, he says:

> And here? What can I expect here? You know the fairy tale about the man who died, don't you? He was waiting in Eternity to find out what the Lord had decided to do with him. He waited and waited, for one year, ten years, a hundred years. He begged and pleaded for a decision. Finally he couldn't bear the waiting any longer. Then they said to him: "What do you think you're waiting for? You've been in Hell for a long time already." That's what it's been like for me here, a stupid waiting for nothing. What could be more hellish? War? The war's going to follow us across the ocean too. I've had enough of it. All I want is to go home.[15]

---

14 See Fehervary, *Anna Seghers*, 170.
15 Seghers, *Transit*, 186.

The plight of the European refugees waiting in hope of escaping to "the New World" is aptly communicated through similar episodes that capture their desire to flee Europe. At the same time, the text is filled with irony since from the first pages we know that *Montreal*, the ship which Marie and the doctor will embark on, has sunk and in the end this is reported casually. There is, therefore, in Helen Fehervary's words, "a cyclical quality" in the narrative, which inflects it with a bitter irony;[16] we follow the intricate bureaucratic processes that the refugees have to go through, while we already know the fate of those who were "lucky" enough to get a berth on the ship, which will sink. The novel, however, concludes in a utopian mode as the protagonist leaves behind his apolitical outlook and decides to join the French *Résistance*.

It is worth noting that the text resorts to a number of anachronisms itself and relates the specific story of forced migration to a series of past European catastrophes with references to ancient Greece, Rome, and the Bible. As mentioned in the introduction, Petzold's adaptation makes use of a different anachronism putting characters from 1944 into the setting of contemporary Marseille to address the rising fascism of the present. But the fascism suggested by Petzold is directly interconnected with the postfascist structures of exclusion of Fortress Europe. It is not the product of an organized reactionary political assemblage, as was the case in the 1940s. The refugee crisis to which the film alludes is rooted in the global imbalance between development and underdevelopment that makes migration to the Global North the only choice for a substantial part of the world population. This contradiction and the political scapegoating of refugees for economic problems produced by neoliberal policies not only make new reactionary movements reemerge but also invite one to consider Tamás's and Traverso's arguments that reactionary practices are embedded in mainstream politics.

But the film's anachronism has further political implications. Its reference to Europe's traumatic past and its portrayal of Europeans with a strong urge to migrate beyond the continent point to the current refugee crisis without following what Thomas Austin calls "benefaction tropes" of benevolent European filmmakers. Austin refers to filmmakers of the likes of Aki Kaurismäki whose films paint a positive image of suffering non-European refugees without, however, evading a Eurocentric understanding of Europe's historical and contemporary role in conflicts outside its borders.[17] By contrast, Petzold's anachronistic retelling of Seghers's

---

16 Seghers, *Transit*, 47.

17 Thomas Austin, "Miserable Journeys, Symbolic Rescues: Refugees and Migrants in the Cinema of Fortress Europe," in *Cinema of Crisis: Film and Contemporary Europe*, ed. Thomas Austin and Angelos Koutsourakis (Edinburgh: Edinburgh University Press, 2020), 203.

European story alludes to contemporary problems beyond and within the European frontiers and implies that they are not to be disconnected from Europe's own problematic past and present. Firstly, the film's anachronism emerges from its relation to the source text, which it slightly modifies to address present concerns. On the one hand, it remains relatively faithful to the narrative of the novel about the persecution of the European refugees by the Nazis; on the other hand, the mise-en-scène problematizes neat distinctions between the years of Nazi rule and the contemporary present. As such, the visual design creates an obvious clash between the past and the present that prevents it from being classified as a period film. Alex Fletcher rightly comments that the conflict between the contemporary setting and the references to camps and deportations that recall the Nazi past, as well as the use of contradictory props—for example, the modern gear of the police force versus the characters' old-fashioned clothes and the décor of the hotels, bars, and offices that signify a past era—create a sense of temporal indeterminacy.[18] The dialectical blending of the past and the present, the fascist past and the post-fascist present, is also highlighted in a part of the film that goes beyond the source text and focuses on the bond between Georg (Franz Rogowski) and Driss (Lilien Batman), the son of Melissa (Maryam Zaree), a North African woman considered to be an illegal resident by the French authorities. Georg's encounter with the young boy and his mother invites further comparisons between the fascist past and contemporary European exclusionary border policies.

Pertinent in this respect is Olivia Landry's assertion that "time is out of joint in this film." Landry cogently argues that the confluence of the past and the present in the film's narrative operates as a means of avoiding the pitfall of producing a museumized image of the past. The film offers instead a "narrative of loss, despair, and death that inexorably resembles our historical present as it also harkens back to the terror of a Nazi past."[19] In comparing the legacy of the Nazi terror to the present, the film points to the most important feature of postfascism, which is the fact that the Enlightenment ambition of universal citizenship according to which the human and the political condition are coextensive has been totally disregarded by contemporary liberal democracies. The latter are keen to publicly condemn "passive populations" and act in ways that deprive them of their social rights. Not unlike the European refugees in Seghers's novel facing the hostility of the French authorities, who press them to exit Marseille, contemporary non-European refugees are similarly deemed unworthy of social rights by the countries of the Global North.

---

18   See Alex Fletcher, "History at a Standstill: Migration and Anachronism in Christian Petzold's *Transit*," *Film International* 18, no. 3 (2020): 83–91.

19   Landry, "The Beauty and Violence of *Horror Vacui*," 95, 103–4.

Petzold's adaptation focuses mainly on the part of the novel following Weidel's death, and the nameless character of Seghers's novel becomes Georg in Petzold's film. The film's link between fascism and postfascism is successfully made via an emphasis on the "techno-securitization" of life through the military-police complex and modes of surveillance.[20] We do not see Swastikas and familiar Nazi insignia, but riot-policemen in contemporary gear and compliant citizens willing to act as informers against vulnerable refugees. This is brilliantly captured early in the film when Georg manages to escape a police blockade. The setting here evokes familiar images of European security forces arresting refugees for lack of identification documents. When Georg escapes, a local woman is portrayed as overly eager to inform on him to the police.

Later, upon his arrival in Marseille, Georg is filmed by a CCTV camera whose point of view temporarily frames the action.[21] This persistent emphasis on modern forms of security and control, as well as the citizens' collaboration with the authorities indirectly raise current issues of development and underdevelopment given that the techno-securitization of life that characterizes liberal democracies has an exclusionary dimension aiming to guarantee the unrestricted movement of capital while restricting the flow of people from places whose economies suffer from conditions of unequal exchange. The adamant desire of the locals to report the displaced people to the authorities complicates matters further by pointing also to repressed histories of French collaboration with the Nazis. This is given full sway in a scene that shows the owner of the hotel, in which Georg resides, accompanying the police, who enter forcefully into his room to check on his identity and residence permit. We have learned from previous conversations that the hotel owner tends to call the police on refugees staying in the premises, to make more profit. When Georg escapes by showing Weidel's documents, she and the policemen are visibly astonished. The scene is interrupted by another incident capturing a woman being forcefully arrested and separated from her children, while the other residents witness this silently.

---

20 For more on techno-securitization, see Darren Ellis, "Techno-Securitisation of Everyday Life and Cultures of Surveillance," *Science as Culture* 29, no. 1 (2020): 11–29.

21 Scholars have noted that the use of CCTV footage is a repeated trope in Petzold's films. Olivia Landry calls it "a trademark quality" in his films. Olivia Landry, *Movement and Performance in Berlin School Cinema* (Bloomington: Indiana University Press, 2018), 37. Other scholars have also commented on the connection between surveillance and late modern forms of state power. See Kurt Buhanan, "What's Wrong with this Picture? Image-Ethics in Christian Petzold's Films," *German Quarterly* 89, no. 4 (2016): 480–95; Andrew J. Webber, "The Seen and the Un-seen: Digital Life-time in Christian Petzold's *Etwas Besseres als den Tod* (2011)," *Oxford German Studies* 46, no. 4 (2017): 345–59.

The style is restrained and places attention to the reactions of the observers of this incident, rather than to state violence. This formal asceticism is also toned down by the third-person voice-over, which overpowers the diegetic protests on the part of the woman and the children. It reads: "He saw the others watching like him. Were they without pity? Relieved that it was not them? . . . And he knew what was making everyone so still and hushed: it was shame." The material is rendered more complex by the fact that Petzold opts for conveying the story in a sparse, undramatic manner that indicates the everydayness and routine aspects of these events. This sets his film apart from familiar, melodramatic depictions of fascism as an excess of evil. At the same time, Petzold's choice for natural summer light and vibrant colors produces an antithesis between mise-en-scène and content that intensifies the Kafkaesque dimension of the story.

Petzold's penchant for saturated colors that highlight Marseille's summer creates a visual surplus in the mise-en-scène, quite in line with what Rosalind Galt describes as an aesthetic of cinematic prettiness that produces a form of visual seduction through a surplus of color and light. Galt contests the canonical view according to which aesthetic beauty is associated with an apolitical and superficial cinematic tradition and draws attention to many modernist filmmakers, including Michelangelo Antonioni, Bernardo Bertolucci, and Ulrike Ottinger, amongst others, whose films are characterized by an excessive imagery that does not lessen their political critique.[22] Galt's point provides an apposite context for thinking about *Transit* as a film whose visual surplus reinforces its political impact, since the style produces some contradictory effects. The mise-en-scène generates an excessive visuality, which is in tension with the film's narrative restraint, subject matter, and slow tempo. The visual excess seems to prefigure a dramatic excess, which does not materialize since the narrative remains minimalist and the acting affectless. If anything, there is a certain degree of irony in the manner in which this transit space for refugees—who are facing imminent danger—is depicted in warm, summer colors. In effect, the richly textured staging generates emotional distance heightened by the fact that the storyline privileges mundane rather than dramatic moments, even registering the imminent arrival of the Nazis in a banal way. Petzold revives modernist techniques inherited from the past, which do not simply engage in the critique of the image as the locus of lies. There is instead a different political critique here that points to the everydayness of some of the most horrific events taking place in the warm Marseille summer. The film thus points to the ways the locals as well as the victims of persecution silently acquiesce to the horrors of fascism; the lack of political organization among the latter, who are busy

---

22 See Rosalind Galt, *Pretty: Film and the Decorative Image* (New York: Columbia University Press, 2011), 194–96.

seeking individual salvation, also anaesthetizes them to the plight of the others. This is a central theme in the source text too. Illustrative from this perspective is the narrator's response upon being asked whether he plans to write something about their experiences as refugees. In the following passage, in which one can sense that Seghers is engaging in an act of self-criticism, the narrator responds:

> As a little boy I often went on school trips. The trips were a lot of fun, but then the next day our teacher assigned us a composition on the subject, "Our school trip." And when we came back from summer vacations we always had to write a composition: "How I spent my vacation." And even after Christmas, there was a composition: "Christmas." And in the end it seemed to me that I experienced the school trips, Christmas, the vacations, only so that I could write a composition about them. And all those writers who were in the concentration camp with me, who escaped with me, it seems to me that we lived through these most terrible stretches in our lives just so we could write about them: the camps, the war, escape, and flight.[23]

This form of self-criticism raises questions not just about France's historical complicity in the persecution of Jews during the German occupation, but also about the absence of wider structures of antifascist resistance.

Petzold's penchant for a restrained style that evades melodramatic clichés points to our contemporary acclimatization to structures of exclusion in contemporary Fortress Europe and is therefore in keeping with Seghers's novel, which also aims for an affectless style that deploys a certain distance both in the narration of the bureaucratic hurdles faced by the people in transit and the more intense moments, such as suicides and arrests. In effect, the novel draws attention not so much to the fascist takeover of Europe but to how that takeover turns into a banal experience, to which both the defeated French side and the persecuted exiles become acclimatized. Similarly, the film's restraint and casual registering of dramatically loaded moments, such as state violence and the suicide of a German Jewish woman (Barbara Auer), allow one to think about the correspondences between the past and the present but particularly in the way individuals can acclimatize themselves to repressive conditions.

It is this feature of Petzold's adaptation that makes us think about questions of everyday fascism, not the spectacular fascism of the twentieth century, but the present political anti-pluralism and the exclusionary identity politics of contemporary Europe that cement the social exclusion of populations deemed to be superfluous. As Tamás writes: "Post-fascism does not need storm troopers and dictators. It is perfectly compatible with

23 Seghers, *Transit*, 214.

an anti-Enlightenment liberal democracy that rehabilitates citizenship as a grant from the sovereign instead of a universal human right."[24] His point addresses a key contradiction of liberal democracy committed to the liberation of the economy, which eventually comes at the expense of universal citizenship; the latter cannot be reconciled with the global division of the world into centers and peripheries. If anything, the associations between the past and the present mentioned by Petzold can be seen in view of the ways that the social exclusion of the "superfluous" populations has been naturalized, as I mentioned in the first section of the chapter. The film's layering of multiple temporalities, enmeshing the fascist takeover of Europe in the 1940s and the contemporary violence of Fortress Europe that seeks to strengthen structures of exclusion of non-Europeans, establishes a sense of continuity between the past and the present. Seghers's story is reworked to point to the current historical contradictions and to counter the idea that only liberal democracy can prevent the repeatability of past horrors, a message that seems to be encoded ad nauseam in films about fascism and the Holocaust.

Commenting on the film's complication of temporality and the dialectic between the past and the present, Petzold suggested that *Transit* "is a bit like a dream between the times, and in this dream between the times the old times are passing and also the present times are passing— and they touched each other, and they understand each other."[25] This rather Benjaminian comment urges us to think about the film's temporal in-betweenness. In these terms, Petzold's adaptation does not just rework a story from the canon of German literature to comment on the present. It is well established in scholarship on Petzold that ghosts occupy a decisive place in his oeuvre;[26] after all, three of his films *Die innere Sicherheit* (*The State I am In*, 2000), *Gespenter* (*Ghosts*, 2005), and *Yella* (2007) form the so-called "Ghost trilogy." The topos of the ghost connects the past with the present, but it also signifies absences and losses. While the phantasmatic features of fascism as implied in the film suggest that there are uncomfortable links between the fascist past and the postfascist present, there is also a visible absence that is emblematic of the defeat of the project of radicalized Enlightenment. Consider, for instance, how the lead character decides to join the French Resistance at the end of the novel:

---

24 Tamás, "On Post-Fascism."

25 Daniel Casman, "A Citizen without Civilization: Christian Petzold Discusses 'Transit,'" accessed November 6, 2020, https://mubi.com/notebook/posts/a-citizen-without-civilization-christian-petzold-discusses-transit.

26 See Marco Abel, *The Counter-Cinema of the Berlin School* (Rochester, NY: Camden House, 2013), 70; Jaimey Fisher, *Christian Petzold* (Urbana-Champaign: University of Illinois Press, 2013), 4.

> I intend to share the good and the bad with my new friends here, be it sanctuary or persecution. As soon as there's a resistance movement Marcel and I intend to take up arms. Even if they were to shoot me, they'd never be able to eradicate me. I feel I know this country, its work, its people, its hills and mountains, its peaches and its grapes too well. If you bleed to death on familiar soil, something of you will continue to grow like the sprouts that come up after bushes and trees have been cut down.[27]

This unexpected turn in the story strikes one as unpersuasive, but it is—in line with Seghers's extra-textual persona as a Jewish, antifascist, Communist—committed to the project of universal emancipation. The plot twist operates as an extra-diegetic comment that exceeds the narrative universe. This passage has been omitted by Petzold, who chose to leave the narrative open and end the film with the Talking Heads' song, "Road to Nowhere." This omission and the song's title point to the limits of our epoch, which lacks a credible alternative and a vision for the future. One may be tempted to proclaim that the ghost of the antifascist author of the source text allows the film to bridge the past with the present, but it also makes us aware of the absence of the radical internationalism of what Traverso calls "Jewish modernity,"[28] to which Seghers and the specters of Kafka, Weiss, and Benjamin (all implicitly referenced in *Transit*) belonged. This absence is further highlighted by the fact that in both the novel and the film, the central character chooses to adopt the identity of the persecuted Jewish author, Weidel, whose figure signifies a bygone era of Jewish radical internationalism. While in the historical context of the novel's publication and setting this could be seen as a signal of solidarity, in the present context of the film's production it operates as a utopian gesture that highlights the eclipse of this culture and the visible lack of an internationalist emancipatory project. Utopia literally stands for absence, and it is this absence of an emancipatory political present that becomes manifested in Petzold's film.

---

27 Seghers, *Transit*, 250–51.

28 Traverso uses the term Jewish modernity to describe the vibrant intellectual and political culture instigated by the global Jewish diaspora across Europe. His understanding of Jewish modernity is shaped by an influential essay by the Marxist, Jewish intellectual Isaac Deutscher titled "The non-Jewish Jew." According to Deutscher, the social experience of discrimination faced by many European Jews made them exceed their own Jewish background and tradition and seek radical universal solutions to the impasses of modernity. Figures such as Baruch Spinoza, Karl Marx, Walter Benjamin, Franz Kafka, Rosa Luxemburg, Leon Trotsky, and Sigmund Freud, among many others, exemplify this tradition. See Enzo Traverso, *The End of Jewish Modernity*, trans. David Fernbach (London: Pluto, 2013).

Herein lies the main difference between the source text and its adaptation. Seghers's novel concludes in an optimistic albeit utopian tone, precisely because of the existence at the time of an antifascist political movement that could offer some hope for a politics of resistance. By contrast, Petzold's film does not share a similar sentiment as manifested in the concluding sequence. As such, the film's reformulation of the novel has an element of historical authenticity because it points to the absence of a political alternative that could challenge the fact that fascist ideas of social exclusion have become part of the political mainstream. For as Tamás explains, the normalization of the postfascist reality is contingent on the absence of a narrative of radical critique and political emancipation. This absence of a political alternative restricts the political horizon and imagination of the present. Taking these into account, it is fair to treat Petzold's film as a work of mourning, although not mourning for a vanished past of political resistance but for a present in which organized political resistance against the prevalent anti-Enlightenment rhetoric remains absent. This characteristic of the film is in keeping with Traverso's argument for a polemical left-wing melancholy that is not just committed to the lament of "a lost utopia" but engages in "a fruitful work of mourning" that seeks to reactivate political thinking and action even when the prevalent historical circumstances do not allow it. Rethinking and reevaluating the legacy of antifascist works and their relevance in the present—as Petzold does in his adaptation of Seghers's *Transit*—might be a significant starting point.[29]

Acknowledgments

Research for this chapter was supported by the Arts and Humanities Research Council, Grant Ref: AH/T005750/1 and by an Alexander von Humboldt Fellowship for experienced researchers. This chapter is a reworked version of my discussion of *Transit* in the last section of an article entitled, "Kafkaesque Cinema in the Context of Post-Fascism," in *Modernism/Modernity* 30, no. 3 (2023).

---

29 See Enzo Traverso, *Left-Wing Melancholia: Marxism, History, and Memory* (New York: Columbia University Press, 2016), 20.

Bibliography

Abel, Marco. *The Counter-Cinema of the Berlin School.* Rochester, NY: Camden House, 2013.

Austin, Thomas. "Miserable Journeys, Symbolic Rescues: Refugees and Migrants in the Cinema of Fortress Europe." In *Cinema of Crisis: Film and Contemporary Europe*, edited by Thomas Austin and Angelos Koutsourakis, 198–214. Edinburgh: Edinburgh University Press, 2020.

Bardan, Alice. "'Europe, Spectrality and 'Post-mortem Cinema': The Haunting of History in Christian Petzold's *Transit* (2018) and Aki Kaurismäki's *Le Havre* (2011)." *Northern Lights*, 18, no. 1 (2020): 115–29.

Bataille, Georges. "The Psychological Structure of Fascism." Translated by Carl R. Lovitt. *New German Critique* 16 (1979): 64–87.

Brunner, Philipp. "Filmkritik: Transit," *Filmbulletin: Zeitschrift für Film und Kino* 3 (2018): 31–32.

Buhanan, Kurt. "What's Wrong with this Picture? Image-Ethics in Christian Petzold's Films." *German Quarterly* 89, no. 4 (2016): 480–95.

Casman, Daniel. "A Citizen Without Civilization: Christian Petzold Discusses 'Transit.'" Accessed November 6, 2020. https://mubi.com/notebook/posts/a-citizen-without-civilization-christian-petzold-discusses-transit.

Conrad, Peter. "Introduction." In Anna Seghers, *Transit*. Translated by Margot Bettauer Dembo, vii–xv. New York: New York Review of Books, 2013.

Ellis, Darren. "Techno-securitisation of Everyday life and Cultures of Surveillance." *Science as Culture* 29, no. 1 (2020): 11–29.

Fehervary, Helen. *Anna Seghers: The Mythic Dimension.* Ann Arbor: University of Michigan Press, 2001.

Fisher, Jaimey. *Christian Petzold.* Urbana-Champaign: University of Illinois Press, 2013.

Fletcher, Alex. "History at a Standstill: Migration and Anachronism in Christian Petzold's *Transit*." *Film International* 18, no. 3 (2020): 83–91.

Galt, Rosalind. *Pretty: Film and the Decorative Image.* New York: Columbia University Press, 2011.

Landry, Olivia. "The Beauty and Violence of *Horror Vacui*: Waiting in Christian Petzold's *Transit* (2018)." *German Quarterly* 93, no. 1 (2020): 90–105.

———. *Movement and Performance in Berlin School Cinema.* Bloomington: Indiana University Press, 2018.

Murthi, Vikram. "Christian Petzold on Transit, Kafka, His Love for Den of Thieves and More." Accessed November 3, 2020. https://www.rogerebert.com/interviews/christian-petzold-on-transit-kafka-his-love-for-den-of-thieves-and-more.

Nelson, Max. "'Our Contemporary Winds': Christian Petzold's *Transit*." *Salmagundi* 204 (2019): 38–48.

Petzold, Christian. "Wartime out of Joint." Translated by Becca Voelcker. *Film Comment* 55, no. 1 (2019): 6.

Seghers, Anna. *Transit*. Translated by Margot Bettauer Dembo. New York: New York Review of Books, 2013.

Tamás, Gáspár Miklós. "On Post-Fascism: The Degradation of Universal Citizenship." *Boston Review*. Accessed August 3, 2022. http://bostonreview.net/world/g-m-tamas-post-fascism.

———. "A Postscript to 'Post-Fascism': Preliminary Theses to a System of Fear." *Details* (2011): 57–62.

Traverso, Enzo. *The End of Jewish Modernity*. Translated by David Fernbach. London: Pluto, 2013.

———. *The New Faces of Fascism: Populism and the Far Right*. Translated by David Broder. London: Verso, 2017.

Webber, Andrew J. "The Seen and the Un-seen: Digital Life-time in Christian Petzold's *Etwas Besseres als den Tod* (2011)." *Oxford German Studies* 46, no. 4 (2017): 345–59.

2: "Her mit dem schönen Leben": Happiness and Access in *Berlin Alexanderplatz* (2020)

Priscilla Layne

Introduction

WHEN ALFRED DÖBLIN WROTE *Berlin Alexanderplatz* in 1929, by creating a protagonist (Franz Biberkopf) who was both a war veteran and a former convict, he intentionally focused on a subject on the margins of society: someone whom society had failed.[1] Furthermore, by making gendered violence such an important part of the narrative, Döblin demonstrated that, due to the misogynist nature of ethnonationalism, even those men on the margins could still justify exploiting others to improve their status in society, rather than fighting for real equality. Rather than transferring this ethnonationalism to his recent adaptation of Döblin's novel, the German director of Iranian descent, Burhan Qurbani, interrogates the entitlement attached to white, male, German identity by placing Franz B. even further on the margins of society. Qurbani updates the narrative to better situate it in a late-capitalist, neoliberal and multicultural Germany: Franz B. is now Francis, a Black, undocumented refugee from Bissau.

By choosing to make Francis both Black and undocumented, Qurbani continues a trend he has established in his previous films of centering narratives on vulnerable people existing on the margins of white, mainstream German society, such as the queer Muslim protagonists in his film *Schahada* (*Faith*, 2010) and the Vietnamese immigrants experiencing the violence of reunification in Rostock in *Wir sind jung, wir sind stark* (*We are Young, We are Strong*, 2014). Qurbani, himself the child of Iranian immigrants, was born in 1980 in North-Rhine Westphalia, then in West Germany. Arguably, Qurbani's films demonstrate his interest in allyship that unites different groups of racialized people in Germany. *Berlin Alexanderplatz* draws viewers' attention not only to the problem

---

1   In this essay, since I will discuss both Döblin's novel and Qurbani's film adaptation, I will refer to Döblin's character as Franz B. and Qurbani's as Francis.

of anti-Black racism in Germany, but also to the unique experience of Black noncitizens. While Black people in Germany experience differing degrees of anti-Black racism, Black German citizens and Black people with legal residency have certain protections under the law ranging from the right to vote (in the case of citizens) to the right to education, legal employment, and housing.[2] For the undocumented, however, there are no such protections or possibilities to legally participate in society. While Francis's biography in Qurbani's adaptation allows the director to make a poignant critique of Germany's current migration politics, critics were not always convinced by his execution. In fact, some argued that the film itself is guilty of exploiting Black bodies and reducing African men to their physicality and sexuality.[3]

Another significant difference Qurbani makes is regarding the narrative's main antagonist, Reinhold. In Döblin's novel, Reinhold is a gangster, part of the very criminal milieu Franz B. is trying to escape. Reinhold not only works for the crime boss Pums by participating in his heists, but he is also engaged in the trafficking of women. Reinhold employs the common tactic of masquerading as the women's boyfriend, only to then request they do sex work in order to earn him money. He first ingratiates himself with Franz B. by asking him to take the women he is finished with "off his hands"; a misogynistic euphemism for asking Franz B. to step into the role of boyfriend so that these women forget Reinhold and no longer expect his protection and support. In Qurbani's film, Reinhold is not just a gangster, but a white German man with a (dis)ability that functions as a "narrative prosthesis."[4] Reinhold has been able to compensate for his lack of physical strength by exploiting people who are undocumented and sell drugs for him. But in this neoliberal society, Reinhold is ultimately just a middleman. He punches down on Francis and the various women he consorts with, while fearing the same treatment from the crime kingpin Pums, who frequently denigrates and abuses him. In this chapter, I consider how Qurbani takes the original themes that Döblin explored, namely masculinity, class, and disability, and tells a narrative that has been updated for Germany's neoliberal present. Because Rainer Werner Fassbinder already provided an update to Döblin's novel in 1980

---

2   For more information on anti-Black racism in contemporary Germany, see Natasha Kelly's book *Rassismus: strukturelle Probleme brauchen struturelle Lösungen!* (Zurich: Atrium Verlag, 2021).

3   Tobias Prüwer, "Kommt ein Flüchtling nach Berlin," *Jungle World*, July 30, 2020, https://jungle.world/artikel/2020/31/kommt-ein-fluechtling-nach-berlin; Julius Vapiano, "Nach der Flucht," *Jacobin*, April 27, 2021, https://jacobin.de/artikel/berlin-alexanderplatz-burhan-qurbani-alfred-doeblin-das-neue-evangelium-milo-rau-mittelmeer-flucht/.

4   David Mitchell and Sharon Snyder, "Narrative Prosthesis," in *The Disability Studies Reader*, ed. Lennard J. Davis (New York: Routledge, 2013), 204–18.

34 ♦ Priscilla Layne

with his fourteen-part adaption for German television, I will occasionally draw comparisons between Fassbinder's and Qurbani's treatments of intersectionality.[5]

In *The Critique of Black Reason*, Achille Mbembe argues that it is no longer Blackness that describes the most subaltern position in the world, but surplus humanity, which one can understand as stateless people, people without a right of residency, who anxiously try to reach fortress Europe for a chance at a new life.[6] But the question of surplus humanity is not just about refugees and citizenship; people with disabilities often live below the poverty line, and are expected to work for lower wages if they are able to find a job at all. Döblin's modernist novel is set in a society ruled by class antagonisms: those with capital exploit those without. Döblin portrayed Franz B. as being unable to escape a system stacked against him, because as someone with a criminal record, he could not seem to escape the criminal milieu. But in Qurbani's film, life operates according to neoliberal principles. To update Döblin's narrative for our contemporary times, Qurbani introduces further intersections into the conflict in addition to class and gender, namely race, citizenship, and (dis)ability.

In Qurbani's film, Reinhold has found a way to be able to exploit others, by controlling people without citizenship. But as it turns out, Reinhold's (dis)ability functions as more of a metaphor than something literal. After Francis loses his arm in an accident Reinhold causes, Reinhold's (dis)ability recedes into the background, now that Francis is visibly (dis)abled and Reinhold feels more powerful than him. Francis's tragedy is that he knows "nothing but that index of projected happiness" Reinhold shows him and he feels "compelled to repeat attachment to the very forms whose failure to secure the basic dignities of ordinary existence is central to the reproduction of the difficulty of their singular stories and lived struggle on the bottom of class society in the first place."[7] His friendship with Reinhold represents such an attachment. Qurbani demonstrates that in a neoliberal society, marginalized people are pitted against each other in a struggle to survive, fighting for the crumbs that have been left behind. Ultimately, despite Reinhold's marginalization, he is still a white German citizen who will always have more power than Francis. As Damani Partridge suggests, the only thing possible for undocumented

---

5   There is an earlier film adaptation of the novel from director Phil Jutzi, *Berlin Alexanderplatz* (1931). But I will not be referencing that adaptation as it is concerned with Weimar Germany and not a modern update of Döblin's novel.

6   Achille Mbembe, *The Critique of Black Reason*, trans. Laurent DuBois (Durham, NC: Duke University Press, 2017), 34.

7   Lauren Berlant, *Cruel Optimism* (Durham, NC: Duke University Press, 2011), 166–67.

refugees is "exclusionary incorporation": a politics that otherwise "attempts to maximize the potential of national bodies via good health care, good education, and a reliable defense" willfully neglects noncitizens whose incorporation in society it makes "a challenging, if not dangerous, act."[8] Francis may finally gain Reinhold's recognition, but he will never be an equal participant in German society.

In *Masculinities under Neoliberalism*, Andrea Cornwall describes the particular anxiety felt by men, as "those who have benefitted the most from a political economy of gender shored up by patriarchal ideology that naturalizes gender inequalities."[9] As women, and particularly immigrant women of color, increasingly work low-paid, contingent service and outsourced manufacturing jobs without benefits, men find themselves increasingly unemployed as the "mostly male manufacturing jobs are on the decline."[10] Therefore, although all workers are suffering under these changes, from a patriarchal perspective, men might see women as having an unfair advantage. Cornwall continues: "it is the very reordering of this [gender] binary, its reconfiguration under pressure of the abject failure of millions of men to live up to its injunctions, that is one of the most striking features of contemporary life."[11] Thus the sense of emasculation felt by Franz B. and Reinhold in the novel is only exasperated by the neoliberal condition in the film. Furthermore, because Qurbani introduces the category of racialization into the narrative, it is not simply the case that Reinhold feels threatened by women; he also feels threatened by Black men, especially Francis.[12]

In *Berlin Alexanderplatz* (2022), destabilized masculinity is conveyed through Francis's suffering as he comes up against the "effect of catastrophic impacts" which better describes the neoliberal condition of a Black man who is stateless, unemployed, and trying to not only survive, but also thrive in Germany.[13] Unlike Franz B., whose identity as a felon

---

8   Damani Partridge, *Hypersexuality and Headscarves: Race, Sex, and Citizenship in the New Germany* (Bloomington: Indiana University Press, 2012), 19.

9   Andrea Cornwall, "Introduction," in *Masculinities under Neoliberalism*, ed. Andrea Cornwall, Frank G. Karioris, and Nancy Lindisfarne (London: Zed Books, 2016), 9.

10   Cornwall, "Introduction," 9.

11   Cornwall, "Introduction," 9.

12   Cornwall's observations about masculinity during neoliberalism resonate with Hester Baer's insightful analysis of Wolfgang Petersen's film *The Boat* (1981). In *The Boat*, destabilized masculinity is conveyed via a crisis of masculinity tied to the Deleuzian crisis of action in films following the Second World War. The Nazi sailors in the submarine are not men of action; they spend much of their time waiting and not knowing what is happening. Hester Baer, *German Cinema in the Age of Neoliberalism* (Amsterdam: Amsterdam University Press, 2021), 23.

13   Berlant, *Cruel Optimism*, 9.

at the start of the novel is the result of his violent actions—murdering his girlfriend—Francis's "crime" is his very existence. As an undocumented immigrant, Francis has no legal rights to be within Germany's—and therefore the EU's—borders. Thus, while Döblin's novel begins with Franz B.'s release from prison, standing in front of the prison's gates and hoping to embark on a new life, Qurbani's film begins with Francis struggling to swim in the Mediterranean, attempting to reach Europe's shores.

How Does It Feel to Be a Problem?

Many of the reasons why Döblin's original protagonist, Franz B., existed on the margins of society stemmed from his time in jail. As a convicted felon, Franz B. has difficulty finding a job, which makes it equally difficult for him to secure housing and establish some stability in his life. During the Weimar Republic, when the novel is set, "prison seemed to be a vehicle for the creation of criminals, not their reformation. Providing them with criminal records barred the way to regular employment had they wished to take it, while the company of other prisoners cemented their sense of criminal identity."[14]

Structurally, Franz B. and Francis are on two completely different planes, due to Francis's status as a Black, undocumented immigrant. Part of how Qurbani changes the narrative is to disrupt its linearity. Döblin's narrator is typical for the genre of new objectivity. He provides us with factual information, while also giving us a glimpse into Franz B.'s thoughts and feelings. Döblin utilizes a narrator to create sympathy for Franz B. The narrator isn't omniscient, but he raises rhetorical questions to encourage readers to contemplate Franz B.'s state of mind. Rather than looking down on him as merely a convicted felon and a murderer, Döblin invites us to try to understand how it might feel for someone like Franz B. to leave prison after so many years and try to establish a life as a free man. Döblin's narrator often raises these rhetorical questions in parentheses: "The awful moment was at hand (awful, why so awful, Franz?), his four years were up. The black iron gates he'd been eyeing with increasing revulsion (revulsion, why revulsion) for the past year swung shut behind him."[15] The questions raised in parentheses are the questions the narrator models for us. We should be asking ourselves the same thing, in order to better understand Franz B.'s psychology.

---

14 Richard J. Evans, "Social Outsiders in German History: From the Sixteenth Century to 1933," in *Social Outsiders in Nazi Germany*, ed. Robert Gellately and Nathan Stoltzfus (Princeton, NJ: Princeton University Press, 2001), 29.

15 Alfred Döblin, *Berlin Alexanderplatz*, trans. Michael Hofmann (New York: New York Review of Books, 2008), 5.

Qurbani attempts to accomplish something similar, only the new beginning that Francis experiences is not leaving jail but migrating from Africa to Europe by crossing the Mediterranean. His migration across the sea is a dangerous journey; there is the possibility that, like so many others, he may not survive. Furthermore, by crossing through water, it also symbolizes a kind of rebirth. Arriving in Europe can bring new possibilities for Francis. But as a result of how this journey is filmed, it is accompanied by an ominous feeling.

Rather than giving us a visual of Francis's passage, the film begins with a silent black screen and white credits, which are suddenly interrupted by heavy breathing. It is disorienting. We don't know who is breathing or what circumstance they find themselves in. Soon after, we hear a woman whisper Francis's name. This woman will be the equivalent of Döblin's Mieze; a woman whom Franz B. meets after his accident, who helps rehabilitate him by making him feel like a man again. In both the novel and the film, Mieze is a sex worker who shares her profits and her apartment with Franz B.; only in the film she works under a name that is the English equivalent, "Kitty." Thus the character has a new *English* name for a new globalized economy. Mieze is both Francis's savior and his downfall, because although meeting her is finally what convinces him to leave crime behind, it will come at a cost: her death while pregnant with his child and Francis's imprisonment. Because Qurbani's film is not linear, he can utilize Mieze's own empathetic voice in place of Döblin's nameless empathetic narrator, as a way to foreshadow what challenges Francis will face. Mieze informs us that Francis comes to Berlin and "stumbles and falls three times. [And] how he always gets up and finally breaks in this city," thus mirroring Döblin's narrative. Because of this non-linear storytelling we know that Francis and Mieze will eventually have a romantic relationship; we also know that Mieze will not survive. By having her narrate his story, in contrast to Döblin's novel, she brings even more empathy toward Francis. But because of how her voice-over mirrors Döblin's rhetorically intrusive narrator, it also has an uncanny effect for viewers.

As the film opens, Francis and an unidentified Black woman speak in a foreign language. The language is neither identified nor translated. Francis refers to the woman as "meu amor," implying that they are lovers and German is not their native language. Francis is very likely speaking Portuguese, the official language of his country of origin, Guinea Bissau. By not translating the Portuguese, Qurbani suggests that we are not privy to Francis's thoughts prior to arriving in Germany. There will always be part of Francis's background that is inaccessible to us. When we finally get our first visuals, Francis and the woman are floating in water in darkness. A red flare in the sky illuminates them, but the perspective is disorienting; they are upside down, as if floating in the sky. They are struggling to keep their heads above the water. She begs Francis to save her. But she goes underwater several times and eventually does not resurface. In later flashbacks we learn that when the woman started struggling to swim, she held onto Francis, pulling him underwater. In order to save himself, he struck her, and she fell unconscious, sinking further in the water after letting him go. While Franz B. is a newly released convicted felon, possibly scarred from mistreatment in prison and worried about what future prospects he has, Francis carries the weight of multiple traumas: whatever forced him to leave his home, his experience of migration, and the fact that he chose to save himself rather than try to save his lover. According to Francis, this is why he is not a good person.

But his arrival in Europe is at first positioned as a possibility for a new life. Francis emerges from the water and walking onto the beach, appearing like someone reborn. As Mieze states in the narration, this was his chance for a new life. And because of the people he lost during his journey, he swears to be good from now on—suffering from a kind of survivor's guilt. Like many people with PTSD who survive a traumatic event, Francis does not understand why he survived and others perished. Promising to be "good" helps him make some sense of his experience. According to his rationalized account of events, the others died because they were not worthy of being saved; if he can be good, he will prove himself worthy of continuing to live. But what does it mean to be "good," especially in a society where one's existence is always already illegal?

Neoliberalism and Happiness

This desire to be "good," or in German to be an "anständiger Mensch" (a decent person), is what unites Francis with his predecessor Franz B. For Franz B. in the 1920s, being "anständig" primarily meant leaving criminality behind him. In 2020, "anständig" also links to Lauren Berlant's description of "the good life." This is not only the fantasy of being decent held by Franz B., it is also about the security people came to know in the postwar 1950s and 1960s. But, as Berlant warns us, this fantasy has atrophied due to the systematic dismantling of the social safety net. As Berlant writes:

> The fantasies that are fraying include, particularly, upward mobility, job security, political and social equality, and lively, durable intimacy. The set of dissolving assurances also includes meritocracy, the sense that liberal-capitalist society will reliably provide opportunities for individuals to carve out relations of reciprocity that seem fair and

that foster life as a project of adding up to something and constructing cushions for enjoyment.[16]

But Francis is not exactly like the film protagonists that Berlant discusses in *Cruel Optimism*, whose "possible desires ha[ve] been pared down to a friend and a job, a state of attaining some bare minimum of social recognition."[17] Francis believes that happiness cannot simply come from the everyday. He wants to stand out. This is why, when we first encounter Francis at the start of the film, Mieze tells us in German: "Franz desires more from life than just a bed and buttered bread"; a line Reinhold will repeat in English, when he tries to recruit undocumented Black men to sell drugs for him. This is a further aspect that sets Francis apart from Döblin's Franz B. In Döblin's novel, Franz B. stumbles into the work of being a pimp. First Reinhold uses him to get rid of girls he is no longer interested in. Then, after Reinhold throws him from a moving car, Franz B. finds life is sweeter when he lives off of Mieze's sex work, rather than selling newspapers.

In contrast to Franz B., Qurbani's Francis does not try to avoid employment, and it is not a criminal act that makes him unemployable. As a refugee and undocumented immigrant, his main obstacle is that he cannot find legal employment even if he wanted it. This is why, when he does find employment, he is perpetually exploited. We see him working the kind of jobs typically available for undocumented workers in a shadow economy, for example working on a construction site, in a tunnel. In such a job, only the view of the Fernsehturm on the horizon reminds Francis that he is in Berlin. He works underground, in the darkness, with other men who are undocumented and scared to speak up against their own exploitation, for fear of being fired or worse: deported. Francis also lives in a home for undocumented migrants who are awaiting decisions on their cases and hope to achieve the "beautiful life" that neoliberal Western societies promise but cannot deliver on.

Masculinity and (Dis)ability

In Döblin's novel, Reinhold, Franz B.'s alter ego, is not someone described with a physical (dis)ability, but he is described as someone who stutters. And this might be the disarming part of his identity that makes someone like Franz B. not initially recognize how dangerous he could potentially be. Qurbani takes this hint of a (dis)ability and turns it into something physical and visually apparent. When we first encounter

16 Berlant, *Cruel Optimism*, 3.
17 Berlant, *Cruel Optimism*, 162.

Figure 2.1. Francis and Otoo enter the elevator where Reinhold is already waiting.

Reinhold in Qurbani's film, he is visiting the asylum seekers' home where Francis lives and he is standing in the elevator, before Francis and his co-worker Otoo enter. Reinhold can be seen facing the camera, holding onto his lower back with his left hand, bent over holding onto the railing in the elevator with his right hand (see Fig. 2.1). He is wearing a baseball cap that is pulled down over his eyes, hiding his face. His physique is lost in his baggy, tan jacket. He is unassuming and non-threatening, especially in contrast to the two Black men stepping onto the elevator who are coming from the communal shower, wearing only towels, and whose muscular torsos present a striking contrast to Reinhold. This is one of several instances in the film where Qurbani plays with German desires for and fears of Black masculinity and compares and contrasts Reinhold with the Black men whom he seeks to dominate for his own feelings of self-worth.[18] But it can also be seen as an instance where Qurbani himself puts Black masculinity on display in a manner that is exploitative.

Reinhold immediately addresses Francis in English: "You are new here. Where you from?" Speaking to Francis in English is a power move, by which Reinhold demonstrates his own cosmopolitanism and his assumption that Francis does not speak German fluently. Otoo snaps back at Reinhold, "Leave him alone. This one isn't for you." By referring to

---

18 In Kaja Silvermann's reading of the dynamic between Franz and Reinhold in Fassbinder's adaptation of *Berlin Alexanderplatz*, Reinhold's desire/hatred for Franz refers to a repressed homosexual desire. I do not doubt that Qurbani reproduces this possibility that can be found in Döblin's novel and Fassbinder's adaptation. However, in Qurbani's film, this desire/hatred for Francis is *also* entangled with racist thoughts and colonial fantasies, such as when Reinhold sends Francis an ape costume to wear to a costume ball, where he then shows up dressed like a colonial explorer.

Francis as "this one" instead of "he," Otoo turns Francis from a subject into an object. His choice of words acknowledges that, for Reinhold, Francis is in fact an object to be exploited and exchanged for money and power; much like the women he will eventually ask Francis for help with. Since Otoo has been at the asylum seekers' home longer than Francis, he knows Reinhold is sizing Francis up like a new specimen at a slave auction. Unfortunately, Francis is not open to receiving Otoo's warnings because at the construction site where they both work, he views Otoo as too weak to stand up for his rights. Reinhold may appear physically weak, but the money he will soon flash in front of Francis and the other African men will be enough to impress them. Reinhold's main strategy for disarming the men at the asylum seekers' home is by using his physicality. His hunched over stance makes him appear smaller. He stutters and states: "I have a funny voice," even inviting the men to "laugh about it."

Thus, though Reinhold is a white, German man, he leads the Black men to believe he is not the kind of white, German man who is more powerful than them or seeks to dominate them. They can tell that they could physically overpower him. Furthermore, he is actually a white German man who claims to be sympathetic to their struggles. He states to them *in English*: "No one deserves to live like this. When I look at you, I see young, strong, proud men who are tired of sitting here and doing nothing. You want a decent life. Ein anständiges Leben." His use of the German phrase "ein anständiges Leben" directly cites Döblin, who uses "anständig" (decent) several times in his novel. Moreover, stating this in German suggests that it is a concept that is not necessarily translatable. Reinhold's statement also appeals to their sense of masculinity. No man wants to feel useless; a feeling that is especially prevalent in a neoliberal society where masculine jobs that require physical labor are on the decline. This is enough to make the Black men be open to his proposition. He never directly tells them what he is proposing—that they sell drugs in the park—he merely flashes a handful of cash and promises them a better life. He knows that the conditions in the asylum seekers' home are so desperate, that some of them may be willing to take a chance on the unknown.

As a (dis)abled, white man, Reinhold can suggest a structural similarity between himself and the undocumented workers he preys on. Just like them, he has a physical difference that leads others to underestimate him, exclude him, and not give him opportunities on the job market. Even the criminal boss he works for, Pums, underestimates and disparages him. By flashing his money and wealth, Reinhold conveys the message that if this white man on the margins could become successful in whatever line of work he is peddling, perhaps these undocumented migrants can, too. And because he is (dis)abled, maybe he will not be as threatening as the German foremen who currently lord over them at their construction jobs.

42 ♦ Priscilla Layne

Yet, despite his apparent (dis)ability, Reinhold still commands the privilege of whiteness and citizenship.

Violence, Gender, and Exchangeability

One of the important connections between Qurbani's film and Döblin's novel is the treatment of women and how women are objectified and exploited for their exchange value. Despite the clear differences between Franz B. and Francis, one thing they do share is a discomfort with women and challenging relationships with women. Franz B. is a rapist, predator, and murderer who is guilty of assaulting several women throughout the novel. Franz B. is not described as conventionally attractive, but there is still something about him that draws women to him. In this manner, Döblin points to not only the prevalence of violence against women in the society, but how much women are both accustomed and drawn to this violence. In contrast, Qurbani's Francis has both charisma *and* good looks and he is generally respectful toward women—aside from two occasions on which he becomes violent. In Qurbani's film, the reason Reinhold even thinks that Francis could be useful for helping him with his "lady troubles" is because women are so clearly sexually attracted to Francis. In this way, Qurbani frequently relies on stereotypes about Black men's virility and hypersexuality, including presenting several intimate scenes of Francis having sex, in order to make Francis even more of a threat to Reinhold. One of the problematic motifs that occurs is, for example, how the editing process often draws comparisons between Francis and a raging bull. Nevertheless, despite the emphasis on Francis's sexuality, he also struggles with it at times.[19]

We first witness that Francis has some trauma around sexual encounters when Amira, one of the Black women from the asylum seekers' home who does sex work, follows him into the woods while he is practicing his pronunciation of German words. As he strolls through the woods, he repeats words to himself like "schwarz" (black) and "Haut" (skin). Her flirtatious behavior, as she coyishly weaves in and out of trees and smiles back at him, is reminiscent of the love scene between the white embodiment of postwar Germany, Maria Braun, and her Black GI lover, Bill, in Fassbinder's *The Marriage of Maria Braun*. That love story had a deadly ending for Bill. Maria was willing to sacrifice their subversive, interracial love for the possibility of power and success within a racist, patriarchal system. Similarly, this scene in *Berlin Alexanderplatz* also has a negative ending, because it is not an "innocent" story of a man and woman falling in love, despite the typical setting of the *locus amoenus.*

---

19 On the perception of Black men's sexuality in German society, see Partridge, *Hypersexuality and Headscarves.*

As undocumented immigrants, Amira and Francis are certainly capable of falling in love with each other; but this possibility is complicated by how they are overdetermined by gender, sexuality, and race in a country where they have little power or stability. Because Francis believes that Amira is attracted to him purely for romantic reasons, he becomes offended when she asks him for money.[20] The reality is that any number of things might be motivating Amira in this moment. She may be both attracted to Francis *and* be using sex work as a way to find some economic security. This is stressed when she states to Francis in English, "I only sleep with men I like," thus asserting her agency. This will prove to be in stark contrast with a later scene, which depicts even Amira falling prey to Reinhold, doing sex work in conditions that are much more dehumanizing and strip her of agency, as she lies motionless beneath a white male customer, with a look of desperation in her eyes.

It is during the scene in the woods with Amira, when she attempts to perform oral sex on Francis, that we get our first inkling that he has experienced trauma around sexual acts. The music grows discordant to mirror his discomfort. Her homophobic comments to him, "Are you gay? Don't worry, I'm going to fix you," only make things worse. She mocks him: "You fucking faggot. You're not a real man." When he stops her by placing his hands around her neck, it is a foreshadowing of how Reinhold will murder Mieze. The mirroring Qurbani establishes suggests that, just as Francis's masculinity is threatened by Amira, Reinhold's masculinity will be threatened by Mieze, and both men use violence as a solution. Amira does not back down, even when Francis lets go and runs off through the woods. She yells "You're not a real man. Run, yes run" and her laugh echoes as he runs through the forest, thus giving this scene the feel of a horror film. The scene introduces one of the central themes that the film borrows from Döblin's novel: hegemonic masculinity, how it is defined, policed, and what happens when someone fails to fulfil the requirements.

Despite Amira's allegations that he must be gay—and the central role homosexuality plays in Fassbinder's film adaptation of the novel—in Qurbani's film one has a sense that Francis suffers under the weight of how his body is overdetermined by race. As Damani Partridge has pointed out, in Germany African men are often objectified and viewed as purely sexual beings. This is how Francis is treated when, at the start of the film's second part, he seeks refuge at Reinhold's place after he beats Otoo in

---

20 When Amira asks him if he works with the other men and does "hard work," he responds in German "Ja, harte Arbeit" (yes, hard work), a line that is reminiscent of another one of Fassbinder's films, *Angst essen Seele auf* (*Ali: Fear Eats the Soul*, 1974). Such citations confirm that Qurbani is citing not only Döblin, but Fassbinder's work as well. This citation therefore foreshadows the fate that will befall Mieze.

a rage and can no longer return to the asylum seekers' home. While in Döblin's novel, Reinhold simply utilizes Franz B. to take women "off of his hands" by distracting them with attention and gifts, in Qurbani's film Reinhold uses Francis's body as a surrogate when he feels he cannot satisfy a woman's sexual desires.

With women, Reinhold also initially adopts the same unassuming stance by resting his (dis)abled, left hand on his hip and crouching over slightly, making himself seem smaller and non-threatening. But we soon learn that this performance of weakness is as much of an act as his earlier appearance in the asylum seekers' home. Once he has successfully taken control of someone he sees as subordinate to him, whether one of the Black male "stash boys" or "cash boys," as he calls them, or a woman, he becomes physically and psychologically abusive. As soon as Reinhold is finished with a woman, he demands that she leaves and becomes violent if she does not. This is what happens on Francis's first night staying with Reinhold, when he hears an altercation while standing outside of Reinhold's bedroom door. This is the first time Reinhold asks Francis to occupy a woman, Anni, once he has grown tired of her. Francis was able to calm Reinhold down, so Reinhold believes he can do the same for Anni. For Reinhold, women are objects to be conquered and collected. Once he is finished with them, he has no desire to have any kind of relationship with them; he simply wants to discard them.

Castration and Emasculation

One of the most important turning points in the novel is when Reinhold pushes Franz B. from a moving car, which results in a life-threatening injury and Franz B. losing his right arm. In pushing him from a car, Reinhold punishes Franz B. for his unconventional masculinity: the latter was too afraid to take part in a heist. In Qurbani's film, however, Francis's relationship with Reinhold is ultimately informed by his intersectional identity as a Black, undocumented immigrant; Reinhold is therefore threatened by Francis's appearance, which he sees as "too masculine," so he chooses to maim him. As soon as Francis moves in with Reinhold, it becomes apparent that Reinhold is threatened by Francis, but he couches his abuse as trying to teach Francis a "lesson"; the lesson that his fantasy of an "anständiges Leben" no longer exists. And even after Reinhold throws him from the car and he barely survives, thanks to a brief hospital stay and both Eva and Mieze's help rehabilitating him, Francis still finds his way back to Reinhold. Francis's relationship with Reinhold is the kind of attachment Berlant describes as "optimistic." Berlant writes:

> All attachments are optimistic. When we talk about an object of desire, we are really talking about a cluster of promises we

want someone or something to make to us and make possible for us. This cluster of promises could seem embedded in a person, a thing, an institution, a text, a norm, a bunch of cells, smells, a good idea—whatever.[21]

The cluster of promises Reinhold represents for Francis are both concrete and abstract. Concretely, Reinhold has promised Francis he will obtain a German passport for him. Due to his undocumented status, a German passport represents a realm of possibilities for Francis; the right to work and to permanently remain in Germany. Abstractly, Reinhold represents the person who will help Francis gain recognition in German society; help him become *human*.

This promise is conveyed in a particular scene, prior to Francis's accident, when he is still living with Reinhold, who gives him his German moniker *Franz*. Francis's foreignness and the exoticization of his person emphasize his femininity, as is articulated when one of Reinhold's female guests, Karie, remarks to him: "Francis, what kind of a name is that? It sounds like a woman." The other woman present, Moni, states, "So heißt doch kein Mensch," which can be roughly translated as "no one is called that," though literally it means: "no person [or human] is called that." The wording in the German is significant. Here, the film thus foregrounds the issue of dehumanization through explicit emphasis in the dialogue. Moni could have easily stated: "So heißt doch keiner" (no one is called that). But she uses the word *Mensch*, and Francis responds to her as if she is questioning his humanity due to his distance from a German, masculine ideal: "Meinst Du, ich bin kein Mensch?" (Do you mean I'm not a person?). This can be understood within a larger, social-historical context regarding the history of scientific racism in Germany. The dehumanization of racialized people, entailed by eighteenth-century philosophical discussions in Europe, helped contribute to the very first theories of race and created a hierarchy of humanity, in which Black people were at the very bottom, considered barely human. Thus, though Francis is being playful in this scene, his question could also be taken more seriously, asking: "Is a Black, undocumented immigrant not seen as a human being in contemporary Germany?" Reinhold's response further emphasizes the racism implied in this conversation. He suggests Francis must become human by receiving a *German* name. This is how Francis becomes *Franz*, further inheriting the "destiny" of his predecessor in Döblin's novel. Reinhold says: "I baptize you Franz, human-being. Amen. Amen." But his repetition of "amen" eventually turns into "a man," thus solidifying the idea that in order for Francis to be fully recognized as not just a human, but

---

21 Berlant, *Cruel Optimism*, 23.

46 ♦ PRISCILLA LAYNE

a man, he must be German.[22] But why would Francis even want to be included in the human ideal as it has been created by white Europeans? Perhaps Francis should instead strive to be something else in the Black diasporic tradition of anti-humanism or post-humanism.

In *Black Skin, White Masks*, Frantz Fanon warns that Black men who seek recognition from white society will never have these desires fulfilled. Fanon writes: "I am overdetermined from the outside. I am a slave not to the 'idea' others have of me, but to my appearance."[23] In Francis's case, it takes Reinhold's murder of Mieze for him to understand that due to the structural differences between them, they can never be equals. In fact, in the second half of the film, after Francis loses his arm, he has to become even more violent in order to assert power and control over those who would otherwise try to dominate him due to his (dis)ability. But, as Francis learns what it means to survive in Berlin's criminal milieu as a (dis)abled Black man, Reinhold's (dis)ability, his *narrative prosthesis*, gradually disappears. He no longer has a limp and no longer slouches or favors his right hand. In the first three parts of the film, Reinhold's (dis) ability stood in as a metaphor for his insecure masculinity: his poor and troubled upbringing, his weakness, his fear of Pums and Francis, and his inability to keep his drug dealers in line. Now that he has brainwashed Francis into being his loyal fighter and murdered Pums in order to take over the business, he feels confident, and this confidence radiates through his body and his upright stature. The Reinhold we encounter toward the end of the film walks with a straight back, not hunched over. He no longer wears a baseball cap to hide his face; rather he shows off a new coiffed and dyed hairdo.

Both in the novel and in Qurbani's film, what ultimately ends Franz B./Francis's opportunity for happiness is Reinhold's interference in his relationship with Mieze. In the film, Reinhold cannot bear to allow Mieze to break his hold on Francis. And it is only when Francis realizes that Reinhold has killed Mieze that he is willing to turn on him. But this change in feeling comes too late, after he is arrested in the park for dealing drugs. Francis, fighting with his guilt and his inner demons regarding what happened to Mieze, fantasizes about doing to Reinhold exactly what

---

22 This naming ceremony could also be read as a subversion of the "Neptune ceremony," a maritime rite of passage performed upon crossing the equator that functioned to constitute sailor masculinity. David Cashman, "King Neptune, the Mermaids and the Cruise Tourists: The Line-crossing Ceremony in Modern Passenger Shipping," *Coolabah* 27 (2019): 92. The assumption was, by crossing the equator, you became someone else. In the case of *Berlin Alexanderplatz*, Francis has crossed the equator from the south to the north, thus he has become another person and now needs a German moniker.

23 Frantz Fanon, *Black Skin, White Masks*, trans. Richard Philcox (New York: Grove Press, 2008), 95.

Reinhold did to Mieze, strangling him to death, a very intimate and personal kind of killing.

But the film does not end with Francis's fantasy of strangling Reinhold in prison, nor with Reinhold's eventual imprisonment for killing a female lover. Instead, the film ends where the novel begins. We see Francis on the day he is released from Tegel prison after he has finished serving time. While Döblin's protagonist does not learn from his second chance, we have more hope for Francis. Francis has something to live for, precisely what, according to Berlant, a person needs in this postcapitalist landscape. His daughter with Mieze survived the brutal attack on her mother, and she waits for him with his Black German friend Eva as he exits the prison. Mieze's narration informs us: "A small miracle bestows upon him fate . . . a new life in a new world."

In Qurbani's film, Francis's idea of a "good life" first means to have a German passport and work, then it comes to mean his child. Francis smiles at the end of the film, either because he believes he can finally achieve "the good life" for the sake of his daughter and/or his daughter represents all of the hopes and dreams he could not accomplish previously. She is born a German citizen and speaks fluent German. Perhaps Francis—now Franz—thinks the doors that were closed to him will be open to her: this is precisely what he suggested to Eva when he compared his racialized status to hers. But the reality is that Franz's daughter will not necessarily be able to live up to these hopes and dreams, because the same neoliberal society that created the circumstances that dehumanized Francis will still be in place for his daughter.

The film ends with Francis sitting at the Neptunbrunnen (Neptune Fountain) in the Park am Fernsehturm (park at the TV tower) near Alexanderplatz in Berlin. When the Neptune Fountain was built in 1891, it was meant to be a symbol of Prussian and therefore German might. The four female statues surrounding Neptune represent the four main rivers of the empire—the Rhein, the Weichsel, the Oder, and the Elbe. But now, thanks to the new borders drawn after the Second World War, one of these rivers is in Poland while one borders Poland. Thus, what was once constructed in honor of German might is now an anachronism. The anachronistic symbolism of the fountain is also reflected in the current debate around its possible relocation.[24] In a twenty-first-century Germany that faces economic woes connected to globalization, rising populism and nationalism, and wars in neighboring countries, the question of where to place this fountain seems unimportant.

---

24 Ulrich Paul, "Katrin Lompscher: Neptunbrunnen am jetzigen Standort gut aufgehoben," *Berliner Zeitung*, January 21, 2017, https://www.berliner-zeitung.de/mensch-metropole/katrin-lompscher-neptunbrunnen-am-jetzigen-standort-gut-aufgehoben-li.34606.

48 ♦ Priscilla Layne

This contentious past, and the association between Neptune and transformation, are perhaps the reasons why the film ends at the Neptune Fountain. In contrast to the beginning of the film, Francis no longer looks like a refugee struggling to survive. He now wears a suit and seems to have a "decent" job that allows him to experience life in Berlin during the day, not at night, underground, or doing something illegal in the park. Prior to the final fissure of their relationship, Reinhold kept his promise and gave Francis a German passport. Francis believes that citizenship will solve the problems of anti-Blackness and therefore, here at the end of this film, he believes he, or at least his daughter and he along with her, have made it. In the film's final shot, therefore, Francis sits at the fountain, looks up, and smiles at the Fernsehturm. The aerial view of the fountain locates it in the middle of a meticulous and orderly garden, perhaps suggesting Francis has adapted to German society. Nevertheless, there is also a certain circularity present. The high angle shot recalls the shot we saw of Francis at the very beginning of the film, when he first arrived in Germany. The Neptune Fountain is also the place Francis brought a fellow worker who was injured on a construction site, an action that resulted in him being fired and having to turn to Reinhold. Thus, with this circularity, the film undermines the happy ending it appears to present us with. By the end, what Francis still fails to comprehend is the effect of anti-Blackness on citizens and noncitizens alike. Rather than the *only* thing standing between Francis and his sought-after happiness, Reinhold was just a symptom of a larger, systemic problem. And there is no reason for us to believe that Francis has learned this lesson. Instead, just like Franz B. at the end of Döblin's novel, Francis joins the ranks of German society—an alignment signified by the aerial shot of others who keep marching along, no match for a system that will keep going with or without them. Qurbani's ending mirrors Döblin's pessimism: "*one stops still, the other falls down, one runs on, the other lies still, widdeboom, widdeboom.*"[25]

25 Döblin, *Berlin Alexanderplatz*, 439.

Bibliography

Baer, Hester. *German Cinema in the Age of Neoliberalism*. Amsterdam: Amsterdam University Press, 2021.

Berlant, Lauren. *Cruel Optimism*. Durham, NC: Duke University Press, 2011.

Cashman, David. "King Neptune, the Mermaids and the Cruise Tourists: The Line-crossing Ceremony in Modern Passenger Shipping." *Coolabah* 27 (2019): 90–105.

Cornwall, Andrea. "Introduction." In *Masculinities under Neoliberalism*, edited by Andrea Cornwall, Frank G. Karioris, and Nancy Lindisfarne, 1–28. London: Zed Books, 2016.

Döblin, Alfred. *Berlin Alexanderplatz*. Translated by Michael Hofmann. New York: New York Review of Books, 2008.

Evans, Richard J. "Social Outsiders in German History: From the Sixteenth Century to 1933." In *Social Outsiders in Nazi Germany*, edited by Robert Gellately and Nathan Stoltzfus, 20–44. Princeton, NJ: Princeton University Press, 2001.

Fanon, Frantz. *Black Skin, White Masks*. Translated by Richard Philcox. New York: Grove Press, 2008.

Kelly, Natasha. *Rassismus: Strukturelle Probleme brauchen struturelle Lösungen!* Zurich: Atrium Verlag, 2021.

Mbembe, Achille. *The Critique of Black Reason*. Translated by Laurent DuBois. Durham, NC: Duke University Press, 2017.

Mitchell, David, and Sharon Snyder. "Narrative Prosthesis." In *The Disability Studies Reader*, edited by Lennard J. Davis, 204–18. New York: Routledge, 2013.

Partridge, Damani. *Hypersexuality and Headscarves: Race, Sex, and Citizenship in the New Germany*. Bloomington: Indiana University Press, 2012.

Paul, Ulrich. "Katrin Lompscher: Neptunbrunnen am jetzigen Standort gut aufgehoben." *Berliner Zeitung*, January 21, 2017. https://www.berlinerzeitung.de/menschmetropole/katrin-lompscher-neptunbrunnen-am-jetzigen-standort-gut-aufgehoben-li.34606.

Prüwer, Tobias. "Kommt ein Flüchtling nach Berlin." *Jungle World*, July 30, 2020. https://jungle.world/artikel/2020/31/kommt-ein-fluecht ling-nach-berlin.

Silverman, Kaja. *Male Subjectivity at the Margins*. London: Routledge, 1992.

Vapiano, Julius. "Nach der Flucht." *Jacobin*, April 27, 2021. https://jacobin. de/artikel/berlin-alexanderplatz-burhan-qurbani-alfred-doeblin-das-neue-evangelium-milo-rau-mittelmeer-flucht/.

3: Negative Futurability and the Politics of Pessimism in Fatih Akın's *Aus dem Nichts* (2017)

Gozde Naiboglu

IN RECENT YEARS, themes of racist violence and far-right terrorism have become prominent in German narrative film and television. Fatih Akın's political drama *Aus dem Nichts* (*In the Fade*, 2017) is the most internationally showcased and prize-winning example of such works, which also include Burhan Qurbani's *Wir sind jung. Wir sind stark* (*We Are Young, We Are Strong*, 2014) and *Berlin Alexanderplatz* (2020), Christian Schwochow's *Je suis Karl* (2021), as well as Christian Alvart's Netflix series *Dogs of Berlin* (2016), ARD Das Erste's three-part miniseries *Mitten in Deutschland: NSU* (*NSU: German History X*, 2016), and several episodes of ARD's *Tatort* (Crime Scene, since 1970).[1] Many of these films and series directly or indirectly reference the murders committed by the neo-Nazi terrorist organization Nationalsozialistischer Untergrund (National Socialist Underground) across Germany between 1998 and 2011, and the subsequent investigations and trials of the case, which concluded in July 2018. In so doing, they pose a range of ethical and political questions pertaining to the issue of racist violence in Germany today; and yet because they largely lack resolution, these films and series refuse to offer reconciliation and thereby ultimately convey a sense of political pessimism. However, the politics of pessimism found in many of these works is far from nihilism, and it is distinct from a pessimistic outlook for a future politics. Instead, it promotes withdrawal, negativity, and a refusal of reconciliation as positive political pursuits: not pessimistic prognoses for politics, but pessimism as politics.

In this chapter, I examine the politics of pessimism in *Aus dem Nichts*, situating the film within the context of Fatih Akın's filmography. I identify a darker turn in his experimentations with the aesthetics of abjection,

---

1   Notable examples of recent *Tatort* episodes that feature themes of neo-Nazism and the extreme right include *Hydra* (dir. Nicole Weegman, 2015), *Sonnenwende* (Solstice, dir. Umut Dag, 2018), and *Borowski und die Angst der weißen Männer* (Borowski and the Anxiety of White Men, dir. Nicole Weegman, 2021).

which Akın has already deployed to various degrees in his earlier films, culminating in his subsequent film, the Fassbinder-inspired, serial-killer biopic *Der goldene Handschuh* (*The Golden Glove*, 2019). *Aus dem Nichts* saturates its cinematic world with negative affect, evoking Germany's recent political past with nonliteral references to the NSU investigations and the ensuing trial. My focus is on the political potentials of this radical pessimism. Adapting the concept of "futurability" from the Italian autonomist philosopher and media theorist Franco "Bifo" Berardi,[2] I argue that *Aus dem Nichts* posits its vision of negative futurability through its protagonist Katja in her search for justice, ultimately ending in murder-suicide. For Bifo, futurability refers to the "multiplicity of immanent possible futures," and it can be traced in the present as a tendency, "a sort of premonition, a vibrational movement of particles that are taken in an uncertain process of continuous combination."[3] Futurability is inscribed in the present in terms of "absolute necessity, relative necessity or probability, tendency, impossibility and possibility."[4] What I call negative futurability here is the troubling process of mobilizing negativity in order to liberate the potentiality of a future that seems to be stuck in the intolerable present as an unlikely possibility or impossibility. *Aus dem Nichts* refuses to imagine an outside to the intolerable regime of violence it forcefully depicts; yet it is precisely this radical pessimism that is set in motion as a vector to shatter the film's morbid vision and escape its world.

Background

Aus dem Nichts was co-written by Fatih Akın and the veteran actor and director Hark Bohm, who is also a trained lawyer. In interviews, Akın has repeatedly stated that the National Socialist Underground investigations and the subsequent trial were the events that prompted him to start the project.[5] Between 1998 and 2011, members of the NSU committed ten murders, three bomb attacks, and fifteen bank robberies, and the connection between these crimes was not discovered by police until November 2011. The shocking failure of the authorities to solve the murders was attributed to the ethnic background of the victims: Eight of the victims were of Turkish and Kurdish background and one was of Greek background. German mainstream media insultingly labelled the case *die Dönermorde* (the kebab murders) for several years, while the police

---

2   Franco "Bifo" Berardi, *Futurability: The Age of Impotence and the Horizon of Possibility* (London: Verso, 2017).

3   Bifo, *Futurability*, 13.

4   Bifo, *Futurability*, 17.

5   Volker Behrens and Michael Töteberg, eds. *Fatih Akın, Im Clinch: Die Geschichte meiner Filme* (Hamburg: Rowohlt E-Book, 2019), 271.

explained away the failings of the case by saying that the families were uncooperative, as they lived in a "parallel society."[6]

Much of the public information available on the NSU trial is provided by the documentation of the NSU-Watch, an anti-fascist initiative formed in 2012. The NSU-Watch activists sat in on more than four hundred trial sessions and published the entirety of the proceedings on their website. In a public speech following the revelation of the verdict in 2018, they summarized the NSU case as such: "The NSU-complex involved authorities who were not merely racist, but actively involved, and hence refused to intervene and stop the killing. [The NSU complex] is about a society who didn't listen to survivors or the victims' families when they suggested Nazi involvement back in 2011. A society whose racism has nurtured the NSU."[7] The society emphasis in this statement is crucial, since it corroborates the central role that cultural and institutional forces played in facilitating the crimes, against the repeated efforts of the media and public discourse to individualize and psychologize the perpetrators and thereby isolate the crimes from the broader issue of systemic racism.

Aus dem Nichts was filmed and released before the conclusion of the NSU trial in July 2018. Akın and Bohm attended the NSU trial sessions twice in Munich while working on the film and they paid close attention to the trial documentation provided by NSU-Watch. The team of script consultants for the film included Andreas Thiel, the lawyer who represented the family of Süleyman Taşköprü, whom the NSU murdered in June 2001.[8] However, Akın also clarified that, despite having paid close attention to the case, the court scenes in the film were meticulously dramatized, departing significantly from the real-life trial sessions.[9] The NSU investigations and trial were considered some of the most significant failings of the German police and secret services in recent years, as they revealed evidence of institutional racism. The conclusion of the trials in 2018 marked the culmination of years of mistrust in the authorities and law enforcement, which was further accentuated by the racist terrorist attack in Hanau in February 2020, in which eleven people, predominantly of Muslim background, were killed. The Hanau attack investigations also revealed failures by the authorities to prevent and solve the crimes, which continue to traumatize the families of the victims.[10]

6   Antonia von der Behrens, "Lessons from Germany's NSU case," *Race & Class* 59, no. 4 (2018): 87.

7   "'We won't stop fighting to get answers.'—speech of 11 July 2018," NSU-Watch, accessed August 1, 2022, https://www.nsu-watch.info/2018/08/we-wont-fighting-to-get-answers-speech-of-11-july-2018/.

8   Behrens and Töteberg, *Akin: Im Clinch*, 274.

9   Behrens and Töteberg, *Akin: Im Clinch*, 276.

10   See Initiative 19. Februar Hanau website, accessed August 1, 2022, https://19feb-hanau.org, and "Racist Terror Attack in Hanau: The Police

The bleak world that Akın creates in *Aus dem Nichts* is firmly embedded within this context of the post-NSU Germany. It can be understood in terms of what Claudia Breger defines as cinematic worldmaking: A process of "multidimensional and multivectoral affective assemblage, configuring interwoven affects, associations, bodies, gestures, memories, objects, perceptions, sensations, topoi, and tropes through images, sounds and words."[11] As Breger argues, these cinematic worlds can saturate fictional tropes and stories "with enough reality" through "nonliteral referentiality" to history and memory, yielding complex affective readings with political orientations.[12] Although the film does not make any explicit references to the NSU, the detailed accounts of the bombing provided in the lengthy court sequences, as well as other narrative details such as the police's persistent insinuation of Nuri's criminal past as the key clue that links the crimes to the ethnic mafia, powerfully connect this cinematic world to Germany's recent history of racist violence and its continuing effects. Scholars have identified *Aus dem Nichts* as important for German film history, precisely because, as Caoduro observes, it is "one of few films addressing far-right domestic terrorism by a major filmmaker."[13] Similarly, Julian Preece considers *Aus dem Nichts* to be "the most gripping recent German film to depict politically motivated violence and counterviolence," and he argues that the ethical and political questions it asks are "more immediate and more comprehensive than was ever achieved in any film about the RAF."[14]

Aus dem Nichts won several awards including Best Actress for Diane Kruger at the Cannes Film Festival and Best Foreign Language Film at the Golden Globes. The reviews were largely positive in Germany, but abroad the film received mixed reviews and even harsh criticism. For example, Peter Bradshaw from the British liberal-left newspaper *The*

Operation," Forensic Architecture, accessed August 1, 2022, https://forensic-architecture.org/investigation/racist-terror-attack-in-hanau-the-police-operation. Initiative 19. Februar Hanau and Forensic Architecture continue to document the Hanau terrorist attack investigations and the evidence of systemic racism that they have so far revealed.

11 Claudia Breger, *Making Worlds: Affect and Collectivity in Contemporary European Cinema* (New York: Columbia University Press, 2020), 10.

12 Breger, *Making Worlds*, 12.

13 Elena Caoduro, "In the Fade: Motherhood, Grief and Neo-Nazi Terrorism in Contemporary Germany," in *Mediated Terrorism in the 21st Century*, ed. Elena Caoduro, Karen Randell, and Karen A. Ritzenhoff (Cham: Palgrave Macmillan, 2021), 210.

14 Julian Preece, "Review of *De-/Konstruktionen der RAF im Post-2000-Kino. Filmische Erinnerungsarbeit an einem Mythos* by Corina Erk, and *Screening the Red Army Faction: Historical and Cultural Memory* by Christina Gerhardt," *German Studies Review* 42, no. 2 (2019): 413.

54 ♦ GOZDE NAIBOGLU

Guardian called the film a "borderline-preposterous liberal drama" and scolded it for focusing on far-right terrorism instead of Islamist terrorism. He wrote, "in 2017, this piously formulated storyline feels evasive when Islamist attacks are the obvious issue, along with the Islamophobe panic they are intended to create. This movie ducks all this."[15] Bradshaw's dismissiveness, however inexcusable, seems to stem from his unfamiliarity with Germany's recent history and NSU terrorism. It is nonetheless symptomatic of a broader sense of oblivion toward the film's central topic, far-right terrorism. As mentioned earlier, the recent strand of films and series which tackle themes of far-right terrorism, and particularly the real-life case of the NSU, provides an audiovisual context for *Aus dem Nichts* in Germany. But the topic of far-right terrorism and violence rarely features within the broader context of mainstream European cinema. There are a few exceptions to this, such as Erik Poppe's *Utøya: July 22* (2018) and Paul Greengrass's *22 July* (2018), both of which are based on the far-right terrorist attacks that took place in Norway in 2012. This relative lack of contextual reference meant that the reception of the film varied significantly beyond Germany.

Depersonalizing the Fascist Apparatus

Aus dem Nichts is set predominantly in Hamburg, where Süleyman Taşköprü was killed in his grocery shop in 2001. The narrative revolves around Katja Şekerci (played by Diane Kruger), who, ten minutes into the film, loses her husband Nuri (Numan Acar) and their young son Rocco (Rafael Santana) in a bomb explosion. Nuri's Kurdish Turkish ethnic background leads Katja to suspect that the killing could be a far-right terrorist attack. But his criminal record as a convicted and rehabilitated former drug dealer is misconstrued by the police as a clue in their attempt to attribute the attack to the Turkish or Kurdish drug mafia. As the plot unfolds, the perpetrators are revealed to be a neo-Nazi couple. The film follows the aftermath of the violence as Katja goes through an intense period of grief, leading her to self-harm with drugs and a suicide attempt, then to a search for justice in court and, finally, a quest for revenge. When the court fails to convict the neo-Nazi murderers, Katja traces them to Greece where they are protected by members of the Greek far right organization Golden Dawn, and kills them in a suicide bomb attack. Throughout the film, Akın and his regular cinematographer Rainer Klausmann tend to focus on Katja as the sole protagonist, as they emphatically convey the space of the film as an externalization of her

15 Peter Bradshaw, "Ninja Heroine Diane Kruger Marooned in Feeble Revenge Drama," *Guardian*, May 26, 2017, https://www.theguardian.com/film/2017/may/26/in-the-fade-review-diane-kruger-fatih-akin-cannes-2017.

interiority through a combination of camera techniques. This tendency to center visually on Katja's psychology contrasts with the plot's refusal to individualize the perpetrators, a decision which in turn emphasizes the complexity of the transnational far-right network which facilitates the crime and protects the perpetrators.

Aus dem Nichts consists of three sections: "Family," "Justice," and "The Sea." Each of these three parts opens with a brief, two-minute video clip, flashing back to happier times. These short clips use a grainy home-made video aesthetic and a smaller aspect ratio than the widescreen used in the three main parts of the film. Each of the three parts is made using a range of different audio recording techniques as well as different camera lenses, yielding a nuanced effect. The first part, "The Family," is shot using a vintage camera lens to create a Super 16mm look on digital. Coupled with the sound mixed in mono, this lens creates an effect of psychological realism, intensifying character emotions captured through a grainy layer, and by medium and extreme close-ups.[16] The second part, "Justice," which follows Katja as she descends into grief and despair, culminating in the devastation caused by the verdict of the court, employs a cool, clinical, blue-dominated color palette, achieved by modernized CinemaScope lenses. In the concluding section, "The Sea," Akın and Klausmann use vintage Panavision optics to achieve warmer and brighter tones as the plot follows Katja on her revenge journey to Greece, reinvigorated by her burning desire for vengeance.[17] In all three parts, the camera invites the spectator to align very closely with Katja's perspective, albeit using different techniques, including Brian De Palma-style split screens and split diopters as seen in Figure 3.1. In this image, the split diopter is used not only to emphasize Katja's face conveying intensified emotion, but also to visualize her growing dissociation from the intolerable reality surrounding her in the courtroom. The frame often centers on Katja's face in close-up or extreme close-up; and at other times, the back of her head is placed in the center of the frame. Even when the image blocks access to her face, the camera invites alignment with Katja's perspective as it follows her from behind, taking up her viewpoint. Katja is present in each sequence and in almost every frame. Diane Kruger's intense, award-winning performance of bereavement and agony also enhances this alignment.

Despite the mixed range of techniques, lenses, and cameras used in the film, *Aus dem Nichts* tends not to draw significant attention to its

---

16 Carlos Aguilar, "Foreign Contenders: Fatih Akin Used Distinct Lenses and Sound Techniques for Each Section of Germany's In the Fade," *MovieMaker*, December 28, 2017, https://www.moviemaker.com/foreign-contenders-fatih-akin-in-the-fade/.

17 Behrens and Töteberg, *Akin: Im Clinch*, 276.

Figure 3.1. The use of split diopter accentuates Katja's emotional turmoil.

form. Its formal adventurousness primarily serves to complement the central goal of the film, which is to generate a cinematic world that accentuates Kruger's performance of Katja's emotional state. For the most part, Akın uses conventional approaches to narrative: the film tells an individualized story. The camera work and the mise-en-scène are invested less in conveying the processes and procedures involved in the aftermath of a terrorist attack than in affectively portraying the debilitating grief of the mourner seeking justice. Akın uses traditional techniques to accomplish a smooth implementation of the logic of identification, ultimately effecting a conventional mode of psychological realism. While the real-life NSU trial sessions were attended by numerous collective initiatives and anti-fascist activists supporting the families of the victims, the film portrays Katja as extremely isolated and lonely, abandoned by her own family and left without a support network. Her only ally is her lawyer and friend Danilo Fava (Denis Moschitto), who features mostly in the second part of the film but is absent from the final part. The CinemaScope lens used in the second part, in which the entirety of the court scenes take place, emphasizes her isolation even further by achieving a wider aspect ratio and sharper depth of field.

Katja's loneliness is particularly contrasted with the global network of support available for the neo-Nazi perpetrators, who eventually escape prosecution due to the false alibi provided by a member of the Greek neo-fascist party, Golden Dawn. As indicated above, the film remarkably refuses to individualize the perpetrators Edda Möller (Hanna Hillsdorf) and André Möller (Ulrich Brandhoff), in stark contrast to Katja's incisive psychological characterization. The couple do not speak a word throughout the film, and their voices are only heard once when they cheer loudly upon hearing the verdict. The members of the defense team, led by an aggressive and hostile lawyer, appear to show no remorse or sympathy for Katja's loss. The only defense witness to demonstrate sympathy for Katja is André's father (Ulrich Tukur), who appears to give a sincere apology to her in the courtroom; yet, moments later, outside the courtroom, he admits to Katja his prior knowledge of André's plan. The perpetrators are thus portrayed as depersonalized agents of a complex transnational network, whose complexity makes it impossible to detect the full extent of its reach. The film's refusal to psychologize or individualize the perpetrators not only contrasts with the mode of psychological realism that defines its logic of identification centering on Katja, but it also accentuates the structural and systemic enabling that the criminals enjoy. The verdict reveals the shocking complicity of the juridical system in the functioning of the far-right network of violence and injustice.

Akın and Klausmann's camera grants Katja's grief the space that the diegetic world denies her. Katja's only close friend Birgit is unable to offer her any meaningful emotional support. This becomes most evident in a sequence where Birgit insensitively showers her newborn baby with gestures of love, while Katja watches them in anguish and yearning. This spectacle of love sharply contrasts with the awkward and aloof words of condolence and support she offers to Katja. Danilo is more attuned to Katja's grief than Birgit is, yet he also appears uncomfortable with her distress and advises her to avoid the court on the day of the medical hearings which list, in painful detail, the injuries inflicted on Rocco during the attack. Danilo's well-meaning advice inadvertently echoes the villainous defense lawyer's initial request for the judge to remove Katja from the trial. During the post-mortem report hearing, Katja is overcome by rage and makes her way out of the courtroom as the excruciating austerity of the room denies her any outlet. On her way out, she physically attacks Edda and threatens to kill her and André, before being removed by the security guards. The judge opens the following court session with a brief warning to Katja, highlighting to her that only "facts" are allowed in the courtroom and that the defendants are innocent until proven guilty. After an abundance of evidence fails to lead to the conviction of the killers, Katja's cathartic desire for revenge takes an ambivalent turn.

The film's use of conventional storytelling techniques, coupled with its implementation of psychological realism, serve to generate a strong spectatorial desire for catharsis. This desire is fully invested in Katja's search for justice through judicial process in the first and second parts of the film. When the verdict fails to deliver catharsis, however, in the final part the film reroutes the spectatorial desire toward revenge. The climax does eventually deliver revenge, yet only after it troubles and frustrates the spectatorial investment in revenge for catharsis. When Katja's revenge finally comes after some hesitation, it takes the form of simultaneous murder and suicide, thereby complicating the association of catharsis with positive spectatorial experience. Nikolaj Lübecker describes this kind of stimulation, and eventual frustration, of spectatorial desire for catharsis as the "feel-bad" film experience.[18] For Lübecker, the political and ethical potential of the feel-bad film lies in the way in which it "creates, then deadlocks, our desire for catharsis,"[19] in order to create a sense of social catharsis, which is "about raising questions and creating debate rather than delivering closure and satisfaction."[20] *Aus dem Nichts'* refusal to deliver a positive sense of catharsis by blocking the possibility of a reparative closure works as a strong provocation, as evidenced by the negative criticism that the film received.

What provoked particularly negative criticism was the brutal conclusiveness of the film's ending. A. O. Scott found the depiction of the neo-Nazi perpetrators shallow and underdeveloped, and the defense lawyer too villainous, even as he acknowledged that the film was aesthetically accomplished. Like many other critics, Scott was particularly dissatisfied by the ending, finding it more puzzling than devastating, and argued that "the political and personal sides of the story, rather than illuminating each other, fight to a stalemate."[21] For Scott, the ending offers no solution to injustice, nor to Katja's grief, and therefore blocks satisfaction for either problem, leaving catharsis undelivered. In an interview, Akın commented on this controversy about the ending of the film, claiming that *Aus dem Nichts* was not shortlisted in the Academy Awards because the ending was challenging for the Academy members in Britain and France. He said that their dissatisfaction mainly stemmed from the ethnicity of Katja, a white German woman, taking brutal revenge: "Sie haben sich daran gestört, dass eine weiße christliche Frau Rache verübt. Das passte nicht in ihr Weltbild, das müsste eigentlich der Dönermesser schwingende Türke machen. Oder die Kopftuch-Ayse" (They were bothered by a white Christian woman taking revenge. That didn't fit into their worldview; that's what the Turk wielding a kebab knife should do. Or the headscarf Ayse).[22] For Akın, the casting of Diane Kruger, a white German with blonde hair and blue eyes, as the surviving family member was a strategic choice made in order to challenge the us-versus-them logic, the presumption that racism only

---

18 Nikolaj Lübecker, *The Feel-Bad Film* (Edinburgh: Edinburgh University Press, 2015), 12.

19 Lübecker, *The Feel-Bad Film*, 12.

20 Lübecker, *The Feel-Bad Film*, 24.

21 A. O. Scott, "Review: 'In the Fade' Is a Tale of Grief and Violence in Modern Germany," *New York Times*, December 26, 2017, https://www.nytimes.com/2017/12/26/movies/in-the-fade-review-diane-kruger.html. For another review critical of the film's ending, see also Mark Jenkins, "'In The Fade': A Fine Central Performance, An Uncertain Ending." *NPR*, December 27, 2017, https://www.npr.org/2017/12/28/574044612/in-the-fade-a-fine-central-performance-an-uncertain-ending.

22 Behrens and Töteberg, *Akin: Im Clinch*, 272. My translation.

hurts and affects people with a migration background.[23] Due to its refusal to cater to racist stereotypes, as Akın suggests, or due to its restraint in not delivering the expected catharsis, *Aus dem Nichts'* ending was provocative and disorienting for some critics and spectators.

From Ambiguity to Pessimism

To explicate further why this calamitous ending matters, it is necessary to situate the film within Akın's filmography, and the context of his auteurship in contemporary German film culture. Akın is one of the most internationally acclaimed directors in German cinema, with an impressive filmography that includes award-winning feature films such as *Gegen die Wand* (*Head-On*, 2004) and *Auf der anderen Seite* (*Edge of Heaven*, 2007). His parents came to Hamburg from Turkey as labor migrants in the mid-1960s and, with a few exceptions, his films tend to focus on the experience of Germans of migrant background. As Berna Gueneli points out, his films signal "the normalization of ethnic minorities in Europe and in European cinema."[24] Owen Evans echoes this sentiment when he argues that Akın is "seen as the purveyor of a new cinema of intercultural dialogue, which reinforces optimism that robust intercultural identities can be forged within ethnically mixed societies."[25] Akın's previous films, to varying degrees, manifest a certain optimism about the potential to change one's circumstances; yet, a directional change has become

---

23   In the same interview with Behrens and Töteberg, Akin continues to explain how this casting choice was seen as a problematic departure from the real life NSU case. "*Aus dem Nichts* ist ein Film, der gegen große Widerstände entstanden ist. Der Cutter-Verband hat bei Andrew Bird angerufen und gesagt, wir können den Film nicht für einen Preis nominieren, weil die Hauptfigur eine Deutsche ist. Bei dem NSU war das ja nicht so . . . Lesen die Leute keine Zeitung? Die Frau von Theodoros Boulgarides, dem NSU-Opfer aus München, ist Deutsche. Meine Frau ist Deutsche. Ich bin auch Deutscher. Alle Opfer waren Deutsche!" (*In the Fade* is a film which came about against the odds. The editors' association called Andrew Bird and said that we couldn't nominate the film for an award since the protagonist is a German woman. That wasn't the case with the NSU . . . Don't people read newspapers? The wife of Theodoros Boulgarides, the NSU victim from Munich, is German. My wife is German. I'm German too. All of the victims were Germans!"). Behrens and Töteberg, *Akin: Im Clinch*, 272. My translation.

24   Berna Gueneli, *Fatih Akin's Cinema and the New Sound of Europe* (Bloomington: Indiana University Press, 2019), 6.

25   Owen Evans, "Building Bridges: Fatih Akin and the Cinema of Intercultural Dialogue," in *Nationalism in Contemporary Western European Cinema*, ed. James Harvey (Cham: Palgrave Macmillan, 2018), 149.

discernable, particularly with *Aus dem Nichts* and his subsequent film, *Der goldene Handschuh* (*The Golden Glove*, 2019).

Akın's filmography can be viewed within the contextual framework of what Thomas Elsaesser calls the new European "cinema of abjection": these are films that rethink the politics and ethics of being European and question core Enlightenment principles such as liberty, equality, fraternity, and freedom in post-secular, neoliberal times.[26] Cinema of abjection takes crises and evils of the world as given, and explores "what remains of us as human beings when none of the traditional bonds . . . can be relied upon to support a sense of self or identity other than the power of negativity itself."[27] Akın's films fit within this category: they always feature dark themes, suicidal protagonists who are trapped in a downward spiral, or protagonists who live on the edges of society, who are political exiles, ex-convicts, punks, sex workers or drug dealers. However, his films prior to *Aus dem Nichts* have open, optimistic endings which point toward a positive, and possibly transformative futurity. This is certainly the case for *Gegen die Wand*, in which one of the two key protagonists Cahit (Birol Ünel) evolves from conveying severe suicidal hopelessness to finding new meaning in life as he embarks on a journey to explore his familial heritage in the south of Turkey. *Auf der anderen Seite* similarly concludes with an open and reconciliatory ending.

In contrast, *Aus dem Nichts* ends with destruction through an extended sequence. Katja plants a nail bomb under the Möllers' campervan and then goes into hiding, watching it from afar. Then she suddenly aborts the plan when she notices a sparrow flapping its wings around the van. Although why Katja retrieves the device is not made clear—is it to avoid killing the bird or is it because of a sudden feeling of mercy triggered by the fledgling bird?—this plot twist misleadingly offers a sense of relief. The ensuing sequence shows Katja noticing that her menstruation has returned after a long pause caused by the shock of the tragedy, followed by a mundane set of sequences showing her buying a pack of tampons before going back to detonate the bomb; this time not remotely, but killing herself along with the couple. The hesitation—the failed initial attempt to murder the couple, which is overturned by the suicide attack a few minutes later—effectively renders the ending even more conclusive and devastating. Akın gives us alternate possibilities in the form of options available to Katja, but he ultimately chooses the most definitive one. After the explosion, the camera lingers on the burning vehicle for a few minutes, then moves in slow motion toward the sky, turns upside down, and moves again toward the sea. With this ending, I argue, Akın turns away

---

26   Thomas Elsaesser, *European Cinema and Continental Philosophy* (London: Bloomsbury, 2018), 130.

27   Elsaesser, *European Cinema*, 131.

from his affirmative politics to a politics of pessimism: from optimism and ambiguous futurity toward negative futurability.

Bifo defines the neologism "futurability" as follows: "The present constitution of the world contains many different (conflicting) possibilities, not only one. Extracting and implementing one of the many immanent futurabilities: this is the shift from possible to real. Futurability is a layer of possibility that may or may not develop into actuality."[28] For Bifo, the relationship between the present and the future can be understood in terms of immanence in the Deleuzian and Bergsonian sense, which means that all the divergent and conflicting possibilities for the future are inscribed in the present. As he argues, futurability "refers to the multidimensionality of the future: in the present a plurality of futures is inscribed."[29] The question then becomes how one of these possibilities emerges as reality. Bifo explores the social futurabilities that emerge from what he calls the madness of the present, giving contemporary examples such as political extremism (particularly that of ISIS), the presidency of Donald Trump, growing racist violence, and the erosion of welfare policies under the seemingly unstoppable forces of the neoliberal offensive. Drawing on Bifo's conception of futurability, I view *Aus dem Nichts* as a film that works through an aesthetics of negativity and abjection with its own vision of futurability. Far from a nihilistic outlook, negative futurability on screen is an attempt to activate imaginaries to force a way out of this entropy. Negative futurability is a form of activism that proposes thinking negativity anew to liberate future imaginaries from the political present stemming from years of neoliberalism as well as from the increasingly clear impunity of racist violence through state complicity, political extremism, xenophobia, homophobia and transphobia, anti-immigrant sentiment, and aggressive surveillance.

This idea of negative futurability is particularly manifest in the closing shot of *Aus dem Nichts*. The explosion is followed by an extended tracking shot of the sky and the sea; as previously seen in Akın's films, the concluding long shot points out to an openness, but this time, an opening into a future is only possible after the deaths of both the protagonist and the antagonists. For Akın, the third part of the film—particularly the ending—was filmed in a way to have a "soft and beautiful" look, and to highlight the "consolation" that comes at the end.[30] This consolation, of course, does not emanate from the revenge-suicide of the protagonist, but the emergent possibility of a future, which stems from a complete withdrawal, on the film's part from the intolerable relations that push Katja to self-annihilation. On a narrative level, the destruction is conclusive, but

28   Bifo, *Futurability*, 3.
29   Bifo, *Futurability*, 20.
30   Aguilar, "Distinct Lenses."

on an abstract and sensory level, it is a vector that shatters the intolerable regime of violence that suffocates Katja, and thus is a way of activating imaginaries of what could be instead of the prevailing regime of racist violence and complicity of the state and legal system. The pessimism of the ending is therefore depicted as an absolute rupture from the destructive forces of a fascist state apparatus.

How can we understand pessimism as political? The politics of pessimism that *Aus dem Nichts* corroborates can be understood within the context of contemporary political and theoretical movements of negation, such as ahumanism, queer negativity, and Afropessimism.[31] These movements of refusal and negation, as Andrew Culp argues, pose no reparative demands, and withdraw from existing political coordinates and identities.[32] The politics of negativity and pessimism are often polemical because, both in scholarly literature and popular understanding, pessimism tends to be conflated with defeatism and despair and is therefore blamed for contemporary social problems. But theorists of pessimism, such as Joshua Foa Dienstag, propose a reconsideration of its potentials, arguing that the strong reaction that pessimism draws to itself is alone a proof of its power; as Dienstag writes, "thought should be given to the question of why this word functions so well as a gesture of dismissal."[33] The politics of pessimism goes against the presumption that politics and activism must always be positive and participatory, instead proffering a vision of outright refusal, which can be generative of new modes of thinking and action. Such new strategies can take various forms of negation and absence, such as "becoming illegible" to avoid aggressive and ubiquitous modes of surveillance, which, as Annie Ring argues, however imperfect, can still offer powerful ways "to withdraw complicity with unethical regimes that leave little room for escape."[34] Negation and absence can be the only effective forms of resistance against such coercive regimes that demand complicity. As Patricia MacCormack puts it eloquently in her book *The Ahuman Manifesto*, what may be seen as negation and absence (in this case, the antinatalist or antitheist demands of ahumanism), results not in "negative

---

31 These political and theoretical projects diverge significantly in aims, methods, and approach, and I do not seek to overlook, or willfully flatten their differences by categorizing them under one umbrella term. Rather, I bring them together in order to explore the different ways in which negativity and refusal can be powerfully deployed in theory and activism.

32 Andrew Culp, *A Guerrilla Guide to Refusal* (Minneapolis: University of Minnesota Press, 2022) 7.

33 Joshua Foa Dienstag, *Pessimism: Philosophy, Ethic, Spirit* (Princeton, NJ: Princeton University Press, 2006), x.

34 Annie Ring, "The Politics of 'Primary Rejection' in Hermann Melville's *Bartleby* and Hito Steyerl's *How Not to be Seen*: Racism, (Il)legibility, Surveillance and Determinate Negation," *German Life and Letters* 74, no. 1 (2021): 72.

emptiness" but a "voluminously creative space that demands unique and singular practices of remodeling the world temporarily and tactically in order to express redistribution of powers and affects."[35]

Theoretical attention to pessimism and negativity can also be found in the work of queer theorists and Afropessimists. For example, Lee Edelman's anti-reproduction theory rejects the centrality of futural temporality to a queer politics. It refuses the primacy of "reproductive futurism": the heteronormative ideology that bases futurity around the nuclear family.[36] For Edelman and other queer negativists, the future is an unattainable temporality, a "fantasy" that sustains the heteronormative illusion of stability and order. Edelman locates the possibility of queer resistance outside the political domain, because queer bodies are outside of the heteronormative social and political order. Queer negativity's refusal to engage with existing political formulations is structurally akin to the Afropessimist argument, particularly outlined in the works of Frank B. Wilderson III and Jared Sexton, as well as the early works of Saidiya Hartman.[37] For Afropessimism, slavery not only continues to exist; but it constitutes the core of Western life and civilization. Afropessimism argues that anti-Blackness is the basis of Western ideology, and any idea of inclusivity and universality not only excludes Black bodies, but also relies on the physical and psychological suffering of the Black body.[38]

The negation in ahumanism, queer negativity, and Afropessimism has been polemical, sometimes prompting strong emotional reactions such as anger and upset, if not quick dismissal. This is because, as Kennan Ferguson argues, such theoretical schools refuse "the presumptions of unity" and "communal experience," and the idea that "we are all in this together"; they assert instead that historical and economic structures exclude certain kinds of people and prevent them from flourishing in the current political environment.[39] For those people, reconciliation is not the goal, nor the solution, since reconciliation presumes that those who

35 Patricia MacCormack, *Ahuman Manifesto: Activism for the End of the Anthropocene* (London: Bloomsbury, 2020) 107–8.

36 Lee Edelman, *No Future: Queer Theory and the Death Drive* (Durham, NC: Duke University Press, 2004).

37 Jared Sexton, "Afro-Pessimism: The Unclear Word," *Rhizomes* 29 (2016), accessed August 1, 2022, http://www.rhizomes.net/issue29/sexton.html. See also Saidiya Hartman's earlier writings, including *Scenes of Subjection: Terror, Slavery, and Self-Making in Nineteenth-Century America* (New York: Oxford University Press, 1997) and "The Position of the Unthought: An Interview by Frank B. Wilderson, III," *Qui Parle* 13, no. 2 (2003): 183–201.

38 Frank B. Wilderson III, *Red, White, and Black: Cinema and the Structure of U.S. Antagonisms* (Durham, NC: Duke University Press, 2010).

39 Kennan Ferguson, "Introduction: No Politics," in *The Big No*, ed. Kennan Ferguson (Minneapolis: University of Minnesota Press, 2021), 18.

are excluded can simply "get over it." Ferguson thus argues that the politics of negativity is about questioning the primacy of reconciliation, which undermines truths "because reconciliation always demands and depends on untruths."[40]

The ending of *Aus dem Nichts* has been polemical and controversial for similar reasons: the film does not offer any solutions, or as A. O. Scott has put it, it ends in a stalemate. *Aus dem Nichts* rejects reparative or reconciliatory readings. On a literal level, this could be read as political defeatism; but on an affective level, as particularly evoked in the soothing final long take, the film points to a negative futurability. Read against this background, death is neither the beginning nor the end, but simply immanent to the political space for those who suffer from its intractable injustices and have no easy solutions to offer. The film does not offer a utopian way out of this regime of violence; yet its critical potential stems from this refusal to imagine an outside and the provocative, and generative power of this refusal. It stands against a reconciliatory move toward solutions, because such a move would trivialize the problem, instead of taking seriously what makes the problem so intolerable. The negative affects in *Aus dem Nichts* are efforts to activate imaginaries rather than offer solutions—as forms of cinematic expression that operate through sensation and abstraction, and beyond signifying systems of representation and recognition.

Bibliography

Aguilar, Carlos. "Foreign Contenders: Fatih Akin Used Distinct Lenses and Sound Techniques for Each Section of Germany's In the Fade." *MovieMaker*, December 28, 2017. https://www.moviemaker.com/foreign-contenders-fatih-akin-in-the-fade/.

Behrens, Volker, and Michael Töteberg, eds. *Fatih Akin, Im Clinch: Die Geschichte meiner Filme*. Hamburg: Rowohlt E-Book, 2019.

Berardi, Franco "Bifo." *Futurability: The Age of Impotence and the Horizon of Possibility*. London: Verso, 2017.

Bradshaw, Peter. "Ninja Heroine Diane Kruger Marooned in Feeble Revenge Drama." *Guardian*, May 26, 2017. https://www.theguardian.com/film/2017/may/26/in-the-fade-review-diane-kruger-fatih-akin-cannes-2017.

Breger, Claudia. *Making Worlds: Affect and Collectivity in Contemporary European Cinema*. New York: Columbia University Press, 2020.

Caoduro, Elena. "In the Fade: Motherhood, Grief and Neo-Nazi Terrorism in Contemporary Germany." In *Mediated Terrorism in the 21st Century*,

---

40   Ferguson, "Introduction: No Politics," 19.

edited by Elena Caoduro, Karen Randell, and Karen A. Ritzenhoff, 201–18. Cham: Palgrave Macmillan, 2021.

Culp, Andrew. *A Guerrilla Guide to Refusal*. Minneapolis: University of Minnesota Press, 2022.

Dienstag, Joshua Foa. *Pessimism: Philosophy, Ethic, Spirit*. Princeton, NJ: Princeton University Press, 2006.

Edelman, Lee. *No Future: Queer Theory and the Death Drive*. Durham, NC: Duke University Press, 2004.

Elsaesser, Thomas. *European Cinema and Continental Philosophy*. London: Bloomsbury, 2018.

Evans, Owen. "Building Bridges: Fatih Akin and the Cinema of Intercultural Dialogue." In *Nationalism in Contemporary Western European Cinema*, edited by James Harvey, 145–68. Cham: Palgrave Macmillan, 2018.

Ferguson, Kennan. "Introduction: No Politics." In *The Big No*, edited by Kennan Ferguson, 9–23. Minneapolis: University of Minnesota Press, 2021.

Forensic Architecture. "Racist Attack in Hanau: The Police Operation." Accessed August 1, 2022. https://forensic-architecture.org/investigation/racist-terror-attack-in-hanau-the-police-operation.

Gueneli, Berna. *Fatih Akin's Cinema and the New Sound of Europe*. Bloomington: Indiana University Press, 2019.

Hartman, Saidiya. "The Position of the Unthought: An Interview by Frank B. Wilderson, III." *Qui Parle* 13, no. 2 (2003): 183–201.

———. *Scenes of Subjection: Terror, Slavery, and Self-Making in Nineteenth Century America*. Oxford: Oxford University Press, 1997.

Initiative 19. Februar Hanau. Accessed August 1, 2022. https://19feb-hanau.org.

Jenkins, Mark. "'In The Fade': A Fine Central Performance, An Uncertain Ending." *NPR*, December 27, 2017. https://www.npr.org/2017/12/28/574044612/in-the-fade-a-fine-central-performance-an-uncertain-ending.

Lübecker, Nikolaj. *The Feel-Bad Film*. Edinburgh: Edinburgh University Press, 2015.

MacCormack, Patricia. *The Ahuman Manifesto: Activism for the End of the Anthropocene*. London: Bloomsbury, 2020.

NSU-Watch. "'We won't stop fighting to get answers.'—speech of 11 July 2018." Accessed August 1, 2022. https://www.nsu-watch.info/2018/08/we-wont-stop-fighting-to-get-answers-speech-of-11-july-2018/.

Preece, Julian. "Review of *De-/Konstruktionen der RAF im Post-2000-Kino. Filmische Erinnerungsarbeit an einem Mythos* by Corina Erk, and *Screening the Red Army Faction: Historical and Cultural Memory* by Christina Gerhardt." *German Studies Review* 42, no. 2 (2019): 411–13.

Ring, Annie. "The Politics of 'Primary Rejection' in Hermann Melville's *Bartleby* and Hito Steyerl's *How Not to be Seen*: Racism, (Il)legibility, Surveillance and Determinate Negation." *German Life and Letters* 74, no. 1 (2021): 67–89.

66 ♦ GOZDE NAIBOGLU

Scott, A. O. "Review: 'In the Fade' Is a Tale of Grief and Violence in Modern Germany." *New York Times*, December 26, 2017. https://www.nytimes.com/2017/12/26/movies/in-the-fade-review-diane-kruger.html.

Sexton, Jared. "Afro-Pessimism: The Unclear Word." *Rhizomes*, 29 (2016), accessed August 1, 2022. http://www.rhizomes.net/issue29/sexton.html.

Von der Behrens, Antonia. "Lessons from Germany's NSU case." *Race & Class* 59, no. 4 (2018): 84–91.

Wilderson III, Frank B. *Red, White, and Black: Cinema and the Structure of U.S. Antagonisms*. Durham, NC: Duke University Press, 2010.

Part II

Rethinking the Evidence: New Documentary Forms

4: Forensic Fallacies

Lutz Koepnick

CONTEMPORARY DEBATES ABOUT the politics of migration, asylum, and exile witness a wide range of conspiracy theories, evidence-free arguments, and post-truth distortions. Social media are quick to present refugees as agents of sexual assault, even serious media outlets can't help to wonder whether migrants are terrorists in disguise, and mass-produced television shows cast immigrant communities in Germany and elsewhere as hotbeds of international drug trafficking and crime. The reasons for installing the immigrant's body as a screen of often paranoid and unfounded projections are manifold; the rise of populist agitation is as much at its roots as the withering of nuanced perspectives—right and often left—amid the bubbles of post-neoliberal, internet-based communication. What might matter more, however, is that in the end free-floating claims about the figure of the migrant tend to untether the very possibility of public discourse and political debate in general: if evidence-free conjecture and blatant lies reign triumphant, then we lose—as Hannah Arendt already argued in the postwar period—the very base of political dialogue and of pluralistic conceptions of democratic life. In representing a feared loss or lack of spatial groundedness, of moored identity, the figure of the migrant thus increasingly turns into what the champions of populist and mostly right-wing identity politics demonize so as to pursue their anti-pluralistic attack on the foundations of democratic institutions altogether.

The same period that has produced the figure of the migrant as a screen of free-floating anxieties and post-truth speculation has also unmoored contemporary art from whatever it still could take for granted after the demise of dominant traditions and normative concepts of art in the twentieth century. As evidenced in recent art events such as Kassel's Documenta 15 (2022), in its timely embrace of discourses of inclusivity, diversity, and decolonization, contemporary art has shed whatever previously remained of the normative frameworks of autonomous art: it prioritizes collaborative practices over the myth of the individual artist, open-ended process over self-contained work, social engagement over aesthetic self-referentiality, gestures of sharing over the reifying power of the market. Amid this, as critics such as Wolfgang Ulrich and Hanno

70 ♦ LUTZ KOEPNICK

Rauterberg argue,[1] efforts to delimit the concept, domains, and borders of art no longer prove adequate. What defines art today as art, instead, is its ability to strike new alliances with other social sectors and discursive arenas, to resist any essentializing definitions, and to host new conversations about ethics and politics or the destructive force of extractive capitalism and neocolonial exploitation. None of this, to be sure, directly relates to post-truth imaginaries of the migrant, except that contemporary art—like the projective image of the migrant—today inhabits a realm in which fact and fiction mix as easily as arguments once associated with separate spheres, such as politics, the law, ethics, and the aesthetic. Untethered from institutional certainties, art today may happen at ever more places of social interaction, but this untethering also causes many to wonder where and in what form to find it at all.

In this chapter, I explore how contemporary film and moving image art engages with the figure of the migrant, not only to express its solidarity with the unmoored, but in challenging the rhetoric of "alternate facts" to restitch the fabric of political life and redefine art's own rather unmoored role in the contemporary. I discuss three recent films and multi-screen installations that address different instances of violence committed against migrants and immigrant communities in Germany in the twenty-first century. Each moving image piece, in its conceptual intervention and formal set up, responds to how post-truth politics uses and abuses the figure of the migrant for certain ideological projects, but in doing so also remaps the place postautonomous art and art cinema may inhabit to engage its audiences and interfere in political struggles. In all three pieces, moving images are meant to provide or correct what the German legal system, in tackling the violence against migrants, has failed to accomplish: each of them investigates different methods of resituating art today as a medium of restoring justice for migrant communities precisely because the law itself, in the context of post-truth uncertainties, no longer seems to meet its task. Based on a 2004 bombing in Cologne, Fatih Akın's *Aus dem Nichts* (*In the Fade*, 2017) includes a prolonged, detailed, and in all its realistic detail gruesome court trial that fails to hold two neo-Nazis accountable for the murder of a Turkish German citizen and his son. Mario Pfeifer's two-channel video installation *Noch einmal* (*Again*, 2018) meticulously reenacts the assault on a Syrian refugee in East Germany, but requires a make-shift jury to pass judgment on the attack because the German court system refused to do so. Finally, Forensic Architecture's *The Murder of Halit Yozgat*, first shown at Documenta 14 (2017), reconstructs the murder of a Turkish citizen in Kassel in 2006 with a wide

---

1   Wolfgang Ulrich, *Die Kunst nach dem Ende ihrer Autonomie* (Berlin: Wagenbach, 2022); Hanno Rauterberg, *Die Kunst und das gute Leben: Über die Ethik der Ästhetik* (Frankfurt am Main: Suhrkamp, 2015).

variety of investigative tools and digital strategies, yet plays out its case in the realm of contemporary art precisely because the German legal system was unable or unwilling to do its job.

What all three pieces in this chapter share is their effort to tackle actual historical events and their legal aftermaths. Each is significantly concerned with processes of forensic reconstruction and fact-finding, yet each chooses fundamentally different ways to negotiate a situation in which forensic facts and material evidence no longer seem to suffice to reinstate justice and repair society's broken fabric. While all these moving image works aspire to make good on the failures of the courts to establish justice, and each of them deliberately deploys a different set of visual, aural, and computational strategies to persuade the viewer of "what really happened," all three in their intense focus on forensic processes and fact-finding procedures express the precarious nature of facts and truths in post-liberal and post-truth societies today. In all three films, the body of the murdered migrant or immigrant thus not only emerges as a site at which contemporary German cinema and video art urges the viewer to expand prevalent understandings of forensic evidence: away from positivistic conceptions prevalent in popular crime and real-crime stories, toward notions attuned to the etymological affinity of "forensis" and "forum." Accordingly, all three films suggest that neither truth nor justice can be established in the absence of a functioning public sphere and media landscape in whose context people struggle over the meaning of right and wrong, fact and fiction. As importantly, all three works, as they present the failure of short-sighted concepts of forensics, seek to model broader understandings of forensic evidence and situate contemporary art as a central medium to restore justice and reevaluate the image of the migrant amid the anti-pluralist frenzy of post-truth media.

Aus dem Nichts

Loosely based on a deadly 2004 attack of members of the National Socialist Underground (NSU) on a Turkish German neighborhood in Cologne, Fatih Akın's *Aus dem Nichts* was released in spring 2017 to largely positive reviews. It won Diane Kruger—a German born-actress who had migrated to the US as a teenager—the Best Actress award at Cannes in May 2017 for her depiction of Katja Şekerci, and the film a Golden Globe award for Best Foreign Film in January 2018. Though the film tells a dramatic, at times violent, at times harrowing tale of xenophobic murder and desperate revenge, its perhaps most captivating sequences can be found during the prolonged court proceedings: the trial against two neo-Nazis—André and Edda Möller—who clearly committed the murder of the Kurdish German citizen Nuri Şekerci and his and Katja's son Rocco, but who in the end walk free because residual traces of reasonable doubt seem to overshadow the weight of forensic evidence.

Precisely because Akın spends considerable screen time capturing the testimonies, cross-examinations, and arguments, the court's verdict certainly comes as a surprise for both the diegetic audience in the court room and the film's viewer. The evidence, at least from a lay perspective, simply appears overwhelming and is further supported by the fact that André's father (played by Ulrich Turkur), deeply appalled by his son's actions and political convictions, testifies in no uncertain terms against his offspring. Detailed forensic analysis matches the bomb that killed Nuri and Rocco with all kinds of materials found in the Möllers' garage; fingerprint tracking offers indexical proof that André and Edda had indeed touched what was used to build the nail bomb. Moreover, André and Edda leave no doubt about their contempt for existing democratic and legal institutions, as well as for the presence of citizens with migratory backgrounds on German soil. What derails the case as a case, however, is the sheer and rather formal possibility that other individuals could have gained access to the stored ingredients for the bomb, and the fact that Katja's occasional drug use disqualifies her statements about the events. Though everyone pretty much knows that André and Edda have committed the crime, their acquittal simply reflects the fact that forensic evidence, like what we call facts and data, still relies on interpretation; that even indexical signs provide no royal road or uncontestable one-way street toward uncontestable truth and, hence, justice.

Akın's staging of the prolonged court room sequence underscores the fragility of legal truth. Due to different juridical traditions and institutionalizations, *Aus dem Nichts* cannot draw on the dynamic heart piece of every American court drama—the theatricality of attorneys, accused, accusers, and witnesses in persuading an assembled jury of lay persons—in order to choreograph the proceedings. Like those of numerous other countries, Germany's legal system does not know of jury trials; it is driven by the assumption that decisions in court should be made by professionals and be informed by the cold facticity of evidence, not the affects and histrionics of rhetorical performances. This also changes the role and relation of State Attorney, Defensive Attorney, and Judge, as all three are meant to engage—at least in theory—in a joint process of fact finding, not one of appealing to the minds (and hearts) of an at once select and random group of lay jurors. People no doubt perform in German courtrooms as much as they do in North America; their audience, however, is less that of general public as embodied by the jury, than of legal experts. As a result, court trials are typically much more technical, procedural, or formal than cinema might afford to stir emotions and tell compelling stories, not least of all because the typical seating arrangements in a German court room avoid the stage-like settings we know from Hollywood court room dramas and hence afford a far less fluid dynamic of gazes and gestures, of seeing and being seen.

Akın's choreography of the Möller trial, rather than bypassing the German court's hostility to theatrics, rigorously focuses on the trial's technical rigor. We hear defensive lawyers raising extensive procedural objections; we listen to expert witnesses detailing their forensic findings. Though emotions flare up repeatedly, the overall atmosphere is one of cold scrutiny and distant evaluation of facts, defining the court more as a seminar room discussing legal problems than a site to assess the brutal murder of a respected immigrant and his son. Throughout all of this, Akın's camera shuttles back and forth between different perspectives and focal lengths, providing a mesh of frontal, lateral, and angular points of view while refusing any classical logic of shot and reaction shot. What the camera does not offer, in other words, is a privileged point of view for the proceedings in general and from which to identify one body or one voice around which the action might pivot. The effect is disorienting, as Akın's editing refuses to stitch his images into a seamless, continuous, and contiguous flow. But what the film's viewer is dealing with here is not a confused representation of a logical procedure, but a stunningly rigorous procedure of representing a confused process, the confusion of a process that fails to reconcile competing truth claims and that, due to the defense's playful use of formal ambivalence, disintegrates into a mere kaleidoscope of contending narratives. In the end, the Möllers will be acquitted not because of too little but of too much logic and reason—a kind of reason that effectively deconstructs the foundation of truth and justice and for which Akın's jumpy editing and heterogenous cinematography during the proceedings provides a perfect allegory.

In the remainder of the film, Katja will take things into her own hands to do—like a modern Michael Kohlhaas—what the law fails to do. The film now generically switches from court room drama to action thriller, while Akın's editing and cinematography regain their fluidity, their ability to orient viewers firmly in space and time and define the protagonist's perspective as the principal lens through which we partake of the action. And yet, Katja's project to restore justice because the pluralization of truths and post-truth society—the limits of forensic evidence, understood as a fundamental crisis of the indexical—prevents the law from doing its work does not yield a happy ending, a clear resolution. After following them to Greece, she blows up the Möllers in their RV with the same kind of self-fabricated bomb they—in their racist effort to keep Germany free of what they perceived as the threat of migration and immigration—used to kill her husband and son. But she knows well enough that in the math of violence and injustice, negating the negative will not produce any positive. Scarred by the traumatic loss of her family as much as the trauma of the inconclusive trial, she decides to use her own body as the bomb's vehicle and hence kills herself along with the two neo-Nazis. Her revenge may restore the unity of body and truth, the indexical and the just, but it can only do so by exploding the personal into the political all the while being quite aware that such acts do not restore the foundations of an operative society.

The film's final shot slowly rises above the bombed RV, the flames of a burning tree, and the black smoke both create, until it reaches the uncontaminated blue of the sky above the Aegean Sea. Then, without any visible cut the image weirdly flips and approaches the inverted horizon line of ocean and sky before it ascends into the water. Projected above the image of the water and its ripples, the concluding titles—"Between 2000 and 2007 in Germany, the 'National Socialist Underground' shot nine people from immigrant backgrounds and a policewoman and carried out multiple bombings. The sole motive behind their attacks was their victims' non-German origin"—leave little doubt that Katja's final act, as well as the film's political intervention, represent no more than mere ripples in Germany's economy of racist violence: outcries that may challenge the perversions of justice from the pivot of the personal and the aesthetic, perhaps even offer some form of cathartic release, but that in the end fall short of righting the wrongs of a world fundamentally out of kilter.

Noch einmal

Mario Pfeifer's *Noch einmal* (2018) is a two-channel, forty-two-minute video installation, first screened at the tenth Berlin Biennale for Contemporary Art in 2018.[2] It projects at once found and carefully staged footage on two rather large screens that connect with each other at an obtuse angle and thereby clearly define the space from which seated audiences can behold the images. The piece was later reedited into a single-screen work to meet the specific demands of classical theater auditoriums and a television broadcast on the German-French *arte* channel in June 2021. With this, the project clearly hoped to extend its potential viewership, moving the gallery to a wide range of public settings and even into people's living rooms. My focus here, however, is on *Noch einmal*'s multi-screen version, not only because it was in this format that Pfeifer's work was first experienced by its audiences, but also because the dual-stream installation and spatial choreography add dimensions to viewing the piece that no single-screen version, whether displayed in a traditional movie theater or on a flat television screen, could adequately

---

2   For a previous and somewhat extended reading of this installation, see Lutz Koepnick "Records in Motion: Migrants and Mobile Spectatorship," in *Gegen\Dokumentation: Operationen-Foren-Interventionen*, ed. Esra Canpalat et al. (Bielefeld: Transcript, 2020), 29–38.

recapture—dimensions critical to the question of how moving image art today can address questions of racist violence and justice in times of post-truth relativism.

What unfolds on both screens of Pfeifer's installation captures and reenacts a widely reported event in May 2016, when four male citizens of Arnsdorf, Saxony, in what they presented as an act of civil courage and self-justice, dragged a refugee from Iraq violently out of a discount super-market and tied him with cable ties to a nearby tree. The traumatized refugee died shortly after this event due to other circumstances, which caused the court proceedings against the four attackers to close without a verdict in 2017.

In a setting clearly marked as a film stage, two hosts, played by well-known German crime-show actors Dennenesch Zoudé and Mark Waschke, reconstruct the events for the audience with the help of photographs and YouTube videos and provide background information about the various people involved. They constantly cross the lines between different diegetic spaces as they oversee a meticulous reenactment of the supermarket incident in the studio setting. On another diegetic level, we also observe ten German citizens who in turn observe the reenactment from a position similar to that of the audience in front of the two screens. They are more than mere witnesses, though. Instead, their role will resemble the function missing in the German court system: that of jurors in an American courtroom drama. For in the video's final minutes, each of them will comment on what they saw during the reenactment of the action and leave little doubt that during the original legal proceedings neither was truth established nor justice served. In the words of the exhibition statement itself: "The citizens are interviewed after the last scene is played. They explain how they judge the action's reenactment considering their own biographical, social, cultural and political experiences." As the installation audience's diegetic and meta-diegetic stand-ins, they—as a tribunal of sorts—restore a sense of justice in face of the law's spectacular failure to do so. Though these ersatz-jurors are not asked to speak in one voice to render a joint judgment, Pfeifer's installation effectively employs the dual-screen set up to draw the viewer into a form of reparative justice—one in which the law seemingly requires the pluralistic perspective of artistic media to overcome its own blind spots and restore some sense of legitimacy.

During the first half of the film, Pfeifer uses the combination of two screens as a quasi-forensic medium to reconstruct the supermarket incident from multiple perspectives, highlight the extent to which our knowledge about real events relies on mediated images, and remind extradiegetic viewers of the different diegetic levels that permeate each other in the video. While we watch our hosts introduce, direct, and review the performance on one screen, the action they help to choreograph unfolds on the other. Repeatedly, we watch the same sequence of events from two different angles. We observe our witnesses witnessing while we are also able to see, from some other point of view, what may unfold in front of our eyes. And we see found footage or newspaper reports about the 2016 incident and its legal aftermath. Through these segments, Pfeifer invites the viewer, less to behold two images at once, but rather to toggle between different ontological levels of representation and continually probe competing and not necessarily compatible views on the past. In so doing, *Noch einmal* clearly wants to communicate the instability and multiplicity of truth in our postmodern and highly mediated present, the need to reread and restage the past because whatever we call the document always already entails acts of interpretation.

Filmmaking, in its efforts to reveal the violence done to a refugee in East Germany, thus takes on what characterizes the life of the migrant and exile on a structural level: a logic of an irreconcilable multiplication of temporalities and spatial orientations, a folding of experience that, in the words of Edward Said, results from "the unhealable rift forced between a human being and a native place, between the self and its true home."[3] With its two screens, *Noch einmal* performs this very rift between here and there experienced by migrants and the painful but at times also potentially productive pluralization of narratives, truths, and stories-to-be-told that marks the existence of those dispelled from their homes. It imprints onto the viewer in the gallery what we, with Said, may count as both the ontology and phenomenology of the refugee—and stages this as the most appropriate form to repair the broken vessels of the law and any fetishistic approach to forensic evidence, fact, and truth.

Remarkably, however, *Noch einmal* in the end somewhat mistrusts its own mistrust in the rhetoric of documentary realism, evidence, and legal proceduralism. In the final minutes of the film, when capturing individual statements of the ten justifiably troubled, at times even traumatized inner-diegetic onlookers, the camera work for both screens tends to focus incessantly on each speaker's face, eyes, and mouth, whereby Pfeifer's prolonged extreme close-ups endow their words, their indictments, with unquestionable authenticity and truthfulness. The sequencing of shots and statements at first clearly blurs lines and confuses the extradiegetic viewer. Does this group of ten function as a group of independent witnesses to provide additional testimonies? Do they serve as stand-in jurors offering what the court failed to provide? As members of a tribunal rendering justice through extra-legal procedures? As concerned citizens—our avatars within the film—commenting on the blindness of the existing legal system? While Pfeifer's piece withholds a clear answer

---

3   Edward M. Said, "Reflections on Exile," in *Reflections on Exile and Other Essays* (Cambridge, MA: Harvard University Press, 2000), 173.

to these questions, what becomes clear quickly, however, is that the film's final minutes are all about anchoring the film's political intervention in the echo chambers of personal responses, in the ethics of moral affection. As if in need to bring its political ambitions safely home, the film in the final minutes repudiates its initial rhetoric of fragmentation and incompleteness as caused by the pluralization of truths in post-truth media societies. In its stead, it yields to a stylized language of synthetic amplification and integration: the language of ethical outrage and unconditional empathy. Accordingly, even if they existed unquestionably, by themselves mere facts or evidence—forensic coldness—cannot generate justice and repair the damage done to both the migrant's body and the body politic in general. Instead, what is needed to remediate sociality are vibrant images and sounds—the touch—of individual moral feelings and humanistic commitments; and, more specifically, art film's unique ability to feature the commons as a site that can celebrate difference and diversity and contain xenophobia and racism precisely because its deliberate images exceed the abstraction of positive laws and juridical procedures.

The Murder of Halit Yozgat

The Murder of Halit Yozgat premiered during Documenta 14 in Kassel in 2017, produced by a multidisciplinary team associated with the London-based research group Forensic Architecture (FA). Though it would be difficult, if not impossible, to reduce the work of FA over the past decade to one single agenda and practice,[4] the group's overall ambition has been to question existing, mostly state-centered monopolies in the production of legal and political truths, to involve non-state actors in generating and circulating evidence in open, participatory networks, and in so doing to make audible the voices of those whose victimization in recent conflicts has been silenced or simply remained unheard. FA's signature practice is to make use of advanced digital tools and techniques of data visualization to generate detailed timelines of specific events, drawing on otherwise untapped video or audio archives to read official accounts about past attacks on individual lives or violations of human rights against the grain.

An immigrant from Turkey, Halit Yozgat was killed on April 6, 2006 in an internet café in Kassel. He was the ninth and last victim in the very series of NSU murders that two years earlier had struck a busy street in Cologne's Mühlheim borough as well and would more than a decade later inform the making of Akın's *Aus dem Nichts*. What caused FA to take on Yozgat's killing in 2007 was the peculiar fact that a German intelligence agent, Andreas Temme, was present in the internet café during

---

4   For an overview, see Eyal Weizman, *Forensic Architecture: Violence at the Threshold of Detectability* (New York: Zone Books, 2019).

the killing, yet did not provide any reasonable account of the killing during the initial investigation. *The Murder of Halit Yozgat*'s ambition was less, in the form of a tribunal, to accuse Temme of being involved with the neo-Nazi assassins, than to explore unaccounted evidence, reconstruct the exact timeline of the murder, and simply disprove Temme's initial statements. In order to meet this ambition, however, FA went as far as to build a physical mock version of the entire internet café, allowing the group's researchers to model the events and gather more accurate data about the café's visual field, the dissemination of sound waves after the shooting, and even the spread of sulfuric clouds and smells as caused by the firing of the gun.

When displayed at Documenta 14, *The Murder of Halit Yozgat* was presented on three adjacent screens, each offering a different aspect of the reconstruction and reenactment, all contributing to developing a timeline down to the second that in the end debunked the validity of Temme's account. The representation's tremendous rigor and care for detail wants to speak for itself. The film's use of hitherto untapped archives—e.g., the terminal login timestamps of various users in the internet café—and of scientifically complex modelling scenarios—e.g., the possible reverberation of sound waves in the building after the shots—documents the artists' uncompromising dedication to due diligence. And the distribution of images across the screens emphasizes at once the collaborative work it takes to carry out this investigation and the actual work it is to watch the reconstruction as the viewer's gaze constantly needs to shuttle between all three screens to follow and synthesize the developments. The fragmentation of possible perspectives across the installation's three screens thus results in a programmatic mobilization of the viewer's gaze: it heightens our sense of alertness and attention, but it also emphasizes the active role of the viewer in what may count as truth and evidence in the first place.

Though *The Murder of Halit Yozgat* ends with a clear sense that Temme lied about his presence in the internet café and that state authorities failed their presumed mission to investigate possible evidence extensively, the installation's ambition is not to cast an extra-juridical verdict, let alone implicate Temme in the murder. Instead, the point is simply to visualize the inadequacy of what had formerly counted as evidence and claim that the case cannot be considered closed yet. Just as importantly, in its efforts to mobilize the viewer's perception across its animated screens and engage us in the process of truth finding, the piece exemplifies one of FA's core ideas: the desire to deconstruct the sanctity and positivism of ordinary understandings of evidence and the ambition to perform in front of our eyes the very fact that facts and truths are nothing but constructions to be negotiated and evaluated in the forum of the public sphere. As Thomas Keenan writes:

It is an arduous labor of truth construction, one employing a spectrum of technologies that the forum provides, and all sorts of scientific, rhetorical, theatrical, and visual mechanisms. It is in the gestures, techniques, and turns of demonstration, whether poetic, dramatic, or narrative, that a forensic aesthetics can make things appear in the world. The forums in which facts are debated are the technologies of persuasion, representation, and power—not of truth, but of truth construction.[5]

Keenan's concept of truth construction will certainly raise some eyebrows as it may be seen as feeding directly into post-truth notions of "alternate facts" and efforts to shape legal and political processes according to one's relativistic understanding of the real; as such, it in fact may be seen as an open invitation to unprecedented forms of self-justice and extra-juridical vigilantisms.[6] This is not the place to discuss this in detail or to complicate and refute such assumptions. What matters more for our context here is that FA's stress on the process in which truths are constructed, debated, and negotiated is designed to remind us of the rhetorical, performative, narrative, and aesthetic aspects of what is typically considered as the facticity of evidence in the first place. As such, it wants to sharpen our awareness for the forums (or the lack of forums) in which different claims about the truths of legal arguments meet each other. To hold on to concepts of unambiguous evidence, we are told, is as problematic as to hold on to naïve notions of the evidentiary nature of photography—the indexical—not just in times of the digital capture, rendition, and dissemination of photographic images, but in general. No truth or evidence can exist today without referencing or rendering transparent the process that allowed one to make certain claims in the first place, and no process in truth construction and finding can be persuasive if it fails to address its own rhetorical qualities, the formal or aesthetic aspects of how we try to reconstruct and visualize the past.

With its deliberate animations spread *and* fractured across three different screens, *The Murder of Halit Yozgat* engages its multi-screen installation setting as an ideal platform to meet these challenges. Each screen possibly comments on the other, each image is in conversation with another (and the viewer), thus dispelling the idea that truth and evidence would reveal themselves if we simply looked hard and clear enough. One can argue about whether FA's use of the art world as the primary arena to reevaluate and publicize possible violations of due process and basic

5   Thomas Keenan and Eyal Weizman, *Mengele's Skull: The Advent of a Forensic Aesthetics* (Berlin: Sternberg Press, 2012), 67.

6   See Zachary Feldman's trenchant analysis in "Art or Artifice: The Role of Documentary in Contemporary Art" (PhD Thesis, Vanderbilt University, 2022), 70–133.

human rights mostly preaches to the already converted. What *The Murder of Halit Yozgat* offers us, however, is a place, a reparative forum, to reposition (post)autonomous art as a contemporary place, a place of contemporaneity, at which to interrogate the performative and aesthetic aspects of evidence and truth; and to realize the extent to which any effort to hold on to naïve, positivist notions of truth and evidence echoes analogous efforts to maintain naïve notions of photographic indexicality and to ground lives and identities in the fixity of space. Ours is an age of mobility, flux, and unmoored identities, as much as it is an age in which neither photographic images nor legal courts provide uncontestable truths based on objectivist notions of forensic evidence. What we need, according to *The Murder of Halit Yozgat*, are robust public forums in whose perimeters we can carry our competing truth claims, drill deep into repressed strata of knowledge and data, and precisely thus live up to the idea that nothing about our present, including the borders between art and society, evidence and interpretation, and the migrant and the native, can be taken for granted anymore.

Pluralism and the End of Aesthetic Autonomy

As we have come to know them over the course of the last decade, post-truth societies do not simply erase reliable boundaries between fact and opinion, evidence and falsehood, but in so doing they erode the very fabric that warrants communality and enables civil forms and forums of political debate, controversy, and dissent. In a world of alternate facts and self-contained social media communities, what gets lost is much more than just the difference between facticity and falsity. What crumbles instead is any shared faith in the vibrancy and desirability of political dialogue, life, and difference. That is why Hannah Arendt, in a famous essay of 1967 entitled "Truth and Politics,"[7] correlated the waning of truth and rigorous political debate in twentieth-century culture with the rise of totalitarian movements and their efforts to erase any instances of difference, otherness, and plurality:

> If everyone lies to you, the consequence is not that you believe the lies, but that no one believes anything at all anymore—and rightly so, because lies, by their very nature, have to be changed, to be "relied," so to speak. So, a lying government which pursues different goals at different times has constantly to rewrite its own history.

---

7   Hannah Arendt, "Truth and Politics," *New Yorker*, February 17, 1967, https://www.newyorker.com/magazine/1967/02/25/truth-and-politics.

That means that people are deprived not only of their capacity to act, but also of their capacity to think and to judge.[8]

In Arendt's view, our faculty to form judgments, understood as our ability to make distinctions, at once required and reinforced the fabric of communality and our capacity to probe other viewpoints and perspectives. To form judgments and opinions, in Arendt's perspective, always aimed at some form of publicness; it relied on the anticipated effort to persuade others from one's perspective, on involving and including those who are not us in our reasoning, however solitary good thinking might be. The totalitarian attack on evidence and facticity, however, its effort to remove truth from the vocabulary of political discourse, could not but result in marking the other as incompatible other. It was inherently anti-pluralist, and it rested on and resulted in a politics of scapegoating, of marginalization, of exclusion—one that in our own times first and foremost directs itself against those who allegedly don't belong: the migrants, the exiles, the refugees.

The films and video installations discussed in this chapter, in drawing on the affordances of their respective media platforms, aspire to nothing less than restoring sociability and judgment: they engage the figure of the migrant and refugee as a figure critical to the future of pluralistic forms of political life. In each of the works, the cutting between different perspectives plays a pivotal role in moving beyond the anti-pluralist stalemates of post-truth society, whether it means to shuttle between different points of view within one and the same cinematic frame (*Aus dem Nichts*), across two screens (*Noch einmal*), or between multiple screens and different modalities of moving images such as computer animation and found footage (*The Murder of Halit Yozgat*). While it is tempting to see in each project a certain anxiety or potential to digress into toothless gestures of relativism and constructivism, or even to secretly mimic post-truth ideas of alternate facts, the point of all three pieces is to insist that we cannot solve the challenge of global mass migration and exile today if we resort to monological perspectives and hence to wide-scale efforts to eradicate the border between truth and lie, fact and fiction. In all three works, the migrant serves as a powerful reminder of the need for us to probe competing viewpoints and interpretations of reality, which in Arendt's view defined the very condition not only for operative political life but also our very capacity to form judgments in the first place.

These projects' concern with forensics, then, provides much more than just a political intervention or form of advocacy. Instead, it situates

---

8   Hannah Arendt, "Interview with Roger Errera," in *Thinking without Banisters: Essays in Understanding, 1953–1975*, ed. Jerome Kohn (New York: Schocken Books, 2018), 491–92.

the art of moving images, in all its different manifestations, as a critical medium to uphold the claims of communality and justice amid the antipluralist, post-truth drain of faith in public life. Art and the aesthetic, they all propose, matter as never before to secure the workings of a diverse social fabric and its ability to engage with the figure of the migrant and refugee, so frequently perceived as Other. In its inherent ability to offer different and pluralistic views of what may count as fact and evidence, the spheres of film art and aesthetic visualization in all three projects shed former claims of self-contained aesthetic autonomy, aspire to build new alliances, and seek to migrate into contested political and legal fields—all this to restore what it might take to extend justice to the precarious position of migrants and refugees in our contemporary world.

Bibliography

Arendt, Hannah. "Interview with Roger Errera." In *Thinking without Banisters: Essays in Understanding, 1953–1975*, edited by Jerome Kohn, 489–505. New York: Schocken Books, 2018.

———. "Truth and Politics." *The New Yorker*, February 17, 1967. https://www.newyorker.com/magazine/1967/02/25/truth-and-politics.

Feldman, Zachary. "Art or Artifice: The Role of Documentary in Contemporary Art." PhD thesis, Vanderbilt University, 2022.

Keenan, Thomas, and Eyal Weizman. *Mengele's Skull: The Advent of a Forensic Aesthetics*. Berlin: Sternberg Press, 2012.

Koepnick, Lutz. "Records in Motion: Migrants and Mobile Spectatorship." In *Gegen\Dokumentation: Operationen-Foren-Interventionen*, edited by Esra Canpalat, Maran Haffke, Sarah Horn, Felix Hüttemann, and Matthias Preuss, 29–38. Bielefeld: Transcript, 2020.

Rauterberg, Hanno. *Die Kunst und das gute Leben: Über die Ethik der Ästhetik*. Frankfurt am Main: Suhrkamp, 2015.

Said, Edward M. "Reflections on Exile." In *Reflections on Exile and Other Essays*, 173–86. Cambridge, MA: Harvard University Press, 2000.

Ulrich, Wolfgang. *Die Kunst nach dem Ende ihrer Autonomie*. Berlin: Wagenbach, 2022.

Weizman, Eyal. *Forensic Architecture: Violence at the Threshold of Detectability*. New York: Zone Books, 2019.

5: The Border as Abjecting Apparatus: *Shipwreck at the Threshold of Europe, Lesvos, Aegean Sea* (2020) and *Purple Sea* (2019)

Randall Halle

Aт тне END OF THE SUMMER on August 18, 2015, a boat capsized in the Aegean carrying migrants from Turkey to Greece. It was not the only boat that had sunk in that turbulent summer. Already five months earlier on April 18, 2015, between 700 and 1,100 people had lost their lives in one of the worst shipwrecks in the Mediterranean when the ship they were on sank in the waters between Libya and Lampedusa. In 2014, over 5,000 and in 2015 almost 7,000 people perished making the crossing.[1] But on August 18, something important for our understanding of the dangerous crossing happened; the filmmaker Amel Alzakout wore a waterproof Contour camera on her wrist that recorded the journey and the tragic shipwreck. Luckily, she survived the ordeal and made it eventually to Berlin, where she was able to settle and begin to work. The visual material she captured chronicled the experience of a wreck, lost lives, and a rescue at sea operation. Alzakout's material has come to serve as key incitement to two recent film projects: *Purple Sea* (Amel Alzakout and Khaled Abdulwahed, 2019) and *Shipwreck at the Threshold of Europe, Lesvos, Aegean Sea* (Forensic Architecture, 2020). This chapter considers these films closely; it also draws from them in its general reflections on the work of the moving image in representing migrant experience and on the work of the border as an abjecting apparatus.

On a certain level, this work joins a series of films about the 2015 migrant wave that includes *Fuocoammare* (Gianfranco Rosi, 2016),

---

1 The Missing Migrants Project of the International Organization for Migration (IOM) estimates that over 24,000 migrants have died in the Mediterranean crossing since 2014. 2016 was the worst year with over 8,000 deaths. Numbers have remained around 5,000 annually depending on the pressures of migration and the conditions of border control in Turkey and North Africa. See Missing Migrants Project, accessed November 11, 2022, https://missingmigrants.iom. int/who-we-are.

Human Flow (Ai Weiwei, 2016), *Sea Sorrow* (Vanessa Redgrave, 2017), and *It will be Chaos* (Lorena Luciano and Filippo Piscopo, 2018). These films have a broader focus and contain images of masses drawn from the twenty-four-hour news reporting cycle. As Karen Remmler noted of these films, "images of overcrowded boats have become iconic for the plight of refugees."[2] We can add that the stories of these films typically begin precisely at the shore; in effect the stories begin with the people framed as a mass of refugees headed to Europe. The so-called refugee crisis presents the migrants as a crisis for their point of destination. Their backstory, where they are from, the rationales that brought them to the journey, and what transpired before they reached the shore typically play little part in the films. The crises they experienced that force them into migration do not enter into the frame of these films. As I have discussed elsewhere, this way of representing the flood of refugees in these films reduces the fellow human to an Other without individuality, without a personal story; they are massified without a particular face.[3] And facelessness has consequences for how we understand our ethical relation to the other.

To a certain extent, this condition of overcrowded boat and facelessness describes the images Alzakout captured. The camera attached to her wrist reveals the boat and the water but does not focalize Alzakout as subject.[4] Yet there is more to this footage than pictures of pitiable abject refugees being helped by Europeans, as Lilie Chouliaraki has discussed.[5] To be sure, Alzakout's film material could have easily become lost in the vast grave that the Mediterranean has become. Indeed, many on Alzakout's boat did indeed perish. They almost fell to the fate that Estela Schindel has poetically lamented in her work on the border crossings of the undocumented, whereby their deaths are traceless and take place out of sight, in the remoteness of seas and deserts, as clandestinely as the journey itself.[6] We are grateful that this fate did not happen. Alzakout's footage

---

2   Karen Remmler, "The Afterlives of Refugee Dead," *EuropeNow* 33, special feature on "European Art, Culture, and Politics," April 28, 2020, https://www.europenowjournal.org/2020/04/27/the-afterlives-of-refugee-dead-what-remains/.

3   Randall Halle, *Visual Alterity: Seeing Difference in Cinema* (Urbana-Champaign: University of Illinois Press, 2021).

4   For in-depth discussions of focalization, see the contributions in Peter Hühn, Wolf Schmid, and Jörg Schönert, eds., *Point of View, Perspective, and Focalization* (Berlin: de Gruyter, 2009).

5   Lilie Chouliaraki, "Between Pity and Irony: Paradigms of Refugee Representation in Humanitarian Discourse," in *Migrations and the Media: Global Crises and the Media*, ed. Kerry Moore, Berhard Gross, and Terry Threadgold (New York: Peter Lang, 2012), 13–31.

6   Estela Schindel, "Border Matters: Death, Mourning and Materiality at the European Borderlands," *EuropeNow* 33, special feature on "European Art, Culture,

now has an important and even singular quality in the documents of the migrant experience. Her material counters the tracelessness of the lost in the border crossing and allows for a new type of analysis of the experience and the conditions that are needed to counter the iconography of the media-constituted flood of Others.

Of the two projects that the material generated, *Purple Sea* is a very personal film, employing the strategy of a personal essay or experimental autobiographical film. It was produced in collaboration with Pong Film, one of Germany's most innovative film teams focused on experimental documentary projects.[7] *Shipwreck* by contrast travels as an installation project, is available as well on the web, and was made by a group at the forefront of the so-called "forensic turn." I will explore this "turn" below, but for now let me underscore that both projects pose powerful critiques of the European border control and rescue operations of that period. They display a border control operation oriented toward expelling migrants, rather than rescuing them. Moreover, they work against dominant images of a European (southern) border as a natural and clearly defined barrier.[8] Forensic Architecture in particular has focused in its work on how the Mediterranean passage has been made difficult or dangerous by an apparatus of border control. Frontex, the European Border and Coast Guard Agency, appears repeatedly in Forensic Architecture's projects as part of an apparatus that separates a European community from a "foreign" other. Indeed, I am interested in these two complexly connected films for precisely what they reveal about the border. The masses of humans seeking passage to safety are not pitiable and abject, rather it is the border as apparatus that seeks to abject them. These films offer a counter-perspective to the abjection inscribed in the current configuration of the European border apparatus.

---

and Politics," April 28, 2020, https://www.europenowjournal.org/2020/04/27/border-matters-death-mourning-and-materiality-at-the-european-borderlands/.

7   For a general discussion of Pong and, in particular, the related film *Havarie*, see Halle, *Visual Alterity*.

8   Fazila Bhimji, *Border Regimes, Racialisation Processes and Resistance in Germany: An Ethnographic Study of Protest and Solidarity* (Cham: Palgrave Macmillan, 2020); Marise Cremona and Joanne Scott, eds., *EU Law Beyond EU Borders: The Extraterritorial Reach of EU Law* (Oxford: Oxford University Press, 2019); Ljudmila Bilkic, "'Everything New Is Born Illegal.' Historicizing Rapid Migration through New Media Projects" (PhD diss., University of Pittsburgh, 2018); Gržinic, Marina, ed., *Border Thinking: Disassembling Histories of Racialized Violence* (Berlin: Sternberg Press, 2018).

The European Border as Abjecting Apparatus

When Alzakout's overloaded wooden boat headed from the Turkish mainland trying to reach the island of Lesbos, it set out on a journey of only twelve kilometers. I want to underscore that there is a direct ferry crossing this very route many times a day, providing a safe alternative for people to move. But the ferry is foreclosed to people without particular papers and, as a result, in order to make the crossing those without such papers have to pay into an active international smuggling economy.[9] At the end of summer 2015, talks between the EU and Turkey had gone public in which the participants discussed terms for the Turkish government to shut the Mediterranean routes down. Smugglers crowded people onto this boat who had become anxious about their status and were thus willing to take greater risks. It was late in the season but the numbers of people seeking passage continued to rise even though the Aegean waters are more difficult and colder at this time. The boat capsized with over three hundred people on board. Forty-three people died and at least seventeen others went missing.

What is of particular interest to me here is that this is the European border, a border that has gone through intense transformation since the 1990s and helps us understand the various possibilities of borders and the juridico-political regimes that draw them. The lifting of the border between the two Germanies in 1991 compelled the end of the Cold War and an end to the oppositional blocs that divided the European continent for almost half a century. The loss of the German-German border transpired almost simultaneously with the formation of the Schengen Zone of the European Union. The proclamation in 1992 of a "Europe without borders" did not of course mean that Europe had no borders, but within the geographical territory demarcated by the states belonging to the Schengen Zone, a liberal order came to reign allowing for the free passage of goods, services, and people.

The malleability and transformation of European borders continued as further response to ongoing shifts in state organization and juridico-political discourses. Indeed, the breakup of the former Yugoslavia and the waves of refugees out of the Balkans in the mid-1990s showed how quickly the rationale of Europe without borders could become

---

9   International Organization for Migration, *Migrant Smuggling Data and Research: A Global Review of the Emerging Evidence Base*, vol. 2 (Geneva: International Organization for Migration, 2018); Ruben Andersson, *Illegality, Inc: Clandestine Migration and the Business of Bordering Europe* (Berkeley: University of California Press, 2014).

"Fortress Europe."[10] Even after the pacification of the Yugoslav crises, the European border continued to transform; the project of European unionization led to waves of new states acceding to the EU—most famously in 2004, the year of Eastern Enlargement. And then as it might have appeared that the geopolitical lines of Europe had approached some stability, since 2014 a number of contestations and further reconfigurations of the geopolitical space designated as Europe have taken place: the annexation of Crimea, Brexit, the Arab Spring and the waves of refugees fleeing Syria, the reassertion of border controls during the COVID-19 pandemic, and the Russian invasion of Ukraine and the opening to asylum seekers fleeing violence there. All of these events have impacted the cartographic and mental maps of Europe.

In this intense history of rapid shifts in the European border, with its almost dialectical tension of an open liberal and a circumscribed protectionist space, we recognize quickly that "where is Europe" is less a question of a "naturalness" of borders, rivers, seas, mountains, etc., and more a question of ideational belonging. Europe's border is not first a geopolitical cartographic delineation, but rather a condition that allows people to feel themselves to be proximate and complexly connected to each other.

Benedict Anderson helped us consider how distant and disconnected peoples are given to feel themselves as part of a common community within the nation-state.[11] Here I am interested precisely in the interconnected but opposite process, in effect the question: by what mechanisms do we fail to recognize our others as being in community or being worthy of our solidarity?[12] The rapidly shifting European border provides important insights into this imagining of non-community, of essential abject difference. The European border, but also borders in general, border regimes, and borders as an apparatus of differentiation and dissociation play a role central to the determination of whom we recognize as our neighbors and whom we consider as foreign and other, even if they live next door. The border designates a psycho-social apparatus for the assertion of inclusion and the exertion of exclusion and expulsion.

In *The Powers of Horror* Julia Kristeva famously described the act of abjection as that process that occurs before a subject/object relation can

---

10 Stephen Gallagher, "Towards a Common European Asylum System: Fortress Europe Redesigns the Ramparts," *International Journal* 57, no. 3 (2002): 375–94.

11 Benedict Anderson, *Imagined Communities: Reflections on the Origin and Spread of Nationalism* (New York: Verso, 2006).

12 See Randall Halle, *The Europeanization of Cinema: Interzones and Imaginative Communities* (Urbana-Champaign: University of Illinois Press, 2014); Halle, *Visual Alterity*.

come into existence.[13] She suggested that before a subject can emerge, the boundaries of a self must first be drawn and thereby that which is other to the self, endangers it, threatens its existence, its ability to exist as subject, must be abjected, expelled to the other side. In that work, Kristeva began by considering waste, death, byproducts which could harm the life of the individual and the community. Such has to be expelled for health and life. Yet Kristeva, also a theorist of intersubjectivity, considered further how the abject likewise provides a point of fascination for the subject, as if the abject is never fully expelled, never completely lost, rather the subject returns to and retains a relation to the abjected. The abject marks an ambiguity of desire and repulsion.

There is an ambiguity in her own writing, a lack of systematicity that results at times in an inversion of her analysis. She writes: "It is thus not lack of cleanliness or health that causes abjection but what disturbs identity, system, order. What does not respect borders, positions, rules."[14] And yet Kristeva considered how prohibitions mark the distinction of the constituted subject and its abject—its point of fascination. The ambiguity in her approach arises, I maintain, because Kristeva failed to distinguish adequately between the biological, psychological, social, and symbolic in her discussion. The law in Kristeva's psychoanalytic approach encompasses these various aspects and is itself understood as stable or, rather, essentializing. I would immediately suggest that the Law, or what I have discussed as juridico-political discourse, does not have this kind of essential stability, rather it exerts an essentializing and stabilizing effect.[15]

To be clear, I understand abjection not as an essential condition of the social political. And as much as cell membranes abject and expel, Kristeva largely ignored that they also allow for transfer, ingestion, incorporation, inclusion, skin for sensing, breathing, feeling. Without the permeability of the membrane, the cell would also die. To my point in this chapter, the geopolitical border and subjective consciousness do not require distinction and difference to be drawn one way or the other. The loss of an abjecting border does not inherently result in the end of life as membrane loss does at the cellular level or flaying at the corporeal. (Sub)conscious abjection of the subject or political and conscious abjection by a state are not permanent, natural, or necessary in form. Geopolitical borders are always permeable. They move and can take on different forms. Arsenic or viral RNA passing a membrane may kill the cell, but humans crossing

---

13 Julia Kristeva. *Powers of Horror: An Essay on Abjection; European Perspectives*, trans. Leon S. Roudiez (New York: Columbia University Press, 1982).

14 Kristeva, *Powers of Horror*, 4.

15 Randall Halle, *Queer Social Philosophy: Critical Readings from Kant to Adorno* (Urbana-Champaign: University of Illinois Press, 2004).

borders are not poison or disease, even if populist media and demagogic politicians often describe migrants as such.

Nevertheless, focusing the paradigm of abjection on geopolitical borders helps us underscore that they are not first and foremost a geographic distinction, a territorial demarcation that separates and inside from an outside. They are not a matter of a given space or culture; rather, they assert sociopolitical space and cultural differentiation. Borders designate what belongs in and outside. Historically, for instance, the Mediterranean has been a space of communication around the entire basin. It is not a matter of distance that separates a space designated Europe from a Mediterranean South. Recall that the distance between the Mediterranean "North" and "South" is quite close geographically. Seventy kilometers separates Tunisia from Italy, the Straits of Gibraltar separate Morocco from Spain by fourteen kilometers. This distance is shorter than Calais to Dover. In the Aegean, where Amel Alzakout set out, the Greek island of Lesbos is twelve kilometers and the island of Kos is even closer, a mere four kilometers from the Turkish mainland. And yet the ideational distance can seem vast. The European imaginative community is not based on geographic proximity.

What is inside and outside Europe in this region has been subject to the same ideational shifting as in Northern and Eastern Europe. Indeed, until recently, policy of the EU to the Southern Mediterranean directed it precisely toward affiliation. It asserted the communicative proximity of the region. In the 1990s, similar to the plans for Eastern Europe, the EU had initiated the EUROMED project to the south to unite this entire region into a free trade, democratic, and culturally coherent zone, preparing to incorporate the Mediterranean rim countries as partners into the EU.[16] However, in the shifting formations of the European border, by 2015 this affiliative assertion of geographic proximity had become an insistence on distance. The Mediterranean became a territory of division and the EU's border apparatus worked to rupture the connectivity once praised and fostered.

The Forensic Turn and the European Border Apparatus

Shipwreck and *Purple Sea* help us understand how the border apparatus is tied fundamentally not to geography but to perception. The perceiving and organizing of difference as fundamental to perception must occur in an interaction of perceiver and perceived positioned somewhere

---

16 Emanuel Adler, *The Convergence of Civilizations: Constructing a Mediterranean Region* (Toronto: University of Toronto Press, 2006); Boening, "Multilateralism South of the Border"; Halle, *The Europeanization of Cinema.*

and somehow in a relation. Both film projects invite us to consider the media of representation as well as the regime that seeks to organize those images. The work of film takes place in an apparatus of material and ideational organization.

The border is a result of perception of boundaries and differentiations. Our technologies of seeing, like film and other visual media, are as much a part of the border apparatus as are our maps and border walls. Seeing is dynamic. Our ability to see the other, visual alterity is a dynamic—but what kind? Is the other a neighbor or threat, a guest we control with our hospitality or a resident with rights, an exhabitant we must excise, a cohabitant whom we tolerate, or an inhabitant who extends our communal existence.

The European border control agency Frontex proudly announced that they had conducted a successful rescue of a large group of refugees together with the Greek Coastguard. Not content with the self-praise of Frontex, after she arrived in Berlin and was able to resume work, Amel Alzakout contacted Forensic Architecture to help her reconstruct the rescue operation with the material she had recorded. *Shipwreck at the Threshold of Europe, Lesvos, Aegean Sea* is the resulting double projection project undertaken by Forensic Architecture, which appeared in 2020.[17]

As an artist collective, Forensic Architecture (FA) began its first projects around 2010 with the work of Eyal Weizman and an ever-growing team of colleagues at Goldsmiths, University of London.[18] Their first published projects were focused on the Israeli-occupied territories but then moved out into various incidents of military abuse, genocide, drone strikes, state sanctioned killing, *and* migrant deaths in the Mediterranean. If the first critical receptions were confused as to the aesthetic value of FA's work, the breakthrough in 2014 with exhibitions at Documenta 14 and the HKW in Berlin brought an appreciation of the possibility of FA to mediate galleries and courtrooms, crime scenes and museums. Since then, no significant survey of modern art seems complete without the inclusion of an FA project.

To date there are over eighty projects on these various topics with *Shipwreck* as project number fifty-two. However, *Shipwreck* can be considered as part of a connected series of investigations of incidents in which people seeking safe harbor and refuge were endangered or died. FA has paid special attention to the perils of those crossing into Europe. Their titles have a style defined by factual specificity, an almost legal language.

---

17 Forensic Architecture, accessed November 11, 2022, https://forensic-architecture.org/investigation/shipwreck-at-the-threshold-of-europe. See also Lutz Koepnick's discussion of Forensic Architecture in this volume.

18 Eyal Weizman, Paulo Taveres, Susan Schuppli, and Situ Studio, "Forensic Architecture," *Architectural Design* 80, no. 5 (2010): 58–63.

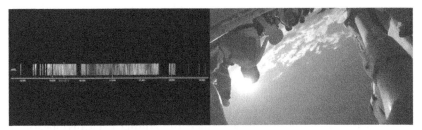

Figure 5.1. Timeline left, image from Alzakout's camera right. *Shipwreck at the Threshold of Europe, Lesvos, Aegean Sea* (Forensic Architecture, 2020).

Listed together they begin to reveal a purposive dynamic. And we can see how the actions of the EU's border apparatus impact a cartographic line: *Pushbacks across the Evros/Meriç River: Analysis of Video Evidence Evros/Meriç River, Greece/Turkey Border 17.09.2019* and *Pushbacks across the Evros/Meriç River: The Case of Ayşe Erdoğan Evros/Meriç River, Greece/Turkey 04—05.05.2019*. The dates, the number of projects, and the increasing frequency of incidents explored indicates an intensification of FA's attention to the problem. But also the work on the topic increased because the violent expulsion and abjection of migrants by the European border apparatus intensified in the period.

FA's projects are available online but also appear installed in galleries, museums, and further contexts. At the 2020 Berlin International Film Festival in the Forum Expanded exhibition "Part of the Problem," *Shipwreck* was one of thirty-nine installations addressing themes of migration, racism, sexism, state violence, and colonialism, among others.[19] Online, the work becomes two-dimensional and informative. Installed it takes on spatial and tactile qualities that draw out other kinds of interaction, not the least of which is collective affect. At the Berlinale *Shipwreck* appeared as two screens at a slight angle to each other. The installation made use of headsets to make the voice over available in the gallery space of Silent Green. Subtitles also allowed access without sonic experience. Indeed, in this project the audio experience plays a very minor role, unlike *Shipwreck's* quasi-companion piece *Purple Sea*, as will be discussed later. A bench afforded individuals an invitation to a collective viewing experience.

The aesthetic of this project as well as the work of Forensic Architecture in general is based in the artifice of digital editing. As with other projects, in *Shipwreck* one of the two screens shows the editing

---

19 "Berlinale Forum and Forum Expanded," accessed November 11, 2022, https://www.arsenal-berlin.de/de/berlinale-forum/programm-forum-expanded/forum-expanded-exhibition.html.

timeline (see Fig. 5.1 above), or the editing timeline runs across the bottom of the two screens while the images under discussion appear above. The viewers can see where the images they are viewing are located in the digital stream, and this makes possible for the viewer to understand other possibilities of montage and hence critically interrogate the ordering of the images FA presents. The format thus makes the connection between image, timeline, editing, and analysis explicit, rather than seeking to produce a series of edited images in which the editing itself disappears. It counters the kinds of seamless image of traditional documentary or those of the news media that are presented as objective. The argument of the project is not bolstered by the impact of images, or by the images edited to fit into an editorial frame; rather, the argument is embedded in the critical analysis of the images and what they show/reveal. This format develops a new type of reflexivity akin to modernist practices of alienation and apparatus display.

We can understand this project and the work of FA in general as part of a larger forensic turn of which FA is only a prominent part.[20] In attempts to expand a culture of human rights and borderless movement, forensic investigation of murder sites and mass graves has proven important to quests for justice in disparate places around the globe, from Argentina to the successor countries of the former Yugoslavia, from South Africa to Myanmar. The broader forensic turn out of which FA emerged typically challenges national narratives of defense, rejects clean war and surgical strike descriptions, and interrogates the culpability of state leadership. It works to counter state narratives disseminated in the mainstream media. In a post-truth era, FA reasserts authenticity, facts, and truth. Against state cover ups, it offers a pedagogy of how to view critically in order to see the truth. I am interested here in the work being produced as part of the forensic turn, especially because as Estela Schindel and others have shown, borders like the European southern border have increasingly

---

20 Jean-Marc Dreyfus and Élisabeth Gessat-Anstett, *Human Remains and Identification Mass Violence, Genocide, and the "Forensic Turn": Human Remains and Violence* (Manchester: Manchester University Press, 2015); Zuzanna Dziuban, *Mapping the "Forensic Turn": Engagements with Materialities of Mass Death in Holocaust Studies and Beyond* (Vienna: new academic press, 2017); Eyal Weizman, *Forensic Architecture: Violence at the Threshold of Detectability* (New York: Zone Books, 2017); James Frieze, *Theatrical Performance and the Forensic Turn* (Oxford: Routledge, 2019); Charles Stankievech, "Exhibit A: Notes on a Forensic Turn in Contemporary Art," *Afterall* 47, no. 1 (2019): 42–55; Cecilia Sjöholm, "Images Do Not Take Sides"; Ljiljana Radonić, "Globalization, Universalization, and Forensic Turn: Postcatastrophic Memorial Museums," in *The Afterlife of the Shoah in Central and Eastern European Cultures: Concepts, Problems, and the Aesthetics of Postcatastrophic Narration*, ed. Anna Artwinska and Anja Tippner (New York: Routledge, 2022), 99–114.

become sites of mass graves and hidden atrocities.[21] And the citizens of the EU have come to accept that the work of the border apparatus is to abject people from entry. (Something similar can be said of the US's southern border.) FA's critical viewing works to "resensitize" audiences to the desensitizing of mainstream images.

In this forensic turn, we can also look to the work of Lawrence Abu Hamdan, Basel Abbas and Ruanne Abou-Rahme, Kader Attia, Sandra Gamarra Heshiki, Philip Scheffner, and Merle Kröger among others. Their work pursues similar goals and increasingly plays a central role in galleries, museums, and art biennales appearing with FA projects. Moreover, the combination of archaeology and forensic science in the forensic turn has had practical juridico-political implications supporting court proceedings and reconciliation work.

In FA's projects specifically, the collective gathers all visual and sonic evidence, written reports from media, police, state and non-state actors, that is, from the entire information apparatus. It is this gathering of evidence, the research into the incidents, that motivates the designation "forensic" in the group's title. Then FA arranges that evidence vis-à-vis the claims typically of the state actor/enforcement agency. It builds it up on the screen to provide an analysis of the veracity of the claims, providing an analytic "architecture," an alternative apparatus.

In the case of *Shipwreck*, FA focused in part on Frontex's claim that it had undertaken a heroic rescue effort. The initial "evidence" for considering the claim was the wrist-mounted Contour camera footage from Alzakout. But additionally, as is typical, the team gathered GPS data, cell phone recordings, thermal imaging, and newspaper and media images as well. They contacted the Greek Coast Guard, combed YouTube, accessed still images and cellphone recordings of Greek and Turkish fishermen, and worked with an Associated Press reporter. They also turned to activist artist Richard Mosse, who had been there recording the incident with a thermal camera. All this evidence builds the architecture on the screen.

The work of FA has of course predecessors. The voice-over strategy is in line with the work of essay filmmaker and installation artist Harun Farocki, who used voice-over narration to guide viewers through new technologies of viewing. In this vein it likewise draws on the strategies of John Berger's 1972 groundbreaking BBC broadcast of "Ways of Seeing,"

---

21   Estela Schindel, "Bare Life at the European Borders. Entanglements of Technology, Society and Nature," *Journal of Borderlands Studies* 31, no. 2 (2016): 219–34; Estela Schindel, "Death by 'Nature': The European Border Regime and the Spatial Production of Slow Violence," *Environment and Planning. C: Politics and Space* 40, no. 2 (2022): 428–46; Estela Schindel, "Deaths and Disappearances in Migration to Europe: Exploring the Uses of a Transnationalized Category," *The American Behavioral Scientist* 64, no. 4 (2020): 389–407.

or Peter Weibel's broadcast of "teleaktionen" on ORF in the same year. It is at core a pedagogy of what we historically called visual literacy. The voice-over reviews and comments on the material falls silent in order to allow the spectator to view or listen to recorded materials, radio communications, and interviews. The voice also works in a coordinated way with animations and graphic markings of visual images. Significant in the strategy of the voice-over in the work of FA is that it engages in a critical accounting relying on the images to prosecute an argument.

In *Shipwreck*, FA "performs" the shipwreck anew to develop a counter to the narrative provided by the EU border patrol agency Frontex. The analysis of the images here reveals that, contrary to their claims of successful search and rescue, the passengers aboard the capsized boat died needlessly. Furthermore, the lives saved were largely a result of local fishing boats and private activist organizations coming out to rescue. FA displays how coastguard boats and Frontex helicopter created swells and waves that created adverse conditions preventing rescue and ultimately extending exposure to the cold and likely increasing the deaths. Moreover, in the reporting the Greek officials sought to locate the boat in Turkish waters to exonerate themselves, but GPS analysis from the camera and the cellphones allowed FA to pinpoint the boat and display the culpability of the agency and the EU's border regime in causing migrant deaths. This work has led to the growing indictment of Frontex and their criminal practice of pushbacks. FA's meticulous documentation has compelled news investigations and has helped force the EU authorities to open an investigation of Frontex.[22]

FA begin and conclude their analysis placing culpability here not just on Frontex but on the heads of government and policies that "intend to police and repel migrants, rather than setting out to assure their safety" (1:35). And again, the voice-over narrator notes factually that "EU agencies continue to treat those still attempting to cross as intruders rather

---

22 Rhal Ssan, "Investigation Claims Frontex Involved in Aegean Sea Migrant Pushbacks," *Euronews*, April 28, 2022, https://www.euronews.com/2022/04/28/investigation-claims-frontex-involved-in-aegean-sea-migrant-pushbacks; Eva Cossé and Kerstin McCourt, "The Hand at the Helm of Frontex," *Human Rights Watch* (blog), July 19, 2022, https://www.hrw.org/news/2022/07/19/hand-helm-frontex; Christian Jakob, "Pushbacks auf dem Mittelmeer: Frontex lügt und mauert," *taz*, April 29, 2022, https://taz.de/!5851450/; Giorgos Christides and Steffen Lüdke, "(S+) Frontex in illegale Pushbacks von Hunderten Flüchtlingen involviert," *Der Spiegel*, April 27, 2022, https://www.spiegel.de/ausland/frontex-in-illegale-pushbacks-von-hunderten-fluechtlingen-involviert-a-086f0e5a-0172-4007-b59c-7bced325cc75; "Illegale Pushbacks: Was macht die EU?" *Europamagazin*, Brussels: ARD, March 15, 2021, https://www.tagesschau.de/ausland/europa/eukommission-frontex-pushbacks-101.html.

than as civilians seeking safe ground" (22:50). The fact that it took almost six years before the mainstream media began to report on the practice shows the important role that the investigative aesthetic played here in filling the silence.

FA does not explicitly construct a counternarrative. It should be clear that the frame of the investigation focuses on the incident. As noted earlier, the footage from Alzakout's wrist camera does not allow us to easily meet our fellow humans at eye level. The story of the people in the boat is limited to the hard evidence of that moment. It helps us understand the peril imposed on them by the border apparatus at the moment of crossing. If the extensive material brought together in *Shipwreck* does not aim to tell the stories of the people in the boat as individual subjects with personal histories, for that we have *Purple Sea*.

The Autobiographical Turn

It is thus the way that *Purple Sea* seeks to provide knowledge of an Other that makes it so profound. If abjection repels the Other, intersubjectivity opens up the possibility of inclusion and makes inhabitation possible. *Purple Sea* begins like *Shipwreck* with a black screen and a voice-over in Arabic. The voice recalls a beautiful day, shining sun, and blue water. And only then do the first images appear. They take us to the moment when the boat is capsizing. The calm voice is replaced by the screaming, yelling sound of emergency whistles being blown, but also the camera going underwater, a condition that dampens the sounds. The image cuts to black, a title card "Purple Sea," and then we return to the camera in the water. For almost two minutes the film itself is submerged in this environment. The images of the boat capsizing and people falling into the water are disorienting rapid movements blurring easy recognition, and it takes time for the eye to account for what the camera recorded. This is almost the opposite of the "architecture" of *Shipwreck* with its visual, analytic clarity. Blues, yellows, oranges, reds appear first as abstract fields almost, and then as the eye adjusts to the proximity, the recognition of bright ropes and lifejackets, hands and bodies, pants and shirts begins to settle in. The camera is proximate to lots of people in the water and where the arm or hand of Amel ends and others begin is unclear.

After what seems a long time, the voice comes back as a voice-over the ambient sounds of the film—largely those from the submerged camera. And it begins to narrate a story that is itself at first disorienting. It takes a while to understand that the narrative past begins in Amel's childhood. For sixty-six minutes the camera maintains the largely submerged position, the ambient sound continues with dampened screams and yelling, and the voice narrates. Without the story the voice tells, this film would appear largely as a documentary of people drowning. Yet the fact

Figure 5.2. Wrist camera recording. *Purple Sea* (dir. Amel Alzakout and Khaled Abdulwahed, 2019).

that the camera, the voice, and the person in the water are connected helps point to survival and infuses the film with a slight sense of hope.

The narrative told in *Purple Sea* requires focus and attention, not unlike the images that seem to remove themselves into abstraction and require an exertion of focus to bring them back into recognition. The narrative moves around in time, while the camera remains largely submerged pressing among ropes, lifejackets, bodies, and debris. The film thus departs radically from the work of FA. It develops more in line with the personal autobiographical film Robin Curtis has discussed extensively.[23] The body in the water and the voice, in Curtis's terms "focalize" the film, producing a self, a subject narrating its life. The film is thus also akin to what Derrida described as otobiography, a production of self for the ear of the other, except I would note that as film it is an ὣς-ὄσσε (ôs-ósse), a narration of a life for the eye and ear.[24] For me, the autobiographical film here offers an important counter to the act of abjection, distinctly important in ways that FA's pedagogical work cannot accomplish. If abjection otherwise rejects the subjectivity of the other, creating its own subjective borders by repelling and violently expulsing the Other, *Purple Sea* presents a subject exposed to that abjection and is nevertheless enduring.

23 Robin Curtis and Angelica Fenner, *The Autobiographical Turn in Germanophone Documentary and Experimental Film* (Rochester, NY: Camden House, 2014); Robin Curtis, *Conscientious Viscerality: The Autobiographical Stance in German Film and Video* (Berlin: Edition Imorde, 2006).

24 Jacques Derrida, *The Ear of the Other*, trans. Avital Ronell and Peggy Kamuf (Lincoln: University of Nebraska Press, 1988).

Derrida reflected largely on the autobiographical text but of course the turn to film indicates that there is not a simple text nor an easy ear and eye in the audiovisual. Robin Curtis and Angelica Fenner presciently discussed the mediated self in autobiographical film.[25] Largely thinking about video and the expansion of handheld cameras, they discussed the "technology of the self."[26] The advent of cellphone cameras and selfies transformed the possibilities of the production of an (audio)visual self in new ways. Lee Humphreys does argue that we should understand the selfie in a long tradition of the daily diary accounting for the quotidian experience.[27] But unlike the selfie shot capturing its moment, the recording possibilities of the wrist-strapped Contour camera have a different result: the length of recording time, its abstraction, and its referentiality to a body and an incident allow for the production of a self as an event, here a self in distress in the middle of a human tragedy.

This self is akin to the self-produced repeatedly during the Arab Spring with the countless cellphone videos held in the hand, documenting the revolutions that began in 2010 and the violent counter-revolutionary oppressions of which the Syrian war is the longest and most violent. Alzakout's camera localized to the wrist requires the voice to produce the self. Not simply a vocalization, the voice focalizes. That voice relates a meeting of a man in Istanbul, a separation, a trip to Germany, the frog pond, the war in Syria, the condition of human smuggling, the passengers on the boat, the capsizing, being part of a family in Syria, reunion with man and daughter in Berlin, and then the encounter with the helicopter discussed in *Shipwreck*. Affective, emotional, sensorial evocations offset the abstraction of the images: the smell of bread, the smell of a lover's hair, the taste of salt. The film proceeds with periods of silence that make us welcome the voice all the more. The narrative it tells relies on flashbacks and flashforwards, moving forward and yet circling back.

The voice-over considers that the lover's flight to Berlin takes three hours and the ferry ride to Lesbos takes an hour and a half. It describes the smuggler-business man, the possibilities of smartphone GPS for rescue operations. And in such information, presented as brief thoughts, it raises the possibility of a different organization of refuge, asylum, hospitality, safety that counters the abjection of the EU border apparatus. But truly the counter to that abjection in this project is the actual production of a self. The extremely localized camera of this project relies on the actualization of the human imaginary of the Other to go beyond the

---

25 Curtis and Fenner, *The Autobiographical Turn*.

26 Curtis and Fenner, *The Autobiographical Turn*, 16.

27 Lee Humphreys, *The Qualified Self: Social Media and the Accounting of Everyday Life* (Cambridge, MA: MIT Press, 2018).

abstraction of the image. We are required to listen to Amel and, as we do, she is raised to the level of subject. Our own subjectivity does not require the abjection of the Other. The film suggests another way of imagining not based on the abjection of the EU border apparatus. It offers another imaginative community to its viewers: one of affiliation. Ultimately, the spectator should ask what forced such a dangerous crossing in a reality of ferries between Kos and Bodrum or airplanes between Istanbul and Berlin. It invites a connection to the subject produced in the film and invites complex connectivity, a concern for human safety and survival, to move to the fore.

The film ends with a black screen and a return to the opening story, a warm sun and a purple sea. The voice indicates human hopes and dreams we all share. The black screen points to end and even death. The credits begin shortly with a brief description of the conditions of the filming. The film offers confirmation that Amel Alzakout survived and that for her life continues. As I noted earlier, the film helps us understand how the border apparatus is tied fundamentally not to geography but to perception; the perceiving and organizing of difference as fundamental to perception must occur in an interaction of perceiver and perceived positioned somewhere and somehow in a relation. In the contemporary mainstream media regime, we are typically given to see borders as lines drawn on geopolitical maps rather than as one of many ways to define communal belonging and foreclose perceptions of connectedness. *Purple Sea* and *Shipwreck* rework the mechanisms of positioning. The meeting of the person Amel Alzakout in *Purple Sea*, along with the display of the border apparatus in *Shipwreck*, together offer other regimes of ordering, other chains of signification, other codes of representation, images not of us and them, a map of another possible world.

Bibliography

Adler, Emanuel. *The Convergence of Civilizations: Constructing a Mediterranean Region.* Toronto: University of Toronto Press, 2006.

Anderson, Benedict R. *Imagined Communities: Reflections on the Origin and Spread of Nationalism.* New York: Verso, 2006.

Andersson, Ruben. *Illegality, Inc: Clandestine Migration and the Business of Bordering Europe.* Berkeley: University of California Press, 2014.

Bhimji, Fazila. *Border Regimes, Racialisation Processes and Resistance in Germany: An Ethnographic Study of Protest and Solidarity.* Cham: Palgrave Macmillan, 2020.

Bilkic, Ljudmila. "'Everything New Is Born Illegal.' Historicizing Rapid Migration through New Media Projects." PhD diss., University of Pittsburgh, 2018.

Boening, Astrid B. "Multilateralism South of the Border: The EuroMed Partnership." *Jean Monnet/Robert Schuman Paper Series 7* No. 1 (2007): no pagination.

Chouliaraki, Lilie. "Between Pity and Irony: Paradigms of Refugee Representation in Humanitarian Discourse." In *Migrations and the Media: Global Crises and the Media*, edited by Kerry Moore, Bernhard Gross, and Terry Threadgold, 13–31. New York: Peter Lang, 2012.

Christides, Giorgos, and Steffen Lüdke. "(S+) Frontex in illegale Pushbacks von Hunderten Flüchtlingen involviert." *Der Spiegel*, April 27, 2022. https://www.spiegel.de/ausland/frontex-in-illegale-pushbacks-von-hunderten-fluechtlingen-involviert-a-086f0e5a-0172-4007-b59c-7bced325cc75.

Cossé, Eva, and Kerstin McCourt. "The Hand at the Helm of Frontex." *Human Rights Watch* (blog), July 19, 2022. https://www.hrw.org/news/2022/07/19/hand-helm-frontex.

Cremona, Marise, and Joanne Scott, eds. *EU Law Beyond EU Borders: The Extraterritorial Reach of EU Law*. Oxford and New York: Oxford University Press, 2019.

Curtis, Robin. *Conscientious Viscerality: The Autobiographical Stance in German Film and Video*. Berlin: Edition Imorde, 2006.

Curtis, Robin, and Angelica Fenner. *The Autobiographical Turn in Germanophone Documentary and Experimental Film*. Rochester, NY: Camden House, 2014.

Dainotto, Roberto M. "Does Europe Have a South? An Essay on Borders." *The Global South* 5, no. 1 (2011): 37–50.

Derrida, Jacques. *The Ear of the Other: Otobiography, Transference, Translation*. Translated by Avital Ronell and Peggy Kamuf. Lincoln: University of Nebraska Press, 1988.

Dreyfus, Jean-Marc, and Élisabeth Gessat-Anstett. *Human Remains and Identification Mass Violence, Genocide, and the "Forensic Turn."* Manchester: Manchester University Press, 2015.

Dziuban, Zuzanna. *Mapping the "Forensic Turn": Engagements with Materialities of Mass Death in Holocaust Studies and Beyond*. Vienna: new academic press, 2017.

Frieze, James. *Theatrical Performance and the Forensic Turn*. Oxford: Routledge, 2019.

Gallagher, Stephen. "Towards a Common European Asylum System: Fortress Europe Redesigns the Ramparts." *International Journal* 57, no. 3 (2002): 375–94.

Gržinic, Marina, ed. *Border Thinking: Disassembling Histories of Racialized Violence*. Berlin: Sternberg Press, 2018.

Halle, Randall N. *The Europeanization of Cinema: Interzones and Imaginative Communities*. Urbana-Champaign: University of Illinois Press, 2014.

———. *Queer Social Philosophy: Critical Readings from Kant to Adorno*. Urbana-Champaign: University of Illinois Press, 2004.

———. *Visual Alterity: Seeing Difference in Cinema*. Urbana-Champaign: University of Illinois Press, 2021.

Hühn, Peter, Wolf Schmid, and Jörg Schönert, eds. *Point of View, Perspective, and Focalization: Modeling Mediation in Narrative*. Berlin: Walter de Gruyter, 2009.

Humphreys, Lee. *The Qualified Self: Social Media and the Accounting of Everyday Life*. Cambridge: MIT Press, 2018.

"Illegale Pushbacks: Was macht die EU?" *Europamagazin*. Brussels: ARD, March 15, 2021. https://www.tagesschau.de/ausland/europa/eukommission-frontex-pushbacks-101.html.

International Organization for Migration. *Migrant Smuggling Data and Research: A Global Review of the Emerging Evidence Base, Volume 2*. Geneva: International Organization for Migration, 2018.

Jakob, Christian. "Pushbacks auf dem Mittelmeer: Frontex lügt und mauert." *taz*, April 29, 2022. https://taz.de/!5851450/.

Jünemann, Anette, Nikolas Scherer, and Nicolas Fromm, eds. *Fortress Europe? Challenges and Failures of Migration and Asylum Policies*. Wiesbaden: Springer, 2017.

Kristeva, Julia. *Powers of Horror: An Essay on Abjection*. Translated by Leon S. Roudiez. New York: Columbia University Press, 1982.

Radonić, Ljiljana. "Globalization, Universalization, and Forensic Turn: Post-catastrophic Memorial Museums." In *The Afterlife of the Shoah in Central and Eastern European Cultures*, edited by Anna Artwinska and Anja Tippner, 99–114. New York: Routledge, 2022.

Remmler, Karen. "The Afterlives of Refugee Dead: What Remains?" *EuropeNow* 33, special issue on "European Art, Culture, and Politics," April 28, 2020. https://www.europenowjournal.org/2020/04/27/the-afterlives-of-refugee-dead-what-remains/.

Schindel, Estela. "Bare Life at the European Borders. Entanglements of Technology, Society and Nature." *Journal of Borderlands Studies* 31, no. 2 (2016): 219–34.

———. "Border Matters: Death, Mourning and Materiality at the European Borderlands." *EuropeNow* 33, special issue on "European Art, Culture, and Politics," April 28, 2020. https://www.europenowjournal.org/2020/04/27/border-matters-death-mourning-and-materiality-at-the-european-borderlands/.

———. "Death by 'Nature': The European Border Regime and the Spatial Production of Slow Violence." *Environment and Planning. C: Politics and Space* 40, no. 2 (2022): 428–46.

———. "Deaths and Disappearances in Migration to Europe: Exploring the Uses of a Transnationalized Category." *The American Behavioral Scientist* 64, no. 4 (2020): 389–407.

Sjöholm, Cecilia. "Images Do Not Take Sides: The Forensic Turn of Images." *The Nordic Journal of Aesthetics* 30, nos. 61–62 (2021): 166–70.

Ssan, Rhal. "Investigation Claims Frontex Involved in Aegean Sea Migrant Pushbacks." *Euronews*, April 28, 2022. https://www.euronews.com/

2022/04/28/investigation-claims-frontex-involved-in-aegean-sea-migrant-pushbacks.

Stankievech, Charles. "Exhibit A: Notes on a Forensic Turn in Contemporary Art." *Afterall* 47, no. 1 (2019): 42–55.

Weizman, Eyal. "Forensic Architecture: Political Practice, Activism, Aesthetics." In *The SAGE Handbook of the 21st Century City*, edited by Suzanne Hall and Ricky Burdett, 630–52. Los Angeles: SAGE, 2017.

———. *Forensic Architecture: Violence at the Threshold of Detectability.* New York: Zone Books, 2017.

Weizman, Eyal, Paulo Tavares, Susan Schuppli, and Situ Studio. "Forensic Architecture." *Architectural Design* 80, no. 5 (2010): 58–63.

6: The Politics of the Machinic Voice in Gerd Kroske's Documentary *SPK Komplex* (2018)

Olivia Landry

GERD KROSKE IS PROBABLY best known for his East German documentary about the anti-regime protests in Leipzig in the weeks leading up to the fall of the Berlin Wall, *Leipzig im Herbst* (*Leipzig in the Fall*, 1989), co-directed with Andreas Voigt. This historically important film was made on the streets, contemporaneous to the movement. Maintaining a commitment to radical political and social topics in his documentary filmmaking, Kroske has more recently turned to West German activist history and the anti-psychiatric Socialist Patients' Collective (SPK). His film titled *SPK Komplex* (2018) documents the collective's emergence in the early 1970s in Heidelberg through the experimental therapeutic practices of Wolfgang Huber, its politicization of the stigmatized perception of illness, and its subsequent dissolution with the imprisonment of Huber and other members.

Influenced by both the historically parallel student and anti-psychiatry movements of the 1960s, the SPK challenged the practice and philosophy of psychiatric determination of mental illness as an individual problem. Such a diagnosis not only stigmatized and institutionalized patients but also criminalized them. In the West German context, the SPK also confronted the practices of the Nazis and their T4 Aktion, which prompted the euthanasia of tens of thousands of people deemed intellectually and physically unfit for life. But the anti-psychiatry movement stretched well beyond national borders. From the publication of Michel Foucault's groundbreaking critique of psychiatry, *Madness and Civilization*, in 1961 to the wide-spread theories and practices of the likes of psychiatrists Franco Basaglia and David Cooper, the SPK contributed to a broad international discourse. Taking a Marxist approach, the collective understood mental illness as the consequence of capitalist society and its unequal power relations of production. Brief but significant, the history of this collective has long been overshadowed by that of the Red Army Faction (RAF). Even the film's title evokes this connection. We are immediately reminded of Uli Edel's 2008 fiction film *Der Baader Meinhof Komplex*.

What does it mean in our neoliberal present to bring such a radical history at long last to the screen through documentary? First, the politics of the SPK clash with the reality of our ever-diminishing public sphere, the increased relegation of feelings and affective life to the confines of the private realm and the family, and the cultural attack on nurture, human dependency, and care.[1] Second, *SPK Komplex* reminds us broadly of West Germany's socialist, militant, and collectivist past in our contemporary moment when it seems that such politics struggle to gain footing or are perceived straightforwardly as relics of a bygone era. Does this film perform politics in response to the present or does it simply present them through a historical lens—of what once was, but is no more? As a filmic mode conventionally invested in exploring, not to mention intervening in political and social issues, what can documentary bring to the history, politics, and legacy of the SPK?

With this film, Kroske implicitly acknowledges the present challenges of political filmmaking. Unlike his earlier *Leipzig im Herbst*, *SPK Komplex* must account for vast divides across time, politics, ideology, and media. As viewers, we find ourselves at a remove. Not only are the crowds missing, so too is the energy of direct politics and the grainy, unsettled aesthetics of filming an event in real time. The object of the film appears at odds with its now crisp, digital image. This is part of the point. Kroske neither attempts to superficially bridge eras nor historicize the SPK as but a moment in the distant past. He approaches this film and its topic with a reflexivity that manifests most prominently in the documentary treatment of historical media objects. *SPK Komplex* reflects on the contemporary possibilities and limits of political filmmaking itself. Against highly political subject matter, the film unfurls as a documentary about contemporary documentary and the challenges of voice, technology, and authenticity in our present age. It asks how media and media representation shape politics, and what role the politics of media itself plays.

Formally unremarkable at first glance, *SPK Komplex* assembles many of the conventional elements of documentary film: talking-head interviews, archival materials, and a narrative frame that unfolds in a notable mode of rhetorical persuasiveness. With its heavy reliance on interviews, Bill Nichols would likely label *SPK Komplex* a participatory documentary, in which interactions rather than observation guide the viewer through the development of a historical account. The third mode in Nichols's earlier typology of documentary, the participatory mode presents a common filmic approach for exploring and portraying histories of events. Social actors serve as eyewitnesses and the director, in this case Kroske, makes

---

1   Ann Cvetkovich, *Depression: A Public Feeling* (Durham, NC: Duke University Press, 2012), 11–12; Julie Stephens, *Confronting Postmaternal Thinking: Feminism, Memory, and Care* (New York: Columbia University Press, 2011), 1.

his own presence felt. In Nichols's words, "when we view participatory documentaries, we expect to witness the historical world as represented by someone who actively engages with others rather than unobtrusively observing, poetically reconfiguring, or argumentatively assembling what others say and do."[2] In participatory documentary, the voice of authority disperses across many figures. Most resonant in the case at hand, however, is the voice of Wolfgang Huber. Recurring scenes feature an audio cassette tape recorder, which plays archival voice recordings of Huber. Allegedly still living underground, he haunts the film through his remediated (audio) presence. In its use of the voice, Kroske's film presents a remarkably novel treatment of the (disembodied) voice through its materiality and referentiality of technology.

Documentary film has long preoccupied itself with questions of the voice. Voice-over narration in documentary film, commonly equated with the voice-of-God technique, emerged as an early establishing component of documentary. In John Grierson's pioneering conceptualization, voice-of-God narration sought to achieve a position of objectivity and detachment from above, with which the audience could align and approach the subject matter of the film with critical detachment. But this approach ultimately proved prescriptive and dogmatic in its presentation of a singular dominant worldview. Within and beyond documentary studies, Paul Bonitzer and Mary Ann Doane have notably addressed what they refer to as the troubling nonreferential charge of the voice-over in film. Disengaged from the body, the voice acquires transcendental dimensions and unquestionable authority. Michel Chion took up this matter of the disembodied voice further and expanded its possibilities to the acousmatic. The acousmatic voice was no longer merely disembodied; its source became nonlocalizable, in other words, not only detached from a body, but from all possible sources of sound as well. I explore this trajectory in an interrogation of the machinic voice of Huber in the film. In the final section of this chapter, I turn specifically to the machine. Not ostensibly acousmatic, the voice does achieve a certain referentiality through the machine, as sound appears to emit from a playback audio cassette recorder. But is this even the real source of sound? The careful staging of machinic sound emission through these scenes furthermore opens up different lines of inquiry. It also reminds us of the temporal, political, and mediatic remove of Huber and the SPK. But this is not a straightforward indexing. Playing with documentary's drive toward historical authenticity and the challenge of achieving this at a remove, *SPK Komplex* presents the complexities of the machinic voice as both emergence and product of

---

2   Bill Nichols, *Introduction to Documentary* (Bloomington: Indiana University Press, 2017), 139.

the documentary mode. Through this mode, the machinic voice sets in motion a politics of its own.

The Voice in Documentary Revisited

Following the opening credits, an initial scene in what appears to be the archive of the University of Heidelberg (the film generally evades identificatory captions) introduces the viewer to Wolfgang Huber by way of his matriculation documents. This scene directly precedes the first sequence of a voice recording on tape. The latter scene begins with a shallow close-up of a Sony audio cassette field recorder. What catches the eye is the machine's rising and falling movement on the twin VU meters. This movement appears to be synchronized with the soundtrack. First, the psychology professor and sympathizer Peter Brückner is introduced to speak about the SPK. After him, Huber's voice emerges. The acoustic quality of the recording suggests that its sound is not diegetic. Indeed, the recorder is not plugged into a speaker or the camera, for that matter; it is impossible that this quality of sound could emit from the player's own small mono speaker. Kroske has apparently synchronized image and sound in order to achieve the highest quality audio experience of these recordings. The recording continues in a subsequent medium shot, which reveals that the machine rests on a damp concrete surface outdoors. Cigarette butts poke through the joints between concrete slabs around it. A final long vertical shot of the machine concludes this scene but the sound bridges to a montage of shots of what appear to be external views of the University of Heidelberg. The soundtrack continues. Grainy archival newsreel footage then eclipses the crisp digital image of the diegesis and fills the frame. We see historical protests outside of the university as well as images of this teach-in. The image of the sonic machine eventually returns; this time the machine rests on a desk of a lecture hall, flanked by another cassette (Fig. 6.1). Against the remainder of Huber's reverberating speech, the image track returns to the present and the digital image of Kroske's camera. The now empty lecture hall, presumably where the teach-in originally took place in 1970, appears desolate and sterile, perhaps a symbol of the contemporary and the reverberating question, similarly evoked by Claudia Breger's contribution to this volume: where are the people? Another external long shot of the university accompanies the conclusion of speech and its recording. In this early, drawn-out sequence, Kroske establishes the importance of the voice and its representation, not simply in the absence of the person as a kind of placeholder, but in its own critical materiality. In doing this, he resists the inclination to recreate a moment from the past and instead invokes a history of the voice and its role in documentary. One cannot explore the voice—any voice—in documentary, without bringing it to

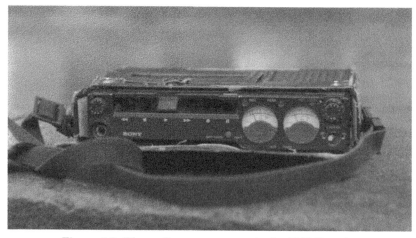

Figure 6.1. The audio cassette recorder in *SPK Komplex* (Gerd Kroske, 2018).

bear on the long history of the voice and the emergence of the documentary mode.

In her critical contemporary work on documentary, Pooja Rangan confirms that the speaking voice has long been taken up as documentary's defining formal feature, not to mention the central metaphor of documentary studies.[3] Originally conceived of and named by John Grierson in the 1920s, the early form of documentary was, according to Nichols's categories, expository in mode and bore a soberly didactic approach. The salient element of these documentaries was the voice-over or voice-of-God narration. In the postwar years this mode and its perceived authoritarian technique of direct address came under suspicion. Pascal Bonitzer famously lambasted what he referred to as the absent "voice-off" of documentary as the essence of stolen power and dogmatism.[4] Documentary filmmakers subsequently developed alternative modes. Nichols discusses this change as the beginning of the "evolution" of the four phases of documentary film.[5] The speaking voice as central feature was not discarded; rather, it became recast as metaphor for different styles of communication and points of view. After the Griersonian mode of direct address came the observational style of *cinéma vérité*, then the direct address or interview

---

3   Pooja Rangan, *Immediations: The Humanitarian Impulse in Documentary* (Durham, NC: Duke University Press, 2017), 134.

4   Pascal Bonitzer, "The Silences of the Voice," trans. Philip Rosen and Marcia Butzel, in *Narrative, Apparatus, Ideology: A Film Theory Reader*, ed. Philip Rosen (New York: Columbia University Press, 1986), 324.

5   Bill Nichols, "The Voice of Documentary," *Film Quarterly* 36, no. 3 (1983): 18.

style of participatory documentary, and finally the reflexive style, which often employed different techniques of investigation and maintained a voice of doubt and uncertainty.[6] Some scholars have criticized Nichols's linear approach and wholesale dismissal of the device of the voice-over with the counterargument that the problem lies not in the voice-over itself but in its early mode of use. Rangan proposes, for instance, that the use of a reflexive, first-person voice-over can also be "transgressive."[7] It is a matter of who is talking and how.

SPK Komplex is a case in point; it applies the voice in a variety of ways. Beyond the voice recordings, to which I will return, the film relies heavily on interviews with five former members of the SPK, former members of the Heidelberg police force, lawyers, a photographer, and a judge who presided over the SPK trials. In this way, the voice of Kroske's documentary strives toward multiplicity in a participatory style of what Nichols describes as a mode of "I speak with them for you."[8] Different voices and accounts of events come together in a single story.[9] Kroske's own direct presence as participant in the film is limited to his voice, which remains on the whole mostly quiet. Twice he reads documents in voice-over and occasionally we hear his low and raspy voice from behind the camera as he asks a follow-up question to an interviewee. The overall promise of the interview-style documentary lies in its performance of a history that does not hew to a singular voice, or narrative for that matter. Yet some voices are more resonant than others. Most frequently heard in the film are the voices of the former SPK members, in particular Edwald Goerlich, Carmen Roll, and Lutz Taufer, who also appear multiple times throughout. Their rapport with the movement may have altered with time, prison (in some cases), and age, but on the whole it retains a sympathetic, even nostalgic, quality.

Among these voices, Huber's own machinic voice stands out. Not among the interviewees, Huber is declared "unauffindbar" (untraceable) in the closing notes of the film. Yet so many traces of him remain and give shape to this film. His photographic likeness clutters the film frame. Grainy archival footage occasionally presents him as a once live and moving body. Finally, in two extended sequences, Huber's speeches at various teach-ins at the University of Heidelberg penetrate the soundtrack. Even in his absence, Huber is almost excessively present in (re-)mediated form. Kroske seeks to recreate Huber's presence through the remediation of archival materials. In a sense, Huber is rendered object: image, voice

6   Nichols, "The Voice of Documentary," 17–18. See also Nichols, *Introduction to Documentary.*
7   Rangan, *Immediations,* 139.
8   Nichols, *Introduction to Documentary,* 138.
9   Nichols, *Introduction to Documentary,* 146.

recording. In remediating voice recordings of Huber, the disembodied voice emerges and Kroske reinvokes the documentary tradition of the voice of God with its authoritative overtones along different lines.

The Disembodied Voice (of the Machine)

Bonitzer's main trouble with the voice-off of early documentary was its lack of referentiality and pretensions to an authority and mastery that cannot be questioned. For without a body, without a subject, and without reference, the voice-off becomes a kind of pure signifier with unrestrictive interpretative powers. Bonitzer and later Mary Ann Doane have pointed to the troubling nonreferential charge of this kind of voice-off or voice-over. If Bonitzer uses the term of "voice-off" to refer to both those instances of speaking of a person from outside the frame and voice-of-God narration, Doane proposes a distinction between the two as cases of "voice-off" and "voice-over," respectively.[10] For her, it is important to recognize that the voice-over has disengaged itself from the body and thereby assumed transcendental dimensions attesting to an unquestionable authority and command of interpretation. Without rejecting Bonitzer's sweeping "voice-off," Doane's more discerning approach and conceptualization of the "voice-over" gets us closer to the qualities of the disembodied voice of the machine.

> It is its radical otherness with respect to the diegesis which endows this voice with a certain authority. As a form of direct address, it speaks without mediation to the audience, by-passing the "characters" and establishing a complicity between itself and the spectator—together they understand and thus *place* the image. It is precisely because the voice is not localizable, because it cannot be yoked to a body, that it is capable of interpreting the image, producing its truth. Disembodied, lacking any specification in space or time, the voice-over is, as Bonitzer points out, beyond criticism-it censors the questions "Who is speaking?," "Where?," "In what time?," and "For whom?."[11]

This unbound voice, detached from the film's diegesis, its image, or even to a body, becomes omnipresent and therefore also omniscient. It "sees" all, "hears" all, and "knows" all. As a result, it also cannot be questioned or doubted. The inviolability of the disembodied voice, according to

---

10 Mary Ann Doane, "The Voice in Cinema: The Articulation of Body and Space," *Yale French Studies* 60 (1980): 37–38.

11 Doane, "The Voice in Cinema," 42.

Bonitzer, is the essence of its power.[12] Charles Wolfe goes as far as to argue that the disembodied voice of documentary is not only unattached from a body, but is also unrepresentable as such: "Disembodied, this voice is construed as fundamentally unrepresentable in human form, connoting a position of absolute mastery and knowledge outside the spatial and temporal boundaries of the social world the film depicts."[13] Such a description conjures up the iconic image of "His Master's Voice" advertising logo for the Gramophone and Typewriter Company: To the left sits an Edison phonograph and to the right the terrier Nipper with his head tilted in confusion as he listens to his dead master's recorded voice resonating from the phonograph funnel. Does the pursuit of the disembodied voice ultimately always bring us to the machinic voice of technology? As ironic as this teleology may sound, discussions raised by Pierre Schaeffer, Michel Chion, Mladen Dolar, and Rey Chow certainly support it.[14] In the film, multiple appearances of the recording and playback device in *SPK Komplex* also takes us in this direction.

The disembodied voice and the machine indeed connect through the concept of the acousmatic voice, whose source is invisible and often nonlocalizable. If the disembodied voice delinks from the body, then the acousmatic voice relinquishes all provenance. Harking back to the philosophical legend of Pythagoras, Pierre Schaeffer first conceptualized the term in his groundbreaking study *Treatise on Musical Objects: An Essay across Disciplines*, first published in French in 1966. Pythagoras believed that his disciples (the *akousmatikoi*, Greek for "auditors" or "listeners") could learn most efficiently free from distraction by listening to his lectures without seeing him in the flesh.[15] He achieved this pedagogical practice by lecturing from behind a curtain. In this way, Pythagoras's disembodied voice assumed an added aura of authority. Marking the founding of the first philosophical school, Pythagoras's approach brought him cultlike status. Chion expanded on and popularized Schaeffer's concept through his work with the voice and cinema. According to Chion, the voice is always elusive: uncategorizable, uncontainable.[16] Yet we are drawn to the voice more than any other sound. Our vococentricism is nowhere more apparent than in the context of cinema. We listen for the voice. It

12   Bonitzer, "The Silences of the Voice," 324.

13   Charles Wolfe, "Historicising the 'Voice of God': The Place of Vocal Narration in Classical Documentary," *Film History* 9 (1997): 149.

14   Rey Chow, "Listening after 'Acousmaticity,'" in *Sound Objects*, ed. James A. Steintrager and Rew Chow (Durham, NC: Duke University Press, 2019), 117.

15   Brian Kane offers one of the most comprehensive descriptions of this history. Brian Kane, *Sound Unseen: Acousmatic Sound in Theory and Practice* (Oxford: Oxford University Press, 2014), 4.

16   Michel Chion, *The Voice in Cinema*, trans. Claudia Gorbman (New York: Columbia University Press, [1982] 1999), 1.

draws us in. Even if this voice is nonlocalizable onscreen, in cinema of course all sound reverberates from the same source. This is what Chion specifically calls "cinema's invention of the *acousmêtre*."[17] Conceptually unique, the acousmatic voice does compare ideologically to the disembodied voice taken up by Bonitzer and Doane. Chion's acousmatic voice similarly has four powers: "the ability to be everywhere, to see all, to know all, and to have complete power. In other words: ubiquity, panopticism, omniscience, and omnipotence."[18] One of his main examples of acousmatic sound in film is in Fritz Lang's *Das Testament des Dr. Mabuse* (*The Testament of Dr. Mabuse*, 1933), whose titular character leads a crime ring solely through the power of his voice, which becomes omniscient by dint of the technology of the recording and playback devices he instrumentalizes and cunningly hides behind thick curtains. As Chion notes, Schaeffer conceptualized the acousmatic voice in response to the inventions of sound technology. Connecting technology with the history of Pythagoras provided an ideological perspective that attested to the power of this nonlocalizable voice.

What does this all say about the disembodied, mechanized voice of Wolfgang Huber in *SPK Komplex*? Does his voice become endowed with the powers of the *acousmêtre*, or at least the disembodied voice, even though the source of his voice is in fact visualized? Kroske's documentary may otherwise avoid the device of voice-of-God narration and with it its troubling ethos of authority and power; however, the iterant employment of the disembodied voice through technology bears remnants of that history and legacy that cannot be ignored. As much as Kroske also localizes the voice through myriad images of Huber, brief archival footage, and the visualization of the playback device, the question of the disembodied voice and its performance and role in the film are provocative. The most reflexive point of the film comes precisely in a moment of contemplation of the voice. In the final scene in which we hear Huber's voice, Kroske lets it play in the home of one of the former SPK members, Edwald Goerlich. A very quiet and reserved character, it is evident that Goerlich struggles to discuss his history with the SPK. While the other former members appear very matter of fact and almost detached, for Goerlich this seems to be a very personal story. In the recording to which he and Kroske listen, Huber discusses the general animosity and wrongful condemnation of his status as a doctor of psychiatry, at once listing the wrongful accusations and providing evidence against them. As the recording continues to play in the background, Kroske tries to engage Goerlich in a discussion of the tone of Huber's voice. He asks Goerlich

17 Chion, *The Voice*, 9.
18 Chion, *The Voice*, 24.

if Huber sounds hurt ("verletzt"). Goerlich hesitates. He appears both grief-stricken and lost in thought:

Goerlich:	"Was wollen Sie wissen?" (What do you want to know?)
Kroske:	"Ob ich da richtig liege in meiner Beurteilung?" (I am wondering if I am correct in my judgment?)
Goerlich:	"Ja, natürlich." (Yes, of course.)
pause	
Goerlich:	'*Un fleur de peau*,' nennt man das auf Französisch. Kann es nicht übersetzen." ('*Un fleur de peau*,' one might say in French. I can't translate it.)[19]

This curious and very personal discussion of the voice gives it "grain," as Roland Barthes would contend; in other words, attaches it to a body, makes it more human.[20] By humanizing the machinic voice through the assignment of human emotions and tones, part of its mystery and even its authority does appear to ebb. Not only does Huber have a face and body we can see in pictures, he also possesses emotions diagnosed through an analysis of his voice. However, Kroske does not let us off that easily; the film does not just attempt to bring us closer to the disembodied voice, or to thwart the troubling authority of the acousmatic. The film's dramatic staging of the disembodied voice of the machine glossed in an earlier section demands further scrutiny.

A Spectral Object:
Fetishism and Authenticity

In the context of German-language documentary, the question of authenticity unleashed a lively debate as recently as 2021, following the discovery that the 2019 documentary *Lovemobil* about the lives of two female sex workers in Lower Saxony working from a mobile home contained scripted scenes. Many were outraged by this revelation. The director, Elke Lehrenkrauss, was even compelled to return her German Documentary Film Prize. I do not draw a comparison between *Lovemobil* and *SPK Komplex*; I simply evoke this slightly later film and the debate it provoked as an example of the uncompromising drive and almost dogmatic conjecture of truth that hangs over documentary film production. In many ways, authenticity itself becomes fetishized. *SPK Komplex* evokes this

19 "Un fleur de peau" might be translated into English as "on edge" or "at the edge."

20 Roland Barthes, "The Grain of the Voice," trans. Stephen Heath, in *The Sound Studies Reader*, ed. by Jonathan Sterne (London: Routledge, [1977] 2012), 504–10.

discourse through its playful, even sleight-of-hand, approach to historical sound and its source.

At first listen, Kroske's staging (for the camera) of the sound machine as an altogether material object could serve as a means of interrogating and ultimately subverting the potential voice-of-God effect, and with it its troubling authority and transcendence. However, there is even more at stake than first meets the ear and eye. The recordings of Huber play on a Sony audio cassette field recorder called the TC-D5. In the film, the machine strikes the viewer as analog. First, it is a cassette playback recorder; second, it has the rugged look of a portable recording machine used in field research or street journalism. One imagines this could have been the device used by journalists during the tumultuous years of the SPK. This image seems authentic. But there is a catch. This machine first came on the market almost a decade later, in 1978. The effect is thus misleading. The staging of the machine sets loose other possibilities, however.

Beyond the ghostly presence of the disembodied voice of Huber, the auditory trace of a man deemed untraceable, we can also invoke Jacques Derrida's influential reading of Karl Marx's *Capital* and open up a discussion of the spectral presence of the machine. In this reading, the spectral object names both the commodity fetish and its phantomized social value.[21] Jonathan Sterne's discussion of the commodity fetishism of musical instruments is particularly instructive here. He examines how instruments become commodities through social relations and in specific contexts.[22] Offering the example of the Stradivarius violin and the "magic" it invokes, Sterne explicates among other things the deeply entangled social status and history of the musical instrument as spectral object. Although it has been proven that even experts cannot tell the difference between the sound produced by a Stradivarius versus any other high-quality standard violin, many still hold the former in higher regard and automatically assume its superiority. The fact that Stradivarius violins are no longer produced further adds to their status as commodity fetishes. They are one of a kind. Sterne brings this example to also bear on the phenomenon of fetishism of analog audio devices in our digital era. Indeed, companies specialize solely in the design and production of replicas of analog audio devices for a consuming public.[23] Older is better because it is more authentic, so the tautology goes. Returning

21 Jacques Derrida, *The Specters of Marx: The State of the Debt, the Work of Mourning and the New International*, trans. Peggy Kamuf (Oxford: Routledge, [1993] 1994), 199.

22 Jonathan Sterne, "Spectral Objects: On the Fetish Character of Music Technologies," in Steintrager and Chow, *Sound Objects*, 96.

23 Sterne, "Spectral Objects," 100.

to the TC-D5 in *SPK Komplex*, one is struck by the performance of the analog sound machine evidently visualized as a means of reproducing an impression of historical authenticity, a specter of an age now past, that is nonetheless historically false. In the same manner that we deem the Stradivarius as superior because of the history and tradition it indexes, we also perceive the cassettes and the audio cassette player as the genuine article because they are analog.

But if the machine is not authentic to that period, then it is likely that the cassettes are also not authentic. The recordings were no doubt first taken on magnetic reels and then re-recorded onto cassette later for preservation and accessibility purposes. In all fairness, Kroske probably acquired access to the cassette tapes and not to the original magnetic reels of speech, and therefore the filmmaker had no choice but to use a playback cassette recorder. Yet the sound that resonates from the soundtrack at the moment of the recordings does not emit from the visualized machine. Instead, it emits from another source off-screen. This invisible source, following Doane, conceals the work of the apparatus and its noise, and creates in its place a clear, crisp sound.[24] It conceals what Doane has called the "archive of noise," a term she coins in engagement with Friedrich Kittler's observation that the invention of new recording machines in the twentieth century brought with it the storage of their own excessive noise.[25] The concept of the archive of noise developed from new technology, such as phonography and cinema, and its inescapable capacity to, in Doane's words, "record indiscriminately."[26] If noise indexes the machine and its history, why is it missing from these scenes in *SPK Komplex*? Why do we not hear the prominent hiss of the cassette and the muffled and garbled voices it likely contains? The staging of the disembodied voice of the machine appears to strive for the effect of authenticity in its fetishization of the analog machine, but the inclusion of more original sound quality would have added to the effect.

Despite its discrepancies, the film might still achieve this effect for some viewers and auditors. Admittedly, on first listen and viewing I did not recognize the historical inconsistency of the machine, nor did I deliberate the "artificial" sound quality. Jaimie Baron might call this a variation of the "archive effect," or what she describes as "an *experience of*

---

24 Doane, "The Voice in the Cinema," 35.

25 Mary Ann Doane, *The Emergence of Cinematic Time: Modernity, Contingency, the Archive* (Cambridge, MA: Harvard University Press, 2002), 64–65. See also Friedrich A. Kittler, *Discourse Networks 1800/1900*, trans. Michael Mettler and Chris Cullens (Stanford, CA: Stanford University Press, [1985] 1990), 218–19.

26 Doane, *Emergence*, 64–65.

reception."[27] Even if the experience falls short, the staging of authenticity through evidentiary archival materials and analog media in the film remains in place. Effective or not, this staging invokes an ongoing discussion in documentary studies. Nichols's early intervention in this matter remains relevant. In *Representing Reality,* he proclaims: "Documentaries do not present *the* truth but *a* truth (or, better, a view or way of seeing), even if the evidence they recruit bears the authenticating trace of the historical world itself."[28] As compelling and authoritative as Nichols's edict rings, however, the question of what is authentic continues to circulate in documentary studies. One might say even a fetishization of truth and authenticity is itself part of a persisting discourse, which, as Stella Bruzzi confirms almost two decades after Nichols continues to preoccupy documentary filmmakers, critics, and scholars. She calls this "the documentarist's putative desire to attain the 'grail' of perfect authenticity."[29] According to Bruzzi, questions and concerns about authenticity have proliferated with developments in technology and the new possibilities of digital media.[30]

The expectation that we will experience things as they *really* are—or were—onscreen has long been the illusory promise of documentary. For even documentary can only hold to impression. This "impression of authenticity," as termed by Nichols, returns us to the audio cassette machine in *SPK Komplex.*[31] The spectral object in this film does not present a mere fiction so much as it reminds us of the politics of representation and documentary. It asserts the slipperiness of seeking the "holy grail" of authenticity, especially in our hyper-mediatized and digitalized world, in which anything can be manipulated. The staging of the machine as speaking object from the past exhorts its own politics of media history and ontology so central to the reflexivity of this film. Kroske does not exchange one politics for another—that is, the radical politics of the SPK for the politics of media history. Rather, he sees them as intrinsically linked. The revival of the SPK archive (or any archive, for that matter) will always be an undertaking of mediation and remediation. Kroske demonstrates this. Yet in this revival he does signal the anti-authoritarian spirit of the SPK for our political present.

In a kind of coda, the otherwise implicitness of this film vis-à-vis the radical politics of the past and the possibility of recovering these

---

27 Jaimie Baron, *The Archive Effect: Found Footage and the Audiovisual Experience of History* (Oxford: Routledge, 2014), 7.

28 Bill Nichols, *Representing Reality: Issues and Concepts in Documentary* (Bloomington: Indiana University Press, 1991), 118.

29 Stella Bruzzi, *New Documentary* (Oxford: Routledge, 2006), 6–7.

30 Bruzzi, *New Documentary,* 8.

31 Nichols, *Introduction to Documentary,* xii.

politics for the present takes a more categorical turn in the final sequence. Accompanying former SPK member Carmen Roll, who since her release from prison in the 1970s for RAF-related convictions lives in Italy, Kroske takes the viewer to an abandoned psychiatric facility. The photographer and former colleague of Roll, Antonella Pizzamiglio, provides a tour. She then talks about her recent project on the Greek island of Leros. There a dilapidated old psychiatric hospital has been converted into temporary quarters for asylum seekers. The ideological link is clear: History repeats itself. Pizzamiglio displays some of her erstwhile photographs of psychiatric patients in the hospital side by side with new photographs of asylum seekers now residing in the hospital for Kroske's camera. Without suggesting that the two groups are commensurable, the film leaves the viewer to ponder the similar mechanisms of stigmatization, criminalization, and de-humanization, what Randall Halle discusses in his contribution to this volume as "juridico-political abjection," of the intellectually disabled and asylum seekers on Europe's shores and elsewhere. The film concludes with the provocation to recognize the continuing relevance of the work and politics of the SPK in today's world.

Conclusion

I came to *SPK Komplex* not with the anticipation to learn more about the SPK, admittedly hitherto unknown to me, but as a recommendation to explore the use of sound and the visualization of sound emission. Despite many viewings, my focus has remained on this singular element, one which in my opinion makes this otherwise formally conventional documentary noteworthy and original. What developed as a result of this focus on the machinic voice is the potential for reflection on documentary history, or its "evolution," to speak with Nichols, and especially its contentious relationship to the disembodied voice and its embroiled ideology of authority and omniscience. We can at the very least speculate that Kroske did not seek to re-create the documentary disembodied voice, known also as the voice of God, or even as the acousmatic voice, wholesale, but instead reflexively plays with its possibilities. He employs the disembodied machinic voice and visually presents its source. But in his raising of the Pythagorean curtain, he further moots questions about the voice in film, and documentary in particular: can we ever really know the source of the voice? Perhaps herein lies what Rangan asserts as its transgressive potential. Nontraditional versions of the voice-of-God device can subvert ideologies of authority. Wolfgang Huber's machinic voice invites this potential.

Remediating the archival recordings of Huber during various teach-ins offers historical authenticity. Visualizing the playing back of these recordings in situ—that is, at the locations where they originally took place—brings forth questions about the possibility of authenticity and the insurmountable disconnect between the present and the past. Not historically accurate, the staging of the machine relies on impression. The machine assumes the quality of a spectral object designed to index an effect of authenticity by means of its fetishized status as analog. Even in its potential deception, however, or precisely because of this, the film raises important questions about documentary's form as a consequence of its ardent pursuit of authentic representation and the challenge this continues to present. Divisions of time, politics, and media shape the film's approach to its subject. Once scenes of noisy, crowded auditoriums, in which politics were directly put into practice, in *SPK Komplex* these restaged teach-ins appear distant, mediated, and empty. Finally, restrained by the imperative of authenticity and the challenges of presenting the past in the present, *SPK Komplex* does not dismiss the radical politics of its subjects—the SPK and the documentary voice—so much as it more forcefully delves into the question of media's role in shaping these politics over history. At the same time, it reminds the viewer of the possibility of collective action as more than just an echo of the past and the exigency of its revival in the present.

Bibliography

Baron, Jaimie. *The Archive Effect: Found Footage and the Audiovisual Experience of History*. Oxford: Routledge, 2014.

Barthes, Roland. "The Grain of the Voice." Translated by Stephen Heath. In *The Sound Studies Reader*, edited by Jonathan Sterne, 504–10. London: Routledge, [1977] 2012.

Bonitzer, Pascal. "The Silences of the Voice." Translated by Philip Rosen and Marcia Butzel. In *Narrative, Apparatus, Ideology: A Film Theory Reader*, edited by Philip Rosen, 319–34. New York: Columbia University Press, 1986.

Bruzzi, Stella. *New Documentary*. Oxford: Routledge, 2006.

Chion, Michel. *The Voice in Cinema*. Translated by Claudia Gorbman. New York: Columbia University Press, [1982] 1999.

Chow, Rey. "Listening after 'Acousmaticity'." In *Sound Objects*, edited by James A. Steintrager and Rey Chow, 113–29. Durham, NC: Duke University Press, 2019.

Cvetkovich, Ann. *Depression: A Public Feeling*. Durham, NC: Duke University Press, 2012.

Derrida, Jacques. *The Specters of Marx: The State of the Debt, the Work of Mourning and the New International*. Translated by Peggy Kamuf. Oxford: Routledge, [1993] 1994.

Doane, Mary Ann. *The Emergence of Cinematic Time: Modernity, Contingency, the Archive*. Cambridge, MA: Harvard University Press, 2002.

———. "The Voice in Cinema: The Articulation of Body and Space." *Yale French Studies* 60 (1980): 33–50.

Foucault, Michel. *Madness and Civilization: A History of Insanity in the Age of Reason.* Translated by Richard Howard. Oxford: Routledge, [1961] 2001.

Kane, Brian. *Sound Unseen: Acousmatic Sound in Theory and Practice.* Oxford: Oxford University Press, 2014.

Kittler, Friedrich A. *Discourse Networks 1800/1900.* Translated by Michael Mettler and Chris Cullens. Stanford, CA: Stanford University Press, [1985] 1990.

Leipzig im Herbst/Leipzig in Autumn. Dir. Andreas Voigt and Gerd Kroske. German Democratic Republic: DEFA, 1989.

Nichols, Bill. *Introduction to Documentary.* Bloomington: Indiana University Press, 2017.

———. *Representing Reality: Issues and Concepts in Documentary.* Bloomington: Indiana University Press, 1991.

———. "The Voice of Documentary." *Film Quarterly* 36, no. 3 (1983): 17–29.

Rangan, Pooja. *Immediations: The Humanitarian Impulse in Documentary.* Durham, NC: Duke University Press, 2017.

Schaeffer, Pierre. *In Search of a Concrete Music.* Translated by Christine North and John Dack. Berkeley: University of California Press, [1952] 2012.

SPK Komplex. Dir. Gerd Kroske. Germany: Realistfilm, 2016–18.

Stephens, Julie. *Confronting Postmaternal Thinking: Feminism, Memory, and Care.* New York: Columbia University Press, 2011.

Sterne, Jonathan. "Spectral Objects: On the Fetish Character of Music Technologies." In *Sound Objects,* edited by James A. Steintrager and Rey Chow, 94–109. Durham, NC: Duke University Press, 2019.

Wolfe, Charles. "Historicising the 'Voice of God': The Place of Vocal Narration in Classical Documentary." *Film History* 9 (1997): 149–67.

Part III

Reassembling the Archives
of Radical Filmmaking

Figure 7.1. Curator Asta Andersen reads Niklas Luhmann's *Art as a Social System* in *Ich will mich nicht künstlich aufregen* (*Asta Upset*; dir. Max Linz, 2014) © Max Linz.

7: Marking Time after Utopia

Richard Langston

WHEN FREELANCE JOURNALIST and film dramaturge Lars Meyer coined "New German Discourse Comedy" in his 2019 assessment of emergent sensibilities among young German filmmakers, he clearly found inspiration in another widely embraced German neologism: "discourse theater."[1] Regarding the "discourse" in "discourse theater," cultural critic Diedrich Diederichsen argued some fifteen years earlier for "a new genre" in German theater, spearheaded above all by Berlin dramaturge René Pollesch, in which the highly "artificial language of academic texts" acquires everyday use value.[2] Tallying the kinds of inscrutable texts in play for Pollesch, Miriam Dreysse went farther by pointing out in detail that it's not just any theory but rather "sociological theories of neoliberal late-capitalist societies," in particular "critical urbanism, postcolonial studies, gender and queer theory," that serve to help Pollesch's actors scrutinize their lives caught within the matrices of heteronormativity and neoliberal labor relations.[3] Far from wanting to intimidate or indoctrinate audiences with such highfalutin discourse, the grounds for taking recourse to theory, Pollesch himself once explained, has to do with the fact "dass wir Sehhilfen bekommen für die Wirklichkeit" (that we acquire visual aids for reality) otherwise disorienting and impenetrable for actors and audiences alike.[4]

At first glance, Meyer's nascent catalogue of films exemplary of his new rubric "New German Discourse Comedy" does recall Pollesch's

---

1 Lars Meyer, "Zu jedem Bett gehört ein Mann," *Die Zeit*, June 22, 2019, https://www.zeit.de/kultur/film/2019-06/das-melancholische-maedchen-film-susanne-heinrich. Unless otherwise noted, all translations are those of the author.

2 Diedrich Diederichsen, "Maggies Agentur," *René Pollesch: Prater-Saga*, ed. Aenne Quiñones (Berlin: Alexander Verlag, 2005), 15, 14.

3 Miriam Dreysse, "Heterosexualität und Repräsentation: Markierungen der Geschlechterverhältnisse bei René Pollesch," *GeschlechterSpielRäume: Dramatik, Theater, Performance und Gender*, ed. Gaby Pailer and Franziska Schlößler (Amsterdam: Rodopi, 2011), 358.

4 René Pollesch, "Ich bin Antiromantiker," in *Liebe ist kälter als das Kapital: Stücke, Texte, Interviews*, ed. Corinna Brocher and Aenne Quiñones (Reinbek bei Hamburg: Rowohlt, 2009), 358.

theater by dint of its films' explicit inclusion of theory. With its gratuitous recitations from theoretical tracts, Meyer's corpus makes no secret of the importance it places on academic discourse. Take, for example, Max Linz's debut *Ich will mich nicht künstlich aufregen* (*Asta Upset*, 2014), which has its heroine reading aloud from Max Horkheimer and Theodor W. Adorno's *Dialectic of Enlightenment* (1947). Or consider the nameless heroine suffering from writer's block in Susanne Heinrich's debut *Das melancholische Mädchen* (*Aren't You Happy?*, 2016–2018) who reads from the German translation of Tiqqun's *Preliminary Materials for a Theory of the Young-Girl* (1999) on an exercise bike. And then there is Irene von Alberti's *Der lange Sommer der Theorie* (*The Long Summer of Theory*, 2017), which not only lifts its title from cultural historian Philipp Felsch's 2015 history of Berlin theory clearinghouse Merve Verlag but also features characters reading from his book. Most recently, Julian Radlmaier's *Blutsauger* (*Bloodsuckers*, 2021) includes readings and discussions of volume one of Marx's *Capital* (1867), from which the film takes its inspiration.

Upon closer inspection, however, the discourses in Meyer's exemplary discourse comedies are quite different from the likes of Giorgio Agamben and Donna Haraway, to name just a few of Pollesch's usual theoretical suspects. While a few discourse films like Heinrich's do incorporate more recent critical incursions into neoliberal subject formation (like Tiqqun's), for example, others like Linz's and Radlmaier's unapologetically incorporate classical dialecticians such as Karl Marx, Horkheimer and Adorno, and Bertolt Brecht. If the various contemporary social theories attractive for Pollesch's discourse theater provide a credible language for diagnosing otherwise mystified experiences in present-day society, what exactly does discourse film seek with these much older theories? Don't Marx, Horkheimer and Adorno, and Brecht require significant transposition to bear fruit for contemporary cultural analysis? After Alberti transposed Pollesch's *Stadt als Beute* (*Berlin Stories*, 2001) into a 2005 anthology film that recycled the play's title—Pollesch's production incidentally lifted its own title from urban sociologists Klaus Ronneberger, Stephan Lanz, and Walther Jahn's 1999 theoretical book of the same name—she grew doubtful as to whether contemporary theory's promise of critical enlightenment was as robust as discourse theater presumed it to be.[5] Originally intended as a sequel to her film inspired by Pollesch's play, *Der lange Sommer der Theorie* queried, Alberti once explained, "ob Theorie heute noch so etwas [wie gesellschaftliche Revolte] leisten kann" (whether

---

5   See Klaus Ronneberger, Stephan Lanz, and Walther Jahn, *Die Stadt als Beute* (Bonn: Dietz, 1999); René Pollesch, "Stadt als Beute," in *Wohnfront 2001–2002: Volksbühne im Prater*, ed. Bettina Masuch (Berlin: Volksbühne am Rosa-Luxemburg-Platz and Alexander Verlag, 2003), 5–41.

theory can still achieve something like [social revolts]).[6] Compared to romantic images of comrades reading theory in public, Alberti began recognizing so many divergent theoretical trends that collective thinking seemed virtually impossible. Writing in what she herself called an "Umbruchszeit" (time of upheaval), Alberti's suspicion raises pressing questions about theory's utility in contemporary aesthetic practice.[7] Was discourse theater's reliance on theory a chimera all along? Has contemporary theory really reached a point of exhaustion on account of its rampant proliferation? What exactly are discourse films doing rummaging around in the dusty annals of old critical theory? And what's with the humor?

Convinced that epochal thinking along with its ontological presuppositions have run their course, cultural anthropologist Paul Rabinow argued in 2008 that what counts as contemporary in the new millennium is not an epoch per se but rather a temporal relation that results from marking time. Grasped alternatively as a *"ratio of modernity, moving through the recent past and near future in a (nonlinear) space,"* this contemporary relation manifests itself, practically speaking, as an ethos.[8] Neither beholden to the golden age of modernity's bygone "search for the shock of the new" nor to its need for historical erasure, the ethos of the contemporary is instead "perplexed by how to treat representation, affect, and reference."[9] This bafflement, Rabinow adds, arises, on the one hand, from the contemporary's keen awareness of its own historical moment and, on the other, from a lingering uncertainty regarding what to make of modernism's doctrines of yore. The contemporary, in other words, is a site where this ethos sets out to work together both old and new into "multiple configurations and variations."[10]

From Rabinow's vantage point, recourse to older theory in, for example, Linz's *Ich will mich nicht künstlich aufregen* or Radlmaier's *Blutsauger* does not necessarily make discourse films any less contemporary. Theory's relevance for the constitution of a ratio of the contemporary in these so-called discourse films emerges not from just reading old theory against present-day socio-cultural conditions either. Rather, these films mark time by bringing the two terms of their ratio of the contemporary—twentieth-century socio-cultural theory and the twenty-first-century search for political praxis—into dialogue. What snarls, however, any carefree constitution of an attendant ethos of the contemporary is, on one hand, the

---

6   Irene von Alberti, "Director's Note," liner notes for *Der lange Sommer der Theorie*, DVD, dir. Irene von Alberti (Berlin: Filmgalerie 451: 2017), 3.

7   von Alberti, "Director's Note," 3.

8   Paul Rabinow, *Marking Time: On the Anthropology of the Contemporary* (Princeton, NJ: Princeton University Press, 2008), 2. Original italics retained here.

9   Rabinow, *Marking Time*, 108.

10   Rabinow, *Marking Time*, 2.

potential artificiality of all theory given the remove of its abstractions from concrete experience and, on the other, the potential exhaustion of independent cinema's political praxis on account of the dwindling availability of unconditional funding sources. Far from dispensing with utopia altogether, this ethos reads for what one of Linz's heroes, Jacques Rancière, regards as an alternative way of using utopia.[11] In lieu of the dialectics of utopia, whereby a nonplace is replaced by a future place inscribed with a sense of community, Rancière motions for heterotopias, "mobile and divided spaces of perception" in which multiple opposing worlds come into view.[12] As shall be established in the following analysis of *Ich will mich nicht künstlich aufregen*, Linz's own heterotopian aspirations seek, in his own words, to forge "improbable connections between components of a shared reality that are no longer perceived as opposites."[13] To this phenomenological end, Linz prioritizes gauging contemporary time by dint of its decidedly anti-nostalgic relationship to seemingly more utopian cinematic pasts. The perplexity arising from this temporal ratio lies in the incommensurabilities uncovered between the archaeological work Linz's film performs on the past—as theory and aesthetic practice—and the challenge of concocting a cinematic heterotopia under the exploitative conditions of neoliberal film funding.[14]

Term A: Theory

Meyer aptly notes in his article heralding new discourse comedy that this nascent body of films is replete with characters reading works of theory aloud. Reading theory on camera is certainly not unique to the new discourse comedy. But if reading theory in new discourse comedies is indeed somehow tied to their allegedly "Brechtian, anti-psychological, anti-consumerist" politics, then this politics of reading must surely be different from older Brechtian, anti-psychological, anti-consumerist films like

11 On Linz's indebtedness to Jacques Rancière, Alain Badiou, and Gilles Deleuze, see Volker Pantenburg, "Class Relations: Diagnoses of the Present in the Films of Julian Radlmaier and Max Linz," *New German Critique* 46, no. 3 (138) (2019): 56.

12 Jacques Rancière, "The Senses and Uses of Utopia," *Political Uses of Utopia: New Marxist, Anarchist, and Radical Democratic Perspectives*, ed. S. Chrostowska and James Ingram (New York: Columbia University Press, 2017), 231.

13 Caroline Pitzen, "Tenacity and Zeitgeist," Arsenal: Institut für Film und Videokunst e.V., Programm Forum, 2014, https://wwwoesw.arsenal-berlin. de/forum-forum-expanded/archiv/programmarchiv/2014/forum-hauptprogramm/ich-will-mich-nicht-kuenstlich-aufregen/.

14 On Linz's critical engagement with the pervasiveness of neoliberalism in present-day film subsidies, see Pantenburg, "Class Relations," 70.

Dziga-Vertov Group's *Le Vent d'est* (*Wind from the East*, 1969), in which reading theory on camera stood as a provocation for the film's own stated desire to write theory.[15] "In this film," Jean-Luc Godard and Jean-Pierre Gorin's female voice-over announces, "the principal task is theory."[16] As Julia Lesage deftly points out, this task involves fashioning—to use Rabinow's language once again—a ratio between (reading) contemporary theory and enacting (revolutionary) praxis.[17] In an exemplary scene, a French union delegate, a stand-in for the Parti Communiste Française, hands a copy of Louis Althusser's *Reading Capital* (1965) to an actor playing a Native American. "What did the revisionist schoolteacher just say?" the voice-over asks dismayed. "He said: 'Read *Das Kapital*.' He did not ask you to use it. Use it."[18] Indicative of the Maoist condemnation of the old left's complacency during and after May 1968, Godard and Gorin's dismissal of reading theory clears room for its own revolutionary ethos. "It is true," the voice-over affirms near the film's conclusion, "that theory becomes a material force once it reaches the people."[19] For Godard and Gorin's spectators, the medium of this force, film, adopts what Peter Wollen once called—using *Le Vent d'est*—counter-cinema's "seven cardinal virtues" in order to battle bourgeois revisionism in the name of armed struggle and Third World liberation.[20] (These virtues include the destruction of narrative transitivity, the breakdown of all identification, foregrounding a film's mechanics, multiple diegeses, open-endedness, unpleasure as provocation and the retreat from fiction in favor of reality.) For Colin MacCabe, this aesthetic ultimately boils down to a political formalism that subverts "traditional relations between image and sound."[21] What's contemporary then about *Le Vent d'est* is the distance it forges between the reactionary dialectic of theory and the revolutionary force it attributes to its own cinematic praxis. In new discourse comedies, this ratio and the political ethos it occasions are inverted. Whereas reading theory was considered reactionary at the apotheosis of European

---

15   On the "Brechtian, anti-psychological, anti-consumerist" politics of the new discourse comedy, see Meyer "Zu jedem."

16   Jean-Luc Godard, *Weekend and Wind from the East: Two Films by Jean-Luc Godard* (London: Lorrimer, 1972), 162.

17   The précis follows: Julia Lesage, "Godard-Gorin's *Wind from the East*: Looking at a Film Politically," *Jump Cut* 4 (1974): 18–23.

18   Godard, *Weekend*, 167.

19   Godard, *Weekend*, 179.

20   Peter Wollen, "Godard and Counter Cinema: *Vent d'est*," in *Film Theory and Criticism: Introductory Readings*, ed. Leo Braudy and Marshall Cohen (Oxford: Oxford University Press, 2016), 365. See also Lesage, "Godard-Gorin's."

21   Colin MacCabe, *Godard: Images, Sounds, Politics* (London: MacMillan, 1980), 63.

political cinema of the late 1960s, the discourse comedy of the 2010s elevates theory as the indispensable basis for marking present time.

Take, for example, Linz's *Ich will mich nicht künstlich aufregen*. His first feature and final project submitted for graduation from the German Film and Television Academy Berlin (DFFB), the film premiered at the 2014 Berlinale and then went on to twelve screenings at European festivals the following year. Hyped in the German-language press, for example, for its "self-reflective and comedic" qualities as well as its allusion to "intelligent political cinema of the late 1960s," Linz's film finds inspiration not so much in French agit-prop of the late sixties as it does in the legacy of political filmmaking in the Federal Republic of Germany that began with the signing of the Oberhausen Manifesto in 1962. (It should thus come as no surprise that the Manifesto also serves as the inspiration for Linz's ten-part web series *Das Oberhausener Gefühl* [*The Oberhausen Feeling*] made in 2012).[22] In an essay-cum-manifesto for the online magazine *Perlentaucher* also from 2012, Linz expressed outrage over the Manifesto's negligible impact on contemporary German media culture:

> Heute kann sich jeder Alt- und Neo-Nazi in Ruhe durch die öffentlich-rechtlichen Fernsehprogramme schalten. Kein Fassbinder, kein Wildenhahn, keine feministischen Filmemacherinnen mehr, die ihm in schöner Regelmäßigkeit die Stimmung verderben. . . . Im Lichte des fünfzigjährigen Jubiläums des Oberhausener Manifests betrachtet ist das ein Skandal, weil sich das Manifest ja gerade gegen die heimatselige Konservierung post-nationalsozialistischer Filmästhetiken gerichtet hatte.

> [Old-school Nazis and neo-Nazis alike can surf Germany's public television stations today in peace. There are no more Fassbinders, no more Wildenhahns or feminist filmmakers who regularly spoil their mood. . . . In light of the fiftieth anniversary of the Oberhausen Manifesto, this is scandalous because the Manifesto was directed against the nativist preservation of post-National Socialist film aesthetics.][23]

22 Jörg Becker, "Bühnen der Arbeit," *Neue Zürcher Zeitung*, February 15, 2014, http://www.nzz.ch/buehnen-der-arbeit-ld.630145. On the origins of Linz's web series, see Frédéric Jaeger, "Im Zweigespräch: was von Oberhausen bleibt—Max Linz über Oberhausen, Feminismus und einen Geldeintreibetext," *critic.de*, April 26, 2012, https://www.critic.de/interview/im-zwiegespraech-was-von-oberhausen-bleibt-3545/.

23 Maximilian Linz, "Liebe Deutschland," *Perlentaucher: Das Kulturmagazin*, April 25, 2012, http://www.perlentaucher.de/im-kino/liebe-deutschland.html. Inspiration for Linz's essay is Georg Seeßlen's "Zehn Thesen zur Zukunft des Films," published in *epd film* in February that same year.

Not only was "Papa's Kino" back with a vengeance fifty years after its demise, but federal film subsidies, which materialized in the wake of the Manifesto and made New German Cinema possible, now also place contractual demands on filmmakers such that their "politische wie ästhetische Freiheiten" (political and aesthetic freedoms) must genuflect to "bürokratischen Konfektionslogiken" (bureaucratic ready-made logic).[24]

Unwilling to resign himself to mourning and melancholy in light of film financing's neoliberal containment in the new millennium, with *Ich will mich nicht künstlich aufregen* Linz sets out to wrestle with the ideologies and political economy responsible for expelling independent film from the Berlin Republic's cinemas and television. The film's narrative centers on Asta Andersen (Sarah Rolfs), an independent Berlin-based curator for contemporary art in search of public funding to realize her exhibition on the precarious future of politically engaged filmmaking entitled "Das Kino. Das Kunst." Subtle wordplay that transposes cinema's neuter article onto the otherwise feminine noun for art, Asta's clever, if not ridiculous title conveys both art cinema's expulsion as well as its awkward, if not precarious accommodation in one of the hallow domains of the visual arts: the gallery. Far from just documenting the historical emigration of independent filmmaking from the black box of the cinematic theater to the white cube of the gallery, Asta's exhibit also plans to query, she explains, whether the institutional spaces of film created in postwar West Germany could be recultivated amphibiously by way of "Rückverzauberung" (reverse enchantment).[25] In the very same radio interview in which she alienates the federal agency backing her unrealized exhibit, Asta infers that film, like many threatened amphibians, could become both aquatic and terrestrial. "Könnten die auch YouTube, wenn man sie ließe?" (Could they also be on YouTube if you let them?) the radio moderator, referring to all amphibians, asks. "Ja sicher" (Sure), Asta replies, "wenn man sie dafür bezahlt, vielleicht" (but only perhaps if you pay them for it). In spite of perilous funding cuts she herself instigated by criticizing cinema's corporate institutions and the neoliberal doctrine they serve in the radio interview, Asta soldiers onward by courting Indian financier Waris Singh (Pushpendra Singh). She soon learns that her nemesis, the head of Berlin's cultural affairs office Wilhelmine Askwitt (Nina Tecklenburg), reauthorized subventions she revoked earlier. *Ich will mich nicht künstlich aufregen* concludes, however, not with this coincidental "happy end" but rather with a ten-minute epilogue of disparate scenes ranging from a street demonstration against capitalism and racism

---

24 Linz, "Liebe Deutschland."

25 On the history of this migration from black box to white cube, see Andrew V. Uroskie, *Between the Black Box and the White Cube: Expanded Cinema and Postwar Art* (Chicago: University of Chicago Press, 2014.)

128 ♦ Richard Langston

to Waris's infomercial "Five Truths about Money," which ends with the warning "Hinter dem Faschismus steht das Kapital" (capitalism lurks beneath fascism). The film concludes with a close-up shot of Asta driving her Saab through the heart of iconic Kreuzberg; whether her exhibit ever materializes remains unclear.

Although money persists as a real threat to Asta's professional liveli-hood, she also spends considerable time reading theory. Unsurprisingly, reviewers were quick to note just how indulgent Linz's film is with its theoretical references. While one reviewer called it "sprachliches-Adorno-Ping-Pong," (linguistic Adorno ping-pong) others insisted on its indebt-edness to Pollesch's discourse theater.[26] Both calls are not wrong, for Asta is as invested in the Expressionism Debate of the 1930s as she is in the discourse on post-cinema. Before she ever lays eyes on Horkheimer and Adorno, she reads Niklas Luhmann's *Art as a Social System* (1995). Awaiting her attention next is a mountain of theoretical texts piled on her desk that includes titles like Walter Benjamin's "The Work of Art in the Age of Its Technological Reproducibility" (1935–1939), Siegfried Kracauer's *Theory of Film* (1960), Bertolt Brecht's *Journals* (1973), Gilles Deleuze's *Cinema II* (1985), a stack of Merve publications, sundry issues of the journal *Frauen und Film,* Hito Steyerl's *The Wretched of the Screen* (2012), and Sulgi Lie's *Towards a Political Aesthetics of Cinema* (2012). What exactly does all this diverse theory accomplish for Asta's curatorial work? For Linz, marking the contemporary is clearly impossible without a firm grasp of intellectual history. But weight is unmistakably placed on Asta's initial recitation from *Dialectic of Enlightenment* on the culture industry's "standardized forms" and Brecht's opposing thoughts on "the social effects of works of art."[27] What Linz calls a historical discourse "der immer noch weiter eingrenzt, was Kino ist" (that continues to narrow down what cinema is), the aesthetic debates from the 1930s and 1940s form one half of the film's ratio, term A of Linz's contemporary ratio if you will, concerned with cinema's ontology.[28] What cinema was for

26 See Michael Kienzl, "Abseits der Norm: *Ich will mich nicht künstlich auf-regen* läuft ab heute im Kino," *Spex: Magazin für Popkultur* 358 (2015): 87; Stephan Haselberger, "Sprachliches Adorno-Ping-Pong," *Der Tagesspiegel*, Feb-ruary 9, 2014, https://www.tagesspiegel.de/kultur/sprachliches-adorno-ping-pong-3544648.html.

27 Max Horkheimer and Theodor W. Adorno, *Dialectic of Enlightenment: Philosophical Fragments*, ed. Gunzelin Schmid Noerr, trans. Edmund Jeph-cott (Stanford, CA: Stanford University Press, 2002), 95; Bertolt Brecht, *Jour-nals 1934–1955*, ed. John Willett, trans. Hugh Rorrison (New York: Routledge, 1993), 130.

28 The so-called Expressionist Debate, also known as the realism debate, is anthologized in the volume: Theodor W. Adorno et al., *Aesthetics and Politics* (London: Verso, 2007). On the significance of Asta's recourse to Horkheimer,

Horkheimer and Adorno as well as Brecht—either barbarism or social-ism—is, however, a dialectical choice Asta's cinematic amphibianism must clearly refuse. In a world full of streaming video, Asta's advocacy of political cinema cannot afford the either/or of older theoretical arguments. Exiled from the traditional theater, engaged film can proliferate between the extremes of lucrative YouTube monetization and the consecrated spaces of the museum only if it devises an appropriate aesthetic praxis, one that Linz himself has called "rather undialectical."[29] To this end, *Ich will mich nicht künstlich aufregen* tells its story while simultaneously working through the term B in its ratio of the contemporary, namely, the legacy of engaged aesthetic praxis that began with the Oberhausen Manifesto.

Term B: Praxis

Asta's story of political resolve despite the state's capricious collusion with the culture industry is easily told. Yet how Linz's film tells her story is remarkably complex, especially given how extensively it references a narrow path through postwar West German film history, one that maps out potential legacies for political filmmaking in the present. It is, however, not enough to describe the aesthetic praxis typical of New German Discourse Comedy as merely "brechtianisch, antipsychologisch, antikonsumistisch."[30] If Brechtian, anti-psychological, and anti-consumerist were political and aesthetic characteristics operative in older agitprop films like the Dziga-Vertov Group's *Le Vent d'est*, then what exactly is historically relevant about these qualities for a film made in 2014? The praxis term in Linz's ratio of the contemporary is thus keenly aware of its relationship to past political filmmaking and the range of political praxes allegedly viable in arenas of aesthetic production beyond filmmaking. "Das Theater, so wie ich es in der zweiten Hälfte der Nuller Jahre in Berlin erleben durfte, ob in Matthias Lilienthals HAU, René in Polleschs Prater oder auf Christoph Schlingensiefs transgressiven Drehbühnen" (Theater as I experienced it in Berlin in the second half of the aughts, whether Matthias Lilienthal's HAU, René Pollesch's Prater or Christoph Schlingensief's transgressive revolving stages), Linz explains in his aforementioned *Perlentaucher* essay, "hatte sich als Ort der ästhetischen Freiheit gezeigt" (proved itself to be a place of aesthetic

---

Adorno, and Brecht, see Max Linz, director's statement, Filmgalerie 451, accessed September 27, 2022, http://www.filmgalerie451.de/de/filme/ich-will-mich-nicht-kuenstlich-aufregen.

29 Pitzen, "Tenacity and Zeitgeist," 4. See also Pantenburg, "Class Relations," 72.

30 Meyer, "Zu jedem."

freedom).[31] Far from abandoning film altogether, what Linz seeks with *Ich will mich nicht künstlich aufregen* is to test whether film, like the theater of Lilienthal, Pollesch, and Schlingensief before it, can also operate as a "Spielraum für Verhandlungen [. . .] wie die Welt, die wir gemeinsam bewohnen, aussehen soll und könnte" (a space for negotiation [. . .] about what the world we inhabit together should and could look like).[32] To this end, *Ich will mich nicht künstlich aufregen* dons various mantles of West German film history.[33]

Already in the film's opening sequences in which the disparity between Horkheimer and Adorno and Brecht is laid bare we encounter the first such citation, namely, Christoph Schlingensief's film and stage work from the late nineties. Pacing through her office while reciting from Brecht's journal entry on the perils of "formalistic criticism" from January 28, 1941, Asta hands her copy over, first to the creative writer (Franz Friedrich) in residence at her office and then to Hannah Husching (Nele Winkler) and Hannah's friend (Zora Schemm).[34] Like René Schappach (who plays the manager of an AV rental company) and Kerstin Graßmann (who plays herself) who appear later in the film, actresses Winkler and Schemm introduce with their Down syndrome an ability/disability binary that the film quickly subverts in ways not unlike Schlingensief's work. While Schlingensief was certainly not the first German director to cast actors with so-called disabilities, Linz's inclusion of Graßmann, in particular, is clearly a deliberate allusion to her affiliation with the "Schlingensief Family," that cadre of differently abled actors regularly featured in Schlingensief's films, theater, and television productions since 1996.[35] As with Linz's frequent use of artificial sets and tableaux vivants, the inclusion of Schappach, Winkler, and Schemm—principal actors from Berlin's integrative RambaZamba Theater—along with Graßmann help shatter all illusions of narrative fiction. And as for their translation of theory into praxis, it turns out that Kerstin and Hannah do more than any other characters in the film to test the present-day limits of theory's use value. Whereas Kerstin doubles as an instructor specializing in "Brecht yoga," an unmistakable fusion of Marxism and neoliberal self-care, Hannah (dressed

31 Linz, "Liebe Deutschland."

32 Linz, "Liebe Deutschland."

33 Christian Blumberg, "'Die Stadt als Set': Im Gespräch Max Linz über sein Debüt," *Der Freitag*, May 7, 2014, https://www.freitag.de/autoren/der-freitag/die-stadt-als-set.

34 Brecht, *Journals*, 130.

35 On the disruptive function of disability within the "Schlingensief Family," see Kati Kroß, "Christoph Schlingensief's *Freakstars 3000*: '. . . Consistently Abused and Forced to Portray Disability!,'" trans. Christoph Nöthlings, in *Disabled Theater*, ed. Sandra Umathum and Benjamin Wihstutz (Zurich: diaphanes, 2015), 180n3 and 195.

as Ulrike Meinhof) later assaults the camera lens, what Godard and Gorin once regarded as theory made manifest, with a cordless drill.[36] "Hannah," Kerstin exclaims, "Um Gottes willen, was machst du denn da? Das nennst du deine neue Arbeit? Das ist Diskursverknappung!" (Hannah, for God's sake, what are you doing? You call that your new job? You're curtailing the discourse!). Neither Kerstin's assimilation nor Hannah's assault on the apparatus ends up impacting Asta's curatorial ambitions. As for Asta's response, the closest she ever gets to foul play is when she flirts with the idea of siccing Wikileaks on Wilhelmine's dubious academic credentials. By film's end this, too, proves superfluous.

Linz's allusion to Schlingensief is just the first of several interrelated domino pieces in *Ich will mich nicht künstlich aufregen* leading backward in time toward the dawn of independent West German cinema. If Schlingensief's film *Die 120 Tage von Bottrop* (*The 120 Days of Bottrop*, 1997), in which Graßmann appears as Sophie Rois's reluctant lover, counts for Linz as the last exemplar of New German Cinema before the neoliberal ruination of film subsidies, then it is the muse for this final Schlingensief film, namely, Rainer Werner Fassbinder, who frames the next cinematic reference.[37] "Gestern Nacht habe ich mal wieder *Acht Stunden sind kein Tag* die fünfte Folge angesehen" (Last night I watched the fifth episode of *Eight Hours Don't Make a Day* again), Asta explains, as she sits dazed and motionless together with five other colleagues. Asta's fixation on the final episode of Fassbinder's television series *Acht Stunden sind kein Tag* (1972–73) has less to do with the narrative's conclusion than with how heroine Marion (Hanna Schygulla) uses the Marxist principles of alienation and accumulation to explain how capitalists acquire more capital. "Und dass das immer so weiter geht, das findet sie nicht richtig" (She doesn't think it's right that things keep going on like this), Asta drones, "und das sagt sie so mitten hinein ins ganze westdeutsche Fernsehen zur Primetime" (and she says this on West German television right in the middle of prime time). Astonishing for millennials like Asta who very likely download Fassbinder's proletarian melodrama on their laptops is the fact that the mass spectacle of Marion's critique of political economy broadcast on public television remained trapped within the apolitical realm of entertainment.[38] Fassbinder's film was a hit, but its politics never made a radical difference in the Federal Republic's public sphere. As with the only other tableau at the close of the film—Asta listens motionlessly to the Joseph Schmidt song "Es wird im Leben / Dir mehr

36 Alessandra Rosen, "Balance, Yoga, Neoliberalism," *Signs and Society* 7, no. 3 (2019): 294.

37 Linz, "Liebe Deutschland." Linz's reference to the "last New German Film" is, in fact, the secondary title to Schlingenseif's *Die 120 Tage von Bottrop*.

38 Blumberg, "'Die Stadt als Set.'"

genommen als gegeben" ("There's More Taken in Life Than Given") featured in Richard Oswald's 1936 film *Heut' ist der schönste Tag in meinem Leben* (*Today Is the Most Beautiful Day in My Life*)—past proletarian experience fails to move the present. Proletarian experience in Asta's present appears to be no different. Despite their outspoken politics, Turkish German artists working under Asta's representation remain helpless pawns in a system of gentrification, precarious labor, and racism.

Linz's next step backward in cinematic history is none other than Alexander Kluge, one of the masterminds of the proletarian public sphere and the co-architect of the Oberhausen Manifesto. Frustrated that broadcasting her low opinions of democracy's neoliberal institutions imperiled her exhibition's external funding, Asta discusses options over dinner with her mother Dagmar (Hannelore Hoger). Hardly surprised by the steep competition for money her daughter faces in a city full of independent curators, Dagmar initially encourages Asta to exploit the legal system to extract the public funding denied to her. She changes her tune, however, upon learning the identity of Asta's adversary Wilhelmine. "Was! Die!" (No way! That woman!), she counters. Dagmar immediately realizes that Wilhelmine will litigate for years and still block Asta's exhibition. Aware of the cultural affairs officer's ruthless ways—she's even commandeered the Ministry of Education-funded Excellence Cluster "Normative Kühe" (Normative Cows)—Dagmar offers to help. After denouncing all theory—"Philosophen! Raus aus der Polis! (Philosophers! Get out of the polis!), she shouts—Dagmar then avows, "Ich hab' Geld" (I have money). This money she promises takes her to Germany's annual Citizen Festival held at Bellevue Palace, where she tries to win the favor of Federal President Joachim Gauck. Nothing less than an allusion to the *cinéma verité* sequence in Kluge's 1979 film *Die Patriotin* (*The Patriot*) where Hoger's character Gabi Teichert, a disenchanted high school teacher, infiltrates the SPD's 1977 annual convention to win political support for teaching a more positive account of German history, Dagmar's efforts to butter up the president go nowhere just like Gabi's direct action succumbed to laborious party protocols.[39]

Digital Archaeology versus Neoliberal Compliance

Are Linz's allusions to German cinema's past aesthetic strategies intended as potential solutions to Asta's financial woes? Are they bedeviled by

---

39 Pantenburg makes the important qualification that Dagmar's appearance is no one-to-one reenactment, for Hoger is recognizable not as Gabi but rather as the chief detective in ZDF's long-running detective series "Bella Block." See Patenburg, "Class Relations," 73.

inherent shortcomings or are they anachronistically out of sync with Asta's present-day conundrum? Might these failures be, in fact, indictments of the Oberhausen Manifesto's value for present-day cinematic praxis? To the contrary, the fact that Linz's references to Kluge, Fassbinder, and Schlingensief all fall short as models for Asta's search highlights all the more how important the film's reflexive relationship to the history of New German Cinema—from its inception in 1962 to its premature demise with the death of Fassbinder in 1982 to its last self-proclaimed gasp in 1997—is for its search for a viable present-day aesthetic praxis. In this respect, Linz's citations are in no way instances of the "random cannibalization" or "pseudohistorical depth" that postmodern critics once associated with pastiche.[40] Rather, *Ich will mich nicht künstlich aufregen* throws into relief the challenges to its desired heterotopian praxis for the present (as played out on the levels of narrative, form, and medium) against a carefully composed foil of German politically motivated films shaped by German historical conditions from a bygone world order when independent film had not yet been exiled from the movie theater. While the legacies of the Oberhausen Manifesto may have indeed become negligible for, say, the Berlin School and its hallmark long takes, Oberhausen stands front and center as a point of orientation for Linz.[41] Making a difference in the present, when past approaches to making a difference prove ineffectual, thus boils down to literally marking time such that the present and the past, as Rabinow argues, "coexist in multiple configurations and variations."[42] How then is such marking of time at all possible when citation fares no better the second time around?

Ich will mich nicht künstlich aufregen draws attention to the nature of this political project by folding digital techniques for marking time into Asta's narrative. Still in the process of courting Singh for financial backing, Asta pays a visit to independent film archivists working in a loft apartment overlooking Berlin's skyline. A brief montage initially shows the team's desktop, excerpts from the student film *Wochenschau Nr. 2* (Newsreel No. 2) made in 1969, Vertov's *Man with a Movie Camera* (1929) and a title card of his manifesto "The Essence of Kino-Eye."[43] "Wir befassen

---

40 Fredric Jameson, *Postmodernism, or, The Cultural Logic of Late Capitalism* (Durham, NC: Duke University Press, 1991), 18, 20.

41 Lutz Koepnick, "Long Takes . . .," in *Berlin School Glossary: An ABC of the New Wave in German Cinema*, ed. Roger F. Cook et al., 195–203 (Bristol: Intellect, 2013) 195. On Linz's antipathy to long takes, see Blumberg. "'Die Stadt als Set.'"

42 Rabinow, *Marking Time*, 2.

43 The title card reads: "Unsere grundlegende und programmatische Aufgabe ist es, jedem Unterdrückten als einzelnem und dem Proletariat in seiner Gesamtheit in dem Bestreben zu helfen, sich in den Lebenserscheinungen der Umwelt zurechtzufinden" (Our basic, programmatic objective is to aid each oppressed

134 ♦ Richard Langston

uns zur Zeit mit der Geschichte der deutschen Hochschulen seit 1945" (We're currently working on the history of German universities since 1945), archivist Noa (Serpil Turhan) explains; "Und jetzt war die Frage, wie kann man [diese Geschichte] darstellen bzw. zugänglich machen" (Our question has been how to represent [this history] and accordingly make it accessible). As Noa's preliminary material suggests, her project is thoroughly political. Post-secondary education in Germany, she goes on to explain, has long been shaped by countervailing pressures to conform or protest. Her case in point is the documentary film *Wochenschau Nr. 2*, shot at Berlin's German Film and Television Academy in May 1968 by students who occupied the school and rechristened it. Pixelated on her computer screen is Thomas Mitscherlich painting the school's new name on a banner. Muted is Mitscherlich's equally important commentary: "Wir haben die Akademie die Dziga-Wertow-Akademie genannt. Durch seine Filme hatten wir gelernt, nicht nur Filme zu machen, sondern politisch zu sein, um politische Filme zu machen, die das System verändern" (We've called the Academy the Dziga Vertov Academy. We learned with his films not only how to make films but how to be political to make political films that change the system). Without such an archive, present-day students are unable to gauge the contemporaneity of their own struggles. Noa's online archive www.astamateri.al—the flattering URL is clearly intended for Asta's exhibition—is designed, Noa concludes, to actualize the past, "eben nicht unverfügbare Erfahrung, als Erkenntnis und Kritik, auf denen man aufbauen kann" (not as unavailable experience, but rather as knowledge and critique that can be built upon). Their online archive, Noa's in-house film theoretician Sulgi Lie interjects, is "eine Nähmaschine, die unsere Gegenwart mit der Vergangenkeit vernäht. Und wenn wir uns eine Zukunft vorstellen können wollen, dann darf die Naht nicht schließen" (a sewing machine that stitches our present with the past. If we want to be able to imagine the future, then the seam must never close).

A sequence with seemingly little in common with the rest of the film's narrative, Asta's introduction to the website www.astamateri.al is, in fact, the kernel to the praxis term in Linz's ratio of the contemporary. In an article in the German-language media studies journal *montage AV* published the same year as *Ich will mich nicht künstlich aufregen* premiered, Linz recounted firsthand the dissolution of co-determination rights that had been guaranteed to students enrolled at the DFFB since 1968. Upon being appointed the new director of the Academy in 2010, Jan Schütte discontinued the Academic Council, in which students, instructors, and

---

individual and the proletariat as a whole in their effort to understand the phenomena of life around them). Dziga Vertov, "The Essence of Kino-Eye," in *Kino-Eye: The Writings of Dziga Vertov*, ed. Annette Michelson, trans. Kevin O'Brien (Berkeley: University of California Press, 1984), 49.

administrators mutually decided on all curricular matters. As a result, executives assumed complete power and students and faculty faced precarity not seen in over forty years. Without any recourse, students turned to Berlin mayor Klaus Wowereit in an open letter, asking the city-state to rectify co-determination as enshrined in the Berlin Higher Education Act.[44] Not willing to hold their breath, Linz and kindred peers enrolled at the DFFB organized a series of film screenings entitled "Spekulative Geschichte(n) der DFFB in Filmen" (Speculative (Hi)stories of the DFFB in Film), including *Wochenschau Nr. 2*, held in the Academy's and the Stiftung Deutsche Kinemathek's archives. In his *montage AV* essay, he explains that they were looking for "die Verbindungslinien zwischen den Zeiten, von Wertow über die Wertow-Akademie in unsere Gegenwart" (connections between Vertov's time, the time of the Vertov Academy and our present).[45] Far from wishing to convey a historical relation with their screenings, Linz and his cohort sought out, in much the same way Noa does, answers to the question: "Halten Filme—gerade aus einer weit entfernt oder gar verloren scheinenden Vergangenheit—selbst ein produktives Moment für aktuelle politische Auseinandersetzungen bereit?" (Do films—especially those from the distant past or even one seemingly lost to history—still hold a productive moment for current political debates?) Linz's provisional response was the creation of an actual digital archive called astamateri.al featured in his film. Inspired, in part, by Steyerl's claim that archaeology, unlike history, is far better able to recognize a document as a building block of positive epistemic architectures, Linz chose to model his project after the Indian video archive pad.ma (Public Access Digital Media Archive) on account of its deliberate articulation of aesthetic and political praxes.[46]

A point of contact between history and the aesthetic, the digital archive proves, however, to be a negligible force within Asta's story. Named after the student government body operative at most German universities—*Allgemeiner Studierendenausschuss* or AStA—Asta is continually torn between her political alliances (with her theory, her subaltern artists, her mother, and her archivists) and the economic and political demands of neoliberalism, to which she eagerly complies. In the age of neoliberal deregulation, privatization, and withering social welfare, female subjects like Asta require for success a heightened sense of reflexivity

---

44 For the student letters to the DFFB administration and Wowereit, see Robert Weixlbaumer, "Streit an der dffb eskaliert," *Tip Berlin*, December 28, 2011, https://www.tip-berlin.de/kino-stream/streit-der-dffb-eskaliert/.

45 Max Linz, "Film-Politik, Studenten-Bewegung, Online-Archiv: Bericht von der Dziga-Wertow-Akademie," *montage AV* 23, no. 2 (2014): 106.

46 Hito Steyerl, *Die Farbe der Wahrheit: Dokumentarismen im Kunstfeld* (Vienna: Verlag Turia + Kant, 2008), 25.

136 ♦ RICHARD LANGSTON

and self-improvement to "conceive of themselves as their own business" and forge transactional "relationships to others as potential 'business-to-business alliances.'"[47] This self-care impacts, above all, how female subjects like Asta view their labor and comport their bodies. In pursuit of a neoliberal work-life balance, she offsets her extreme workload and sacrifice of everyday leisure by participating in "Brecht yoga," which exhorts her to shut her eyes and contemplate not only society as history but also her body as a "Konstruktionsleistung" (construction site).[48] This body work is, however, not a Marxist intervention so much as Asta's comportment to the new flexible economy's "fashion-beauty-complex," what Angela McRobbie calls the entreaty to individual self-beautification that maintains appropriate patriarchal gender relations.[49] "Welche Schuhe passen besser zu meinem Outfit?" (Which shoes match my outfit better?) Asta later asks fellow curator Franz Beil (Viktor von Wozogen) who, in turn, decries his own inability to curate his everyday life aesthetically. Asta's compliance to neoliberalism's demands does not, however, neutralize altogether her politics or her ability to recognize neoliberalism's threat. After listening, for example, to Wilhelmine's assistant Marc Möbius (Daniel Hoevels) use theory speak to devalue Asta's roster of artists as "Vorzeigesubjekte des Neo-Individual-Liberalismus" (model subjects of neo-individual liberalism), the precarity of their "Kritikalität" (criticality) and the inevitable transcoding of all "Künstlerkritik" (artistic critique) into "kulturelles Lifestyle-Kapital" (cultural lifestyle capital) since 1968, Asta doesn't miss a beat: "Das ist doch totaler Kapitalistenkitsch" (That's total capitalist kitsch), she fires back in disgust. Asta's struggle is indeed similar and different from the one that faced the Vertov Academy. Even though she intuits the artificiality of neoliberal arguments against her contemporary work, her own neoliberal entanglements preclude her from accessing the requisite tools for marking off her present fight from past political struggles. Like Linz and his peers who were disappointed and mobilized when the DFFB suspended their right to co-determination in 2011, Asta pushes forward with her exhibition plans even though she's fully ensnared in the conditions that ensure its precarity.

The Ethos of Comedy

"The ethos of the contemporary," Rabinow writes, "[is] concerned with the emergence and articulation of forms within which old and new

47 Rosen, "Balance, Yoga, Neoliberalism," 293.
48 Rosen, "Balance, Yoga, Neoliberalism," 295.
49 Angela McRobbie, *The Aftermath of Feminism: Gender, Culture and Social Change* (London: Sage, 2009), 10.

elements take on meanings and functions."[50] In Linz's *Ich will mich nicht künstlich aufregen*, the outlines for a ratio between theory and praxis of the contemporary do come into view; the ratio itself, however, never wholly materializes. Old and new resist seamless articulation. Neither the oppositional theories of realism nor the retrieval of past cinematic models produces a robust term required for each side of the ratio. That political cinema in the neoliberal age falls short of forging a definitive historical relation from the legacies of anti-fascist aesthetic theory (Horkheimer, Adorno, Brecht) and anti-fascist aesthetic praxis (Kluge, Fassbinder, Schlingensief) leads not, however, to abject failure. On the contrary, an ethos of bafflement arises that Linz shrouds in humor. Laughter, he once explained, "ist zumindest Folge einer Verfremdungsästhetik. Die Künstlichkeit meines Films formt ein tragikomisches Modell. Alle künstlerischen Verfahren, die mich interessieren, arbeiten mit genau dieser Oszillation" (is, at the very least, the result of an alienation aesthetic. The artificiality of my film forms a tragicomic model. All artistic processes that interest me work with exactly this oscillation).[51] From Brecht yoga to the Excellence Cluster "Normative Cows" to a ridiculous international phone call with Waris about the American sitcom *Seinfeld*, *Ich will mich nicht künstlich aufregen* repeatedly traffics in humor that draws attention to the ubiquity of neoliberalism's tragedies. Brecht's engaged literature becomes operationalized for yoga's neoliberal logic. An actual beneficiary of the neoliberalization of German higher education, the Excellence Cluster "Normative Orders" based at Frankfurt's Goethe Universität is spoofed ("Normative Cows" in German sounds like "normative dimwits"). And an Indian financier keenly aware of the nature of global capital, Indian modernization, the power of fascist myth, and the trajectory of world history, binges on *Seinfeld* while at the same time insisting, like an extra in Godard and Gorin's *Le Vent d'est*, that "Der Kampf um Befreiung ist international" (the struggle for liberation is international). The tragedy of the neoliberal present lies in the fact that nothing in this world is spared from these neutralizing contradictions.

To conclude, however, that *Ich will mich nicht künstlich aufregen* is a defeatist film is to overlook all the aforementioned ways it does mark time by yoking the entangled heterotopian present with a political, seemingly utopian past. Of critical importance are the subtle ways in which difference is introduced into the relationship between past and present. Arguably the most important such difference comes at the very close of Linz's film when we see Asta, with bouquet in hand, emerge from a Kreuzberg florist and climb into her Saab. Schmidt's melancholy song gives way to composer Tamer Fahri Özgönenc's simple electronic beats

---

50 Rabinow, *Marking Time*, 24.
51 Blumberg, "'Die Stadt als Set.'"

and pulsing synths while Carlos Andrés López's camera shoots Asta in profile as she drives with eyes fixed on the street. Unmistakably reminiscent of the identically composed shot in Kluge's *Die Patriotin* when Gabi, entirely paralyzed by her pedagogical pursuits, drives through the streets of Frankfurt crying, Asta's demeanor at the wheel could not be more different. Compared to Gabi's melancholy and mourning—she finally realizes her utopian project is impossible—Asta's cool and composed facial expressions convey focused determination.[52] "Meiner Meinung nach" (in my opinion), Linz declared in his *Perlentaucher* essay, "ist es für mediale Melancholie und Trauerarbeit noch zu früh" (it's too soon for media melancholy and mourning). Asta, too, makes no secret of her political commitment. "You know," she exclaims in English in an earlier sequence in the film's epilogue, "I think this whole discourse of post-cinema and all that, I don't know, I think it's intellectual kitsch." If the future of cinema is indeed to be more amphibian (and thus less dialectical), then it will, on the one hand, continue to subject itself to the disarticulation of politics and the aesthetic on neoliberal streaming platforms like YouTube, on which struggling artists can disseminate their work free of charge.[53] On the other, it will work to mark its contemporaneity as a moving ratio of modernity by bringing not only new and old but also east and west into relation with one another such that spectators recognize, to quote Linz one last time, "improbable connections between components of a shared reality that are no longer perceived as opposites."[54] The archaeological component of this work not only orients future political struggles vis-à-vis past aesthetic strategies but also opens the potential for networking multiple counter-publics otherwise segregated into different medial spheres. These may be YouTube users watching streaming videos on their smartphones, activists accessing online film archives (like www.astamateri.al or pad.ma) from their laptops, museumgoers taking in a cinematic installation like "Das Kino. Das Kunst," or moviegoers watching an independent film like *Ich will mich nicht künstlich aufregen* at Berlin's Kino Arsenal. Apprehending neoliberalism's conditions of possibility across these media is just as essential for Linz's heterotopic use of utopia as is the cinematic marking of time.

52 See Richard Langston, *The Patriot* (Rochester, NY: Camden House, 2021), 47–51.

53 Linz, "Film-Politik," 117.

54 Pitzen, "Tenacity and Zeitgeist," 4. Pantenburg rightly adds to this list Linz's recourse to "farce and earnestness" as well as "artificiality and documentary realism." See Pantenburg, "Class Relations," 73.

Bibliography

Adorno, Theodor W., Walter Benjamin, Ernst Bloch, Bertolt Brecht, and Georg Lukács. *Aesthetics and Politics*. London: Verso, 2007.

Alberti, Irene von. "Director's Note." Liner Notes for *Der lange Sommer der Theorie*. DVD. Dir. Irene von Alberti. Berlin: Filmgalerie 451, 2017.

Becker, Jörg. "Bühnen der Arbeit." *Neue Zürcher Zeitung*, February 15, 2014. http://www.nzz.ch/buehnen-der-arbeit-ld.630145.

Blumberg, Christian. "'Die Stadt als Set': Im Gespräch Max Linz über sein Debüt." *Der Freitag*, May 7, 2014. https://www.freitag.de/autoren/der-freitag/die-stadt-als-set.

Brecht, Bertolt. *Journals 1934–1955*. Edited by John Willett. Translated by Hugh Rorrison. New York: Routledge, 1993.

Diederichsen, Diedrich. "Maggies Agentur." *René Pollesch: Prater-Saga*, edited by Aenne Quiñones, 7–26. Berlin: Alexander Verlag, 2005.

Dreysse, Miriam. "Heterosexualität und Repräsentation: Markierungen der Geschlechterverhältnisse bei René Pollesch." In *GeschlechterSpielRäume: Dramatik, Theater, Performance und Gender*, edited by Gaby Pailer and Franziska Schlößler, 357–70. Amsterdam: Rodopi, 2011.

Godard, Jean-Luc. *Weekend and Wind from the East: Two Films by Jean-Luc Godard*. London: Lorrimer, 1972.

Haselberger, Stephan. "Sprachliches Adorno-Ping-Pong." *Der Tagesspiegel*, February 9, 2014. https://www.tagesspiegel.de/kultur/sprachliches-adorno-ping-pong-3544648.html.

Horkheimer, Max, and Theodor W. Adorno. *Dialectic of Enlightenment: Philosophical Fragments*. Edited by Gunzelin Schmid Noerr. Translated by Edmund Jephcott. Stanford, CA: Stanford University Press, 2002.

Jaeger, Frédéric. "Im Zwiegespräch: was von Oberhausen bleibt—Max Linz über Oberhausen, Feminismus und einen Geldeintreibetext." *critic.de.*, April 26, 2012. https://www.critic.de/interview/im-zwiegespraech-was-von-oberhausen-bleibt-3545/

Jameson, Fredric. *Postmodernism, or, The Cultural Logic of Late Capitalism*. Durham, NC: Duke University Press, 1991.

Kienzl, Michael. "Abseits der Norm: *Ich will mich nicht künstlich aufregen* läuft ab heute im Kino." *Spex: Magazin für Popkultur* 358 (2015): 87.

Koepnick, Lutz. "Long Takes. . . ." In *Berlin School Glossary: An ABC of the New Wave in German Cinema*, edited by Roger F. Cook, Lutz Koepnick, Kristin Kopp, and Brad Prager, 195–203. Bristol: Intellect, 2013.

Kroß, Kati. "Christoph Schlingensief's *Freakstars 3000*: '. . . Consistently Abused and Forced to Portray Disability!'" Translated by Christoph Nöthlings. In *Disabled Theater*, edited by Sandra Umathum and Benjamin Wihstutz, 179–97. Zurich: diaphanes, 2015.

Langston, Richard. *The Patriot*. Rochester, NY: Camden House, 2021.

Lesage, Julia. "Godard-Gorin's *Wind from the East*: Looking at a Film Politically." *Jump Cut* 4 (1974): 18–23.

Linz, Max. "Director's Statement." Filmgalerie 451. Accessed September 27, 2022. http://www.filmgalerie451.de/de/filme/ich-will-mich-nicht-kuenstlich-aufregen.

———. "Film-Politik, Studenten-Bewegung, Online-Archiv: Bericht von der Dziga-Wertow-Akademie." *Montage AV* 23, no. 2 (2014): 105–21.

———. "Liebe Deutschland." *Perlentaucher: Das Kulturmagazin*, April 25, 2012. http://www.perlentaucher.de/im-kino/liebe-deutschland.html.

MacCabe, Colin. *Godard: Images, Sounds, Politics*. London: MacMillan, 1980.

McRobbie, Angela. *The Aftermath of Feminism: Gender, Culture and Social Change*. London: Sage, 2009.

Meyer, Lars "Zu jedem Bett gehört ein Mann." *Die Zeit*, June 22, 2019. https://www.zeit.de/kultur/film/2019-06/das-melancholische-maedchen-film-susanne-heinrich.

Pantenburg, Volker. "Class Relations: Diagnoses of the Present in the Films of Julian Radlmaier and Max Linz." *New German Critique* 46, no. 3 (138) (2019): 53–78.

Pitzen, Caroline. "Tenacity and Zeitgeist." Arsenal: Institut für Film und Videokunst e.V. Programm Forum, 2014, 2–4. https://www.arsenal-berlin.de/forum-forum-expanded/archiv/programmarchiv/2014/forum-hauptprogramm/ich-will-mich-nicht-kuenstlich-aufregen/.

Pollesch, René. "Ich bin Antiromantiker." In *Liebe ist kälter als das Kapital: Stücke, Texte, Interviews*, edited by Corinna Brocher and Aenne Quiñones, 375–64. Reinbek bei Hamburg: Rowohlt, 2009.

———. "Stadt als Beute." In *Wohnfront 2001–2002: Volksbühne im Prater*, edited by Bettina Masuch, 5–41. Berlin: Volksbühne am Rosa-Luxemburg-Platz and Alexander Verlag, 2003.

Rabinow, Paul. *Marking Time: On the Anthropology of the Contemporary*. Princeton, NJ: Princeton University Press, 2008.

Rancière, Jacques. "The Senses and Uses of Utopia." In *Political Uses of Utopia: New Marxist, Anarchist, and Radical Democratic Perspectives*, edited by S. Chrostowska and James Ingram, 219–32. New York: Columbia University Press, 2017.

Ronneberger, Klaus, Stephan Lanz, and Walther Jahn. *Die Stadt als Beute*. Bonn: Dietz, 1999.

Rosen, Alessandra. "Balance, Yoga, Neoliberalism." *Signs and Society* 7 no. 3 (2019): 289–313.

Seeßlen, Georg. "Zehn Thesen zur Zukunft des Films." *epd film* (2012): 35–39.

Steyerl, Hito. *Die Farbe der Wahrheit: Dokumentarismen im Kunstfeld*. Vienna: Verlag Turia + Kant, 2008.

Uroskie, Andrew V. *Between the Black Box and the White Cube: Expanded Cinema and Postwar Art*. Chicago: University of Chicago Press, 2014.

Vertov, Dziga. "The Essence of Kino-Eye." In *Kino-Eye: The Writings of Dziga Vertov*, edited by Annette Michelson. Translated by Kevin O'Brien, 49–50. Berkeley: University of California Press, 1984.

Weixlbaumer, Robert. "Streit an der dffb eskaliert." *Tip Berlin*, December 28, 2011. https://www.tip-berlin.de/kino-stream/streit-der-dffb-eskaliert/.

Wollen, Peter. "Godard and Counter Cinema: *Le Vent d'est*." In *Film Theory and Criticism: Introductory Readings*, edited by Leo Braudy and Marshall Cohen, 365–73. Oxford: Oxford University Press, 2016.

8: Remediations of Cinefeminism in Contemporary German Film

Hester Baer

IN THE OPENING SCENE of Susanne Heinrich's 2019 film *Das melancholische Mädchen* (The melancholy girl; released in the Anglosphere as *Aren't You Happy?*), a young woman is framed in profile against a patently artificial backdrop, a tropical scene of palm trees, sandy beach, and turquoise-blue ocean. Naked under a fluffy white coat, she stands in a rigid pose, smoking a cigarette, as she begins to recite a monologue. A cut frames the woman in medium close-up, and she rotates to look directly into the camera as her metacommentary turns to questions of cinematic representation:

> Wenn dies zum Beispiel ein Film wäre, würden wir schon alle die verlieren, die sich mit einer Hauptfigur identifizieren wollen. Im Film muss immer etwas passieren. Melancholischen Mädchen passiert nichts. . . . Es gibt keine Höhepunkte, keine Entwicklung, keine Katharsis. . . . Man kann von ihnen nichts lernen. *Außer über die Zeit und den Ort, die sich in ihnen spiegeln.*

> [For example, if this were a film, we'd already lose all those who need to identify with the protagonist. In a film, something always has to happen. Nothing ever happens to melancholic girls. . . . There are no climaxes, no development, no catharsis. . . . One can learn nothing from them, *except about the time and place mirrored within them.*][1]

As her monologue concludes, the woman suddenly asks, "Schläfst du?" (Are you asleep?), and a reverse shot reveals the diegetic audience of her speech in the form of a naked man. Filmed from a high angle, he lies in repose on a futon, occupying a position typically reserved for women in western visual culture. Underscoring the sequence's exaggerated

---

1   Quoted from the German dialogue and English subtitles on the DVD release of the film, my emphasis. *Das melancholische Mädchen*, dir. Susanne Heinrich (Berlin: Salzgeber & Co. Medien GmbH, 2020).

Figure 8.1. Shot/reverse-shot sequence in *Das melancholische Mädchen* (dir. Susanne Heinrich, 2020).

attention to gendered cinematic conventions, he proceeds to pick up a Polaroid camera, train its lens directly on the eye of the film camera, and snap a picture, creating a relay of images and looks between the diegetic characters and the audience of the film.

An apt prologue to the episodic narrative that follows, this scene introduces the film's remediation of feminist film theory and women's cinema as well as its engagement with the ideologies and effects of neoliberal culture. *Das melancholische Mädchen* self-reflexively attends to the perennial questions taken up by cinefeminism, including the disruption of viewer identification; the subversion of classical narrative; and the critique of woman's status as image and object of the male gaze. The opening scene's metacommentary further encapsulates the film's presentation of the melancholy girl as a seismograph of our contemporary "time and place," an emblematic figure deployed to register and make visible the aesthetic and political impasse of the present.

This impasse has been the target of a resurgence of feminist activism over the past decade that has sought to mobilize Germany's substantial women's film heritage while also addressing the underrepresentation of women, gender-nonconforming, LGBTQ+, and BIPOC workers in the film and media industries.[2] Owing to the institutional and financial successes of the women's film movement of the 1970s, (West) Germany became a key national locus for a diverse feminist filmmaking praxis that was, however, ultimately short lived. Following decades of neoliberal cultural policies that reversed previous gains, contemporary activists have sought new ways of combatting the sidelining of both political cinema and

---

2   See also Hester Baer and Angelica Fenner, "Introduction: Revisiting Feminism and German Cinema," in *Women's Film Authorship in Neoliberal Times: Revisiting Feminism and German Cinema*, ed. Hester Baer and Angelica Fenner, special issue of *Camera Obscura: Feminism, Culture, and Media Studies* 33, no. 3 (2018): 1–19.

women and minoritized filmmakers. Two key tendencies have emerged that complement but sometimes stand in tension with one another: the campaign for a quota system waged by the feminist organization Pro Quote Film (PQF, "For a film quota"), and an engagement with feminist film theory and the history of women's cinema by contemporary feminist auteur-directors. In this chapter, I offer a brief snapshot of these two intertwined tendencies, arguing that, despite their different approaches, they both hinge on remediations of cinefeminism.

Remediation—understood here as an explicit engagement with and transformation of aesthetic and theoretical precursor texts in order to draw attention to the history, materiality, and representational practices of media—figures prominently in a range of contemporary German cinematic projects that cast critical light on the politics of the present.[3] *Das melancholische Mädchen* shares key traits with the production trend referred to as the discourse comedy, films that humorously interrogate the status of contemporary culture in the face of its neoliberal cooptation and marketization. Exemplified by Max Linz's *Ich will mich nicht künstlich aufregen* (*Asta Upset*, 2014) and Julian Radlmaier's *Selbstkritik eines bürgerlichen Hundes* (*Self-Criticism of a Bourgeois Dog*, 2017)—both of which, like Heinrich's film, were co-produced by the Deutsche Film- und Fernsehakademie Berlin as their directors' respective graduation films— the discourse comedy sends up the art world and the urban intellectual milieu via a unique amalgam of slapstick scenes and direct quotations from critical theory.

Das melancholische Mädchen also shares significant affinities with works by other contemporary feminist filmmakers, especially Irene von Alberti's mockumentary *Der lange Sommer der Theorie* (*The Long Summer of Theory*, 2017) and Tatjana Turanskyj's *Top Girl oder la déformation professionnelle* (*Top Girl*, 2014).[4] Remediation forms a crucial component of their overtly critical take on the neoliberal present, which focuses on the

---

3   First theorized by Jay David Bolter and Richard Grusin to describe the simultaneous proliferation and erasure of mediation in the digital age, *remediation*, in Olivia Landry's elegant formulation, "distills a unique twofold process and structure. First, it entails the dynamic rendering of (particularly) older forms of media by newer media. . . . Second, remediation involves hypermediality and the composition of multimedia forms as a way to revive immediacy." See Jay David Bolter and Richard Grusin, *Remediation: Understanding New Media* (Cambridge, MA: MIT Press, 1999), and Olivia Landry, "Searching for a Storyteller, Remediating the Archive: Philip Scheffner's *Halfmoon Files*," *New German Critique* 46, no. 3 (138) (2019): 116.

4   These three films also share formal-aesthetic and thematic affinities with the oeuvre of Nicolette Krebitz, especially her recent film *AEIOU—Das schnelle Alphabet der Liebe* (*AEIOU—A Quick Alphabet of Love*, 2022), which space precludes me from considering in detail here.

responsibilization of young women amidst intensifying precarity and gentrification, the demand to self-optimize and perform happiness, and the quest for feminist sociality in an atomized society. Evident in their explicit citation of feminist precursor films and theoretical texts, their focus on the representational possibilities offered by cinema vis-à-vis digital culture, and their concerted redoing of feminist aesthetics, remediation facilitates the development of a structural critique of gender-based oppression in these films.

The renewed embrace of cinefeminism by Heinrich, Alberti, and Turanskyj suggests a sea change at hand in contemporary German film culture. While women filmmakers in the first decade of the twenty-first century (including the important women directors of the Berlin School) were reluctant to claim feminism—even as their work often reflects a sophisticated engagement with the intersections of gender, sexuality, race, class, and citizenship—feminist auteur-directors are increasingly attending to the inequities and limitations of postfeminist media culture, not only through interventions into the material conditions of production but also within the diegeses of their films.[5] Whereas Berlin School films often focus on individuals who are frustrated in their expectations as individuals, these more recent cinematic projects explore relationality—addressing questions of collectivity and solidarity as well as relations between individuals and structures—in both content and form, an exploration that takes place not least through the aesthetic relationality generated by strategies of remediation.

By redoing feminist cinema with particular attention to this *aesthetic* dimension, *Das melancholische Mädchen, Der lange Sommer der Theorie*, and *Top Girl* mobilize the potential of a past moment that has been foreclosed upon. Revivifying strategies pursued by cinefeminist filmmakers in the 1960s and 1970s allows contemporary directors to reclaim cinema as an oppositional space vis-à-vis the predominant platforms of (post)feminist culture, in particular social media and television. Heinrich, Alberti, and Turanskyj notably engage the medium specificity of film within their narratives, through a differentiated portrayal of non-cinematic media culture—including casting sessions, performance art, and ubiquitous digital self-representations—and through their often-playful metafictional attention to narrative style, documentary, and autoethnographic practice, as well as through the question of how film funding figures form.

---

5   As I have argued previously, directors associated with the Berlin School (including Maren Ade, Valeska Grisebach, and Maria Speth) have made formal-aesthetic and material interventions into contemporary German cinema that are legible as feminist. See Hester Baer, "The Berlin School and Women's Cinema," in *The Berlin School and Its Global Contexts*, ed. Marco Abel and Jaimey Fisher (Detroit, MI: Wayne State University Press, 2018), 25–48.

Remediation as a strategy also facilitates the overt critique of neoliberalism in these films, which participate in a broader cultural interest in looking back at the roads not taken in the aftermath of the 1960s in order to reflect on and imagine alternatives to the present.[6] Rather than pursuing less direct strategies of "making neoliberalism visible," these films address it metadiscursively, via the remediation of (critical) theory and through the historical repurposing of (aesthetic) paradigms that interrupt it.[7]

Remediating Cinefeminism

As B. Ruby Rich explains in her 1998 book *Chick Flicks*, cinefeminism is

> a term that was sometimes used to describe the broad field of feminism and film that began in the seventies with the flourishing of film festivals and the simultaneous invention of theoretical approaches to classic Hollywood representations of women, eventually expanding to other films as well. It's a discipline that began as a movement, drawing its strength from the political breakthroughs of the women's liberation movement as well as from the intellectual and ideological lessons of the New Left.[8]

Cinefeminism, in Rich's usage, invokes a moment defined by the dialectical interplay of feminist activism and filmmaking, of theory and practice, that proved crucial for the development of the psychoanalytically oriented and academically situated feminist film theory that emerged in its wake. Due to its drive for a coherent methodology and academic legitimacy, feminist film theory ultimately abdicated the multivalent concerns of cinefeminism, which had brought "a chaotic and

---

6 This interest, driven in part by the fiftieth anniversary of 1968, gave rise to an array of retrospectives, exhibits, and publications around 2018. Particularly relevant here are Phillipp Felsch's widely-read *Der lange Sommer der Theorie: Geschichte einer Revolte, 1960–1990*, which provided an impetus for Alberti's film; Cristina Perincioli's *Berlin wird feministisch. Das Beste, was von der 68er Bewegung blieb*, and Helke Sander and Iris Gusner's *Fantasie und Arbeit: Biografische Zwiesprache*.

7 On making neoliberalism visible in German cinema, see Hester Baer, *German Cinema in the Age of Neoliberalism* (Amsterdam: Amsterdam University Press, 2021). In contrast to the strategies employed by films discussed there, all of which were released between 1980–2010, the more recent films considered here address neoliberalism as an economic, political, and cultural formation much more explicitly, while also placing a special emphasis on the representation of neoliberalism's reformatting of individual subjectivities, emotions, and affects.

8 B. Ruby Rich, *Chick Flicks* (Durham, NC: Duke University Press, 1998), 1–2.

diverse arsenal of approaches" to bear on the problem of women's cinematic representation.[9] German cinema figures prominently in Rich's account, and her conception of cinefeminism helps to capture the aesthetic and political affiliations of the West German feminist film movement, which in the 1970s was equally devoted to rectifying the gender imbalance in the film industry and developing new narratives and forms for women's cinema.

Following its founding in 2014, Pro Quote Film took up where this earlier feminist film movement left off. PQF's promotion of legislation to mandate equitable funding and staffing in German film and television builds on similar recent efforts in Sweden and France, efforts that gained traction not least due to the resonance of hashtag campaigns like #TimesUp and #MeToo, which raised new awareness in the public sphere about gender and representation and about widespread sexism in the global film and media industries. While its approach draws on and resonates with transnational feminist film activism in the present day, PQF also self-consciously styles both its political organizing strategies and its particular demands on an earlier German campaign for the equitable redistribution of federal film subventions to women filmmakers undertaken by the Association of Women Film Workers, a feminist activist group founded in 1979.[10] In their Manifesto from that year, signed by over eighty women film workers from the Federal Republic and West Berlin, the group proclaimed:

We demand:
1. 50 per cent of all funds for films, production facilities, and research projects;
2. 50 per cent of all jobs and training places;
3. 50 per cent of all committee seats;
4. Support for distribution, sale and exhibition of films by women.[11]

Under the motto "50/50 by 2020," PQF has likewise pursued a hard-fought lobbying effort for a 50 per cent gender quota in public film funding; it has subsequently begun to advocate for a 30 per cent diversity quota as well.[12] Engaging social media and digitally oriented activism to remediate demands first articulated by the Association of Women Film

---

9   Rich, *Chick Flicks*, 292.

10   See also Sebastian Heiduschke, "Women's Interventions in the Contemporary German Film Industry," in Baer and Fenner, *Women's Film Authorship in Neoliberal Times*, 147–55.

11   Quoted in Julia Knight, *Women and the New German Cinema* (London: Verso, 1992), 113.

12   See Pro Quote Film, "Forderungen," accessed July 15, 2022, https://proquote-film.de/#/ziele/forderungen/object=page:263.

Workers, PQF has also actively solicited participation on both digital platforms and in live events by that organization's founding members, including filmmakers Helke Sander, Ula Stöckl, and Jutta Brückner, thereby bringing new recognition to their role in the history and development of cinefeminism and contributing to a resurgence of interest in their films among a new generation of feminists. PQF has thus helped to drive a renewed focus on the historical legacies of feminist cinema, visible for instance in the 2019 Berlin Film Festival retrospective "Selbstbestimmt: Perspektiven von Filmemacherinnen" (Self-Determined: Perspectives of Women Filmmakers), which facilitated the restoration and digitization of many important women-directed films from both East and West Germany, some of which have become available to global audiences for the first time via festival screenings and on streaming services. In support of its demand for equitable representation, PQF draws on "Zahlen und Fakten" (numbers and facts),[13] especially quantitative studies that provide statistics about the number, age, and physical appearance of women characters in feature films and publicly funded television series.[14] Although it has registered some marked successes, PQF has sometimes come under criticism for its embrace of normative modes of political representation and its commitment to equality politics realized through quantification, orientations that share commonalities with neoliberal policies like gender mainstreaming.

While she has lent her support to the efforts of PQF, for example, Heinrich has also explicitly noted her attempt to find a different way of engaging with cinefeminism, one that runs counter to the focus on women's numerical representation. The emphasis on representation proclaimed by PQF's motto "Mehr Frauen* vor und hinter der Kamera" ("More women* in front of and behind the camera") and encapsulated by the Bechdel test[15] holds, for Heinrich, "so wenig emanzipatorisches Potenzial wie Sex oder Kleidungsstile" (as much emancipatory potential as sex or clothing styles).[16] Instead, Heinrich's *Das melancholische Mädchen*—like Alberti's *Der lange Sommer der Theorie* and Turanskyj's *Top Girl*—pursues a different set of artistic and political commitments

13 Pro Quote Film, "Die Studien," accessed July 15, 2022, https://pro-quote-film.de/#/status-quote/die-studien/object=page:61.

14 Pro Quote Film, "Fakten," accessed July 15, 2022, https://proquote-film.de/#/status-quote/fakten/object=page:57.

15 This motto has been broadly used by PQF on social media and at live events. See, for example, Pro Quote Film, "Die Studien." The Bechdel test, named after the queer comics artist Alison Bechdel, measures the representation of women in narrative film and fiction.

16 Quoted in Lars Meyer, "Zu jedem Bett gehört ein Mann," *Zeit Online*, June 22, 2019, https://www.zeit.de/kultur/film/2019-06/das-melancholische-maedchen-film-susanne-heinrich.

through its deliberate remediation of feminist film history and theory. By attending to cinefeminism in particular—all three films make reference to the work of Sander, Stöckl, and Ulrike Ottinger—Heinrich, Alberti, and Turanskyj pick up on the structural critique of dominant cinematic conventions for portraying gender and sexuality first articulated in the 1960s. In so doing, they reassert cinema's significance as a critical form, while also highlighting the historical differences between the moment of second-wave feminism's emergence and the neoliberal present.

(At the End of) Neoliberalism and (Post) Feminism

Arising from and aiming to make visible the underlying collective pathologies that produce individual crises in the context of late-stage capitalism, *Das melancholische Mädchen* employs melancholy as a structural metaphor for discontent with the atomization of the present and as a paradigm for the film's skewering of postfeminism. In a widely-circulated director's statement, Heinrich—a literary author who published four novels before she began studying directing at the age of twenty-seven—describes her film's autofictional genesis:

> *Das melancholische Mädchen* ist aus einem tiefen Unbehagen in der Gesellschaft entstanden. Ich war Mitte 20, hatte eine Karriere als Schriftstellerin und eine Ehe hinter mir und litt unter einer Depression. Warum konnte ich nicht einfach glücklich sein? Ich war doch frei und gleichberechtigt, ich hatte doch alle Möglichkeiten, oder?

> [*Das melancholische Mädchen* emerged from a deep discontent in society. I was in my mid-twenties, had a career as a writer and a marriage behind me, and was suffering from depression. Why couldn't I just be happy? I was free and equal, I could do anything, couldn't I?][17]

Heinrich stresses her personal experience of the widespread postfeminist dilemma that Angela McRobbie memorably describes in *The Aftermath of Feminism*: young women are offered a "notional form of equality, concretised in education and employment, and through participation in consumer culture and civil society," but they are held responsible for achieving this equality through personal choices rather than through social

---

17 "Kommentar der Regisseurin," in *Das melancholische Mädchen*, Pressebroschüre (Berlin: Salzgeber & Co. Medien, GmbH, 2019).

provisions, which the neoliberal state aims to dismantle.[18] McRobbie diagnoses a range of "post-feminist disorders" emerging from this paradoxical situation—among them *melancholia*—that are experienced by young women who find themselves "confined to the topographies of an unsustainable self-hood, deprived of the possibilities of a feminist sociality."[19] For Heinrich, consciousness of the relation between collective structures and individual symptoms arose from the galvanizing experience of encountering theoretical texts (by Eva Illouz, Byung-Chul Han, and others) that laid bare the links between the economic and emotional spheres of contemporary life: "Ich begann, individuelle Krisen nicht mehr als persönliches Versagen zu betrachten, sondern als gesellschaftliche Pathologien, die von Subjekten ausgetragen werden" ("I began to see individual crises not as the result of personal failure, but rather as social pathologies that are borne by subjects").[20] Perceiving links between individual stories and broader social structures illuminated the absurdity of neoliberal discourse for Heinrich and led to her rejection of its hegemonic mindset of "no alternatives"; ultimately, as she concludes, "Durch die Arbeit am *Melancholischen Mädchen* [habe ich] selbst aufgehört, eins zu sein" (Through my work on *Das melancholische Mädchen* I stopped being a melancholy girl myself).[21] Accordingly, Heinrich has described how her film "unseren Blick auf Strukturen lenkt" (trains our gaze on structures), seeking to provide viewers with a vocabulary to think about and recognize how dominant gender and sexual relations are imprinted by social norms and economic formations, a critical capacity that we have unlearned in the context of neoliberalism.[22] Heinrich's pedagogical approach to cultivating this capacity foregrounds the remediation of earlier feminist ideas and images.

Via this historical repurposing of cinefeminism, *Das melancholische Mädchen* and other recent feminist films deliberately aim to reverse the postfeminist dynamic whereby "seeing and hearing a safely affirmative feminism in spectacularly visible ways often eclipses a feminist critique of structure, as well as obscuring the labour involved in producing oneself according to the parameters of popular feminism."[23] As Sarah

18   Angela McRobbie, *The Aftermath of Feminism: Gender, Culture, and Social Change* (London: Sage, 2009), 2.

19   McRobbie, *The Aftermath of Feminism*, 120.

20   "Kommentar."

21   "Kommentar."

22   "Regisseurin über Das melanscholische Mädchen," *Spiegel Online*, June 26, 2019, https://www.spiegel.de/video/susanne-heinrich-ueber-szene-aus-das-melancholische-maedchen-video-99028003.html.

23   Sarah Banet-Weiser, Rosalind Gill, and Catherine Rottenberg, "Postfeminism, popular feminism and neoliberal feminism?," *Feminist Theory* 21, no. 1 (2020): 9.

Banet-Weiser has argued, the remarkable visibility of feminism in twenty-first-century popular culture has led to a paradoxical situation in which the visual or material consumption of feminism (via digital media or market culture) is perceived as itself synonymous with the transformation of patriarchal structures, thereby underscoring neoliberalism and heteropatriarchy as the seemingly natural and inevitable order of things.[24] By contrast, Heinrich, Alberti, and Turanskyj contest affirmative and consumer-driven forms of feminism by insisting on a differentiated history of feminist theory and aesthetics that brings a feminist political critique of structure back to the fore.

Produced for €25,000, *Das melancholische Mädchen* garnered widespread attention when it won the Max Ophüls Prize for best debut feature in 2019. Told in fourteen vignettes that are introduced with title cards, the film follows the eponymous protagonist, played by Marie Rathscheck, as she moves through a series of anonymous urban spaces. While we witness her seeking work at a casting call, searching for intimacy in encounters with men, and attempting to write a novel (she is stuck on the first sentence of the second chapter), her true quest is for respite from the precarity and "habitual forms of individual self-management and self-regulation"[25] demanded by the 24/7 economy of the present, summed up in the film's tagline, which describes her as "Auf der Suche nach einem Schlafplatz" (searching for a place to sleep).[26]

Alberti's *Der lange Sommer der Theorie* similarly focuses on how precarious working and living conditions shape the lives of young white women in Berlin. The film intertwines narrative and documentary strands as it follows three characters—filmmaker Nola (Julia Zange), actress Katja (Katja Weilandt), and photographer-singer Martina (Martina Schöne-Radunski), the frontwoman for punk band the Cuntroaches—all members of the creative class, who are searching for employment while trying to defend their apartment from predatory real-estate developers (and at the same time running an informal subleasing service to earn money by renting out rooms to tourists). The metafictional storyline of *Der lange Sommer der Theorie* is structured around a film Nola is shooting on "Selbstoptimierung und kollektives Bewusstsein" (self-optimization and collective consciousness), for which she undertakes a series of documentary-style interviews with prominent feminist and cultural theorists.[27] *Der*

---

24 Sarah Banet-Weiser, *Empowered: Popular Feminism and Popular Misogyny* (Durham, NC: Duke University Press, 2018).

25 Jonathan Crary, *24/7: Late Capitalism and the Ends of Sleep* (London: Verso, 2013), 47.

26 *Das melancholische Mädchen*, Pressebroschüre.

27 Quoted from the German dialogue and English subtitles on the streaming release of the film. *Der lange Sommer der Theorie*, dir. Irene von Alberti (Berlin:

lange Sommer der Theorie was produced by the independent production and distribution company founded by Alberti and her partner Frieder Schlaich, Filmgalerie 451, which has played a significant role over the past thirty years in the creation and circulation of non-mainstream German films, including Berlin School films and the works of feminist directors.

Turanskyj's *Top Girl* also examines postfeminist discourses of empowerment and agency through the story of Helena (Julia Hummer), a single mother keeping herself afloat in gentrifying Berlin through sex work. The second installment in a planned trilogy about women and work that remains unfinished following Turanskyj's untimely death in 2021, *Top Girl* was independently produced by Turanskyj & Ahlrichs, the company co-founded by the filmmaker and her business partner Jan Ahlrichs to facilitate the creation of independent feminist films. Like *Das melancholische Mädchen* and *Der lange Sommer der Theorie*, *Top Girl* offers a feminist metacommentary on how neoliberal mandates for self-optimization disproportionately affect women and a concerted emphasis on performances of gender and sexuality.

Redoing Feminist Film Aesthetics

Das melancholische Mädchen, *Der lange Sommer der Theorie*, and *Top Girl* assemble new images of the present through the repurposing of found materials. All three films deploy a pronounced citational aesthetic, foregrounding their relationality with cinefeminism as a key component of their critique of neoliberalism. While their citations of feminist precursors are multiple and varied, they all establish a formal and narrative relation to Stöckl's recently revived feminist classic *Neun Leben hat die Katze* (*The Cat Has Nine Lives*, 1968). Predating organized second-wave feminism, Stöckl's film presents an important aesthetic and political precursor to subsequent feminist cinema, but it is perhaps equally noteworthy for offering provocations that were not widely taken up by feminist filmmakers in the 1970s and 1980s.[28] In this regard, *Neun Leben* embodies the "chaotic and diverse" approach that Rich identifies in emergent feminist filmmaking, qualities that are reflected in its uptake by Heinrich, Alberti, and Turanskyj. They draw on Stöckl's commitment to pop aesthetics, her ironic take on gendered structures of looking, her embrace of the analytical possibilities of the episode film, as well as her emphasis on the process of women's creativity and her imaginative rupturing of normative regimes of sexuality.

Filmgalerie 451, 2020), vimeo.com/ondemand/derlangesommerdertheorie/387469929.

28   See Hester Baer, *The Cat Has Nine Lives* (Rochester, NY: Camden House, 2022), 9.

Heinrich has referred to the opening sequence of *Das melancholische Mädchen*, discussed at the outset of this chapter, as a kind of "Bedienungsanleitung," or user's guide, for her film.[29] This instruction manual immediately alerts viewers to the film's remediation of feminist aesthetics, intensifying form in order to denaturalize cinematic conventions and alert us to the absence of realism. In addition to the self-reflexive monologue and the mise-en-abyme of lenses and gazes that humorously draw attention to the cinematic apparatus and gendered representation, the sequence flags the film's pop style via its glowing color palette of pastel pinks and blues as well as the overt artifice of its costumes and settings, including the obviously fake digital backdrop and the DIY props visible in the frame.

This attention is extended in Episode 1 of *Das melancholische Mädchen*, introduced with a title card that reads "Feminismus zu verkaufen . . ." (Feminism for sale . . .), in which the protagonist attends a casting call where she and another aspiring actor audition for an advertising campaign. An over-the-top send-up of the gender politics of contemporary marketing rhetoric, this episode simultaneously enacts and reflects on the hypersexualization of bodies and the injunction to perform happiness, key traits of neoliberal media culture that serve as analytical throughlines in Heinrich's film. Like the opening sequence, the metadiscursive construction of this episode employs diegetic cameras, screens, and performances, creating a relay of gazes. Drawing on strategies of remediation, Episode 1 both calls viewers' attention to and asserts a distinction between cinema and other forms of media representation, which the film posits as more instrumentalizing in their commodification of women.

The assertion of cinema's relative autonomy vis-à-vis postfeminist media culture is reiterated in Episode 2, which establishes an overt relationality between *Das melancholische Mädchen* and feminist precursor films. The melancholy girl tells her interlocutor, a new parent (Mira Partecke) who is participating in a synchronized mother–baby exercise class, that she has recently watched a Helke Sander film—she is referring to *Die allseitig reduzierte Persönlichkeit—Redupers* (*The All-Around Reduced Personality—Redupers*, 1977)—whose characters appeared, as she puts it, "aufgeklärter, weniger unterdrückt und irgendwie nicht so blutleer wie wir" (more emancipated, less oppressed, and somehow not as bloodless as we are). Directly invoking Sander's feminist classic, this scene also explicitly references Turanskyj's oeuvre through the casting of Mira Partecke, who played the eponymous "flexible woman" in *Eine flexible Frau* (*The Drifters*, 2010), a film that itself cites and reworks both

---

29 See "Regisseurin über Das melancholische Mädchen."

Sander's film and Ulrike Ottinger's *Bildnis einer Trinkerin* (*Ticket of No Return*, 1979).[30]

Again and again, *Das melancholische Mädchen* employs strategies of remediation to question women's (and also men's) ability to access and experience desire amidst the marketization of sex and the mandate to self-optimize. While Stöckl's *Neun Leben* develops a cinematic language for imagining alternatives to heteropatriarchy, Heinrich cites this language to highlight the neoliberal cooptation of pleasure (including in its transgressive and non-normative manifestations). "Mein Körper ist ein Kriegsgebiet, auf dem alle Welt ihre Kämpfe austrägt" (My body is a battleground on which the world's wars are being waged), proclaims the protagonist at one point, citing feminist photographer Barbara Kruger's 1989 work of protest art (itself a famous example of collage) in order to explain why she eschews sex. Later, after a highly stylized sexual encounter with a carpenter she meets on the street, she suggests that her only freedom in life consists of the freedom to fake an orgasm, before reading aloud from the radical philosophical collective Tiqqun's *Preliminary Materials for a Theory of the Young-Girl* (1999), a work that examines—also in the form of a collage—the figure of the young-girl as the idealized model-citizen of advanced capitalism. *Das melancholische Mädchen* weaves an elaborate, even dizzying web of references. These include: a shaving sequence reminiscent of both Valie Export's *Unsichtbare Gegner* (*Invisible Adversaries*, 1977) and Charlotte Roche's novel *Feuchtgebiete* (*Wetlands*, 2008; adapted to the screen by David Wnendt in 2013); the protagonist's costumes, which recall the dresses and Doc Martens of 1990s Riot Grrl style; and animation effects that add gold crowns and glitter to characters, invoking both Disney princess movies and the pop-art stickers of Lisa Frank.

These references recombine and mash up significant moments not only from film history, but also from feminist creative work and girl culture more broadly. In this regard, *Das melancholische Mädchen* might be understood within the tradition of German popfeminism, a movement that has been instrumental in revivifying both gender-based activism and creative work in millennial Germany, but which has arguably found predominant expression in the realms of literature, music, and digital culture

---

30 On Turanskyj's reworking of feminist precursor films, see Barbara Mennel, "From Utopian Collectivity to Solitary Precarity: Thirty Years of Feminist Theory and the Cinema of Women's Work," *Women in German Yearbook* 30 (2014): 125–37; Baer, *German Cinema in the Age of Neoliberalism*, 157–92; and Alice Bardan, "Shoes, Drunk Women, and Phallic Girls: Tatjana Turanskyj's Feminist Interventions in German Cinema," in *The Singular Plural of Feminist Film Practice*, ed. Angelica Fenner and Barbara Mennel, special issue of *Feminist German Studies* 38, no. 1 (2022): 182–201.

rather than in cinema.[31] Like other (mostly non-cinematic) popfeminist projects, *Das melancholische Mädchen* "uses feminism to recode pop culture and pop to rewrite feminism," an approach that also describes *Der lange Sommer der Theorie*.[32]

Alberti's film offers audiovisual appeal in the form of candy-colored costumes, a densely layered mise-en-scene, and a synthpop soundtrack, qualities reminiscent of the distinctive style of *Neun Leben*, whose pop aesthetics were crucial to Stöckl's denaturalization of femininity (but also a source of the film's negative reception, since they contrasted sharply with the muted color schemes and narrative realism that predominated in other critical filmmaking projects of the era). *Der lange Sommer der Theorie* intersperses documentary-style scenes in which Nola conducts interviews for her film with highly stylized performative sequences taking place in the apartment that she shares with Katja and Martina. These sequences, which often include cameos by artists and intellectuals, feature lengthy, often comic conversations on topics ranging from cinematic representation and gender roles to gentrification.

Der lange Sommer der Theorie establishes a specific aesthetic relationality with Stöckl's pop style and episodic narrative form in order to highlight and assert the difference between the feminist rupturing of gender norms pursued by *Neun Leben* and postfeminist media culture's re-naturalization of normative femininity. Unlike the political circularity that Smith and Stehle identify as inherent in popfeminism's no-holds-barred approach to mash-up, Alberti's use of remediation facilitates the overt contestation of neoliberal gender politics in her film. In one early sequence, following an audition Katja has attended for the role of Eva Braun in a "Gefühlsdrama im Führerbunker" (sentimental drama set in the Führer's bunker), the group discusses German audiences' penchant for heritage films as a symptom of their investment in retrograde gender roles. In a moment that condenses the film's problematization of contemporary discourses of women's representation, Martina notes ironically that, unlike most recent German films, at least the production Katja auditioned for would pass the Bechdel test—whose premise the three women are then compelled to explain to their male friend, who has never heard

---

31 Two key works on German popfeminism, Carrie Smith and Maria Stehle's *Awkward Politics: Technologies of Popfeminist Activism* (Montreal: McGill-Queen's University Press, 2016) and Maggie McCarthy's *Mad Mädchen: Feminism and Generational Conflict in Recent German Literature and Film* (New York: Berghahn, 2017), both offer important readings of popfeminism in the context of cinema. However, the films they consider are mostly either adaptations of what began as popfeminist literary texts, or films that are more immediately legible in the context of their other affiliations (e.g., the Berlin School) rather than as "popfeminist" films per se.

32 Smith and Stehle, *Awkward Politics*, 56.

of it. Exasperated, Martina turns to speak directly into the camera, breaking the fourth wall as she sums up the feminist standpoint of Alberti's film: "Also, das wird hier nicht frauenfeindlich, aber auch nicht sonderlich männerfreundlich" (This isn't going to be misogynistic, but it won't be very kind to men either). Later, the women jokingly experiment with "the sexy lamp test"—a thought experiment that, like the Bechdel test, aims to expose the one-dimensional representation of women in media through the substitution of decorative lamps for women characters. *Der lange Sommer der Theorie* humorously turns the tables by applying the test to several nameless male characters who are replaced via jump cut by attractive retro lamps.

While the politics of representation forms a running gag in the fictional episodes of Alberti's film, they become a key focal point of the interviews that Nola undertakes for her film-within-a-film. Dressed in a pantsuit imprinted with newspaper-style headlines including, prominently, the interrogative "Zukunft?" (Future?), Nola poses questions to a series of theorists about the possibilities for living a good life and creating social change amidst the impasse of the present. As Alberti explains in the press kit for *Der lange Sommer der Theorie*, her film was motivated by questions about what theoretical standpoints might drive political action today: "Gibt es eine neue Idee oder eine neue Utopie für das Politische?" (Is there a new idea or a new utopia for politics?).[33] Nola's interviewees, whose responses are excerpted within the diegesis of the film, offer different approaches to this search. The interviews are also available to view in their entirety on YouTube, and the film's credits incorporate a lengthy bibliography of suggestions for further reading.[34] *Der lange Sommer der Theorie* employs the digital space of YouTube as a cinematic supplement, a kind of hyperlink that offers viewers the possibility for expanded engagement with critical theory, foregrounding the participatory function of digital culture vis-à-vis what emerges by contrast as cinema's more aesthetically developed form. Ultimately, *Der lange Sommer der Theorie*, which takes its title from cultural historian Phillipp Felsch's study of Merve, the independent publishing house that played an instrumental role in shaping the intellectual life of West Germany through the publication of theoretical texts (many of them translated from the French), emphasizes the interplay of theory and practice as a starting point for the renewal of feminist political cinema as a project.

---

33 Interview with Irene von Alberti by Inga Behnsen, Presseheft, *Der lange Sommer der Theorie*, Filmgalerie 451, 2017, 5, https://grandfilm.de/wp-content/uploads/2020/01/presseheft_derlangesommerdertheorie.pdf.

34 Nola's interview partners are Phillipp Felsch, Rahel Jaeggi, Lilly Lent & Andrea Trumann, Carl Hegemann, Jutta Almendinger, and Boris Groys.

Turanskyj's *Top Girl* similarly draws on feminist theory in its approach to the problem of women's aesthetic and political representation in contemporary media culture. In an extended and highly disturbing metaphor for women's objectification and lack of social solidarity at present, protagonist Helena seizes the opportunity to become a "top girl" by hiring four of her fellow sex workers to perform as prey in a hunting performance held at a corporate retreat—a performance that serves as a team-building exercise for the firm of one of Helena's clients—where a group of businessmen target the women as they run naked through the woods, shooting blank bullets at them and conquering them like game animals. The film's title *Top Girl* refers to Helena's ambiguous status relative to the women she contracts for the performance, but it also references McRobbie's critique of postfeminism (*The Aftermath of Feminism* was published in German as *Top Girls*), which directly influenced Turanskyj's conception of the film.

Turanskyj has explained that McRobbie's work helped to bring into focus for her how "the mainstreaming of feminism may have resulted in more media representations of women, but it hasn't changed the underlying social structures that are perpetuated in those stories."[35] Like Heinrich, Turanskyj sought to call attention to precisely those structures, a project that she maintained could only be achieved through close attention to form, since postfeminist media culture has thoroughly coopted feminist content, rendering its political critique largely illegible. As in *Das melancholische Mädchen* and *Der lange Sommer der Theorie*, this attention to form manifests in *Top Girl* not least via shots and sequences that call attention to cinema's capacious aesthetic possibilities relative to other forms of media. In an early sequence, four of the women who work at the bordello introduce themselves: one at a time, they walk into the frame, strike a pose, and say their names, before rearranging themselves, *Charlie's Angels*-style, into a different configuration of poses. Looking directly into the camera, each woman recites what seems to be a rehearsed line designed to cater to a particular client's desires. Similar to the casting call at the outset of *Das melancholische Mädchen*, this scene introduces a metadiscursive reflection on agency and subjectivity vis-à-vis the postfeminist hypersexualization of women's bodies that the film positions within the pointed representational framework of sex work.

Top Girl also employs the diegetic insertion of digitally mediated images on screen in order to critically reflect on women's struggle, failure, or refusal to self-optimize. In one sequence, Helena and her co-workers attend a lecture that advocates for cosmetic surgery as an empowering

---

35 Cited in Hester Baer and Angelica Fenner, "Representation Matters: Tatjana Turanskyj on Women's Filmmaking and the Pro Quote Film Movement," in Baer and Fenner, *Women's Film Authorship in Neoliberal Times*, 140.

feminist practice. The lecturer recites the feminist mantra "My body belongs to me" before launching into a sales pitch for vaginoplasty. She stands in front of a large screen on which the title of her lecture is projected: "die frau ohne alter: weibliche selbstoptimierungsstrategien für das 21. jahrhundert" (the ageless woman: feminine strategies of self-optimization for the 21st century). Because of her positioning within the frame, the images are projected directly onto her body, so that a comically large vulva is superimposed onto her chest. This stylized layering of media, screens, and images offers an exemplary critique of the paradoxical rhetoric of postfeminism and the corporeal consequences of neoliberal exhortations for women to self-improve.

Conclusion

Referring to feminist films of the 1960s and 1970s, Turanskyj has pointed out that "these films contain primarily women protagonists in a process of emancipation. That's a key difference from today, where there is this neoliberal appearance of emancipation that Angela McRobbie describes."[36] Turanskyj's filmmaking project aimed to unmask this illusion of emancipation and find a way back to a feminist political critique through attention to form, specifically strategies of remediation that critically reflect on postfeminist media culture while also developing an overt aesthetic relationality with earlier feminist filmmaking. The hunting performance that frames *Top Girl*, for instance, cites directly from the visual style of *Neun Leben* in its depiction of nude women in a pastoral landscape and its reflection on male fantasies in the context of women's sexual empowerment. Whereas these erotic images form part of Stöckl's quest to forge a new path for cinematic representations of non-phallocentric desire, in Turanskyj's film they signal the bankruptcy of the "neoliberal appearance of emancipation" for women, in both the sexual realm and the world of work.

The motto of *Neun Leben*—"Women have never had as many possibilities to do what they want as they have today, but do they know what they want?"—describes the 1968 film's search to find new images of women, their relationships, their desires, and their social possibilities at a transformative moment for gender and sexual relations in the west. This search is indexed by the process-based "cut-up-style narrative form" of Stöckl's film, which Turanskyj has praised for enabling its complex depiction of women's biographies and its simultaneous critique of the conditions in which they develop.[37] In remediating Stöckl's approach, *Das*

---

36   In Baer and Fenner, "Representation Matters," 139.
37   Turanskyj, "Fanpost," in *Ula Stöckl*, ed. Claudia Lenssen (Munich: edition text + kritik, 2019), 37.

melancholische Mädchen, Der lange Sommer der Theorie, and *Top Girl* reassert the significance of feminist creativity and process in response to the ongoing dilemma of imagining alternatives to the hegemony of heteropatriarchy—now in an era when narratives of individual freedom and self-determination no longer signify as emancipatory. These films challenge the emphasis on rights-based frameworks and representational politics that was formalized by second-wave feminism and is taken into account as second nature in the context of postfeminism. In this regard, they complicate and complement PQF's campaign for a gender quota. Despite their differences, however, both approaches engage the remediation of cinefeminism as a strategy for responding to neoliberalism's cooptation of feminist film and media culture.[38] For both PQF and the filmmakers discussed here, a return to the period of cinefeminism enables a rethinking of the commonplaces and the received genealogies of film history and opens up renewed aesthetic and political possibilities for feminist cinema beyond postfeminism and neoliberalism.

Bibliography

Alberti, Irene von. Interview by Inga Behnsen. Presseheft, *Der lange Sommer der Theorie,* Filmgalerie 451, 2017, https://grandfilm.de/wp-content/uploads/2020/01/presseheft_derlangesommerdertheorie.pdf.

———, dir. *Der lange Sommer der Theorie.* Berlin: Filmgalerie 451, 2020. vimeo.com/ondemand/derlangesommerdertheorie/387469929.

Baer, Hester. "The Berlin School and Women's Cinema." In *The Berlin School and Its Global Contexts,* edited by Marco Abel and Jaimey Fisher, 25–48. Detroit, MI: Wayne State University Press, 2018.

———. *The Cat Has Nine Lives.* Rochester, NY: Camden House, 2022.

———. *German Cinema in the Age of Neoliberalism.* Amsterdam: Amsterdam University Press, 2021.

Baer, Hester, and Angelica Fenner. "Introduction: Revisiting Feminism and German Cinema." In *Women's Film Authorship in Neoliberal Times: Revisiting Feminism and German Cinema,* edited by Hester Baer and Angelica Fenner, special issue of *Camera Obscura: Feminism, Culture, and Media Studies* 33, no. 3 (2018): 1–19.

———. "Representation Matters: Tatjana Turanskyj on Women's Filmmaking and the Pro Quote Film Movement." In *Women's Film Authorship in Neoliberal Times: Revisiting Feminism and German Cinema,* edited by Hester Baer and Angelica Fenner, special issue of *Camera Obscura: Feminism, Culture, and Media Studies* 33, no. 3 (2018): 129–45.

Banet-Weiser, Sarah. *Empowered: Popular Feminism and Popular Misogyny.* Durham, NC: Duke University Press, 2018.

---

38 In this regard, it is important to note that Turanskyj was a co-founder of PQF and one of its chief strategists.

Banet-Weiser, Sarah, Rosalind Gill, and Catherine Rottenberg. "Postfeminism, popular feminism and neoliberal feminism?" *Feminist Theory* 21, no. 1 (2020): 3–24.

Bardan, Alice. "Shoes, Drunk Women, and Phallic Girls: Tatjana Turanskyj's Feminist Interventions in German Cinema." In *The Singular Plural of Feminist Film Practice*, edited by Angelica Fenner and Barbara Mennel, special issue of *Feminist German Studies* 38, no. 1 (2022): 182–201.

Bolter, Jay David, and Richard Grusin. *Remediation: Understanding New Media*. Cambridge, MA: MIT Press, 1999.

Crary, Jonathan. *24/7: Late Capitalism and the Ends of Sleep*. London: Verso, 2013.

Felsch, Phillipp. *Der lange Sommer der Theorie: Geschichte einer Revolte, 1960–1990*. Munich: C. H. Beck, 2015.

Heiduschke, Sebastian. "Women's Interventions in the Contemporary German Film Industry." In *Women's Film Authorship in Neoliberal Times: Revisiting Feminism and German Cinema*, edited by Hester Baer and Angelica Fenner, special issue of *Camera Obscura: Feminism, Culture, and Media Studies* 33, no. 3 (2018): 147–55.

Heinrich, Susanne, dir. *Das melancholische Mädchen*. Berlin: Salzgeber & Co. Medien GmbH, 2020. DVD.

———. *Das melancholische Mädchen*. Pressebroschüre. Berlin: Salzgeber & Co. Medien, GmbH, 2019.

———. "Regisseurin über Das melanscholische Mädchen." *Spiegel Online*, June 26, 2019. https://www.spiegel.de/video/susanne-heinrich-ueber-szene-aus-das-melancholische-maedchen-video-99028003.html.

Knight, Julia. *Women and the New German Cinema*. London: Verso, 1992.

Landry, Olivia. "Searching for a Storyteller, Remediating the Archive: Philip Scheffner's *Halfmoon Files*." *New German Critique* 46, no. 3 (138) (2019): 103–24.

McCarthy, Margaret. *Mad Mädchen: Feminism and Generational Conflict in Recent German Literature and Film*. New York: Berghahn, 2017.

McRobbie, Angela. *The Aftermath of Feminism: Gender, Culture, and Social Change*. London: Sage, 2009.

Mennel, Barbara. "From Utopian Collectivity to Solitary Precarity: Thirty Years of Feminist Theory and the Cinema of Women's Work." *Women in German Yearbook* 30 (2014): 125–37.

Meyer, Lars. "Zu jedem Bett gehört ein Mann." *Zeit Online*, June 22, 2019. https://www.zeit.de/kultur/film/2019-06/das-melancholische-maedchen-film-susanne-heinrich.

Perincioli, Cristina. *Berlin wird feministisch. Das Beste, was von der 68er Bewegung blieb*. Berlin: Querverlag, 2015.

Pro Quote Film. "Fakten." Accessed July 15, 2022. https://proquote-film.de/#/status-quote/fakten/object=page:57.

———. "Forderungen." Accessed July 15, 2022. https://proquote-film.de/#/ziele/forderungen/object=page:263.

———. "Die Studien." Accessed July 15, 2022. https://proquote-film.de/#/status-quote/die-studien/object=page:61.

Rich, B. Ruby. *Chick Flicks*. Durham, NC: Duke University Press, 1998.

Sander, Helke, and Iris Gusner. *Fantasie und Arbeit: Biografische Zwiesprache*. Marburg: Schüren, 2009.

Smith, Carrie, and Maria Stehle. *Awkward Politics: Technologies of Popfeminist Activism*. Montreal: McGill-Queen's University Press, 2016.

Tiqqun. *Preliminary Materials for a Theory of the Young-Girl*. Translated by Ariana Reines. Pasadena, CA: Semiotext(e), 2012.

Turanskyj, Tatjana. "Fanpost." In *Ula Stöckl*, edited by Claudia Lenssen, 37–40. Munich: edition text + kritik, 2019.

———, dir. *Top Girl, oder la déformation professionnelle*. Berlin: Neue Visionen Medien, 2016. DVD.

9: A Few Takes toward Reassembling (the Dream of) the People: Julian Radlmaier's *Selbstkritik eines bürgerlichen Hundes* (2017)

Claudia Breger

Introduction: The "Missing People" in the New German Discourse Comedy

IN *CINEMA* 2, Gilles Deleuze famously observed that "*the people are missing*" in postwar Western cinema.[1] This is in contrast to "classical cinema": in the earlier twentieth century, the modern medium of film had been closely associated with the modern phenomenon of the crowd on more than one level.[2] Film and cultural theory circled around the moral dangers and political potentials of collective reception, and on-screen crowds featured prominently in the political aesthetics of socialism as well as fascism and nation-building Hollywood.[3] In the aftermath of Hitler and Stalin, however, these crowds all but disappeared in Western political cinema: visually imagining the masses as a collective actor became exceedingly difficult.[4] As indicated by several contributions across this volume,

---

1   Gilles Deleuze, *Cinema 2: The Time-Image*, trans. Hugh Tomlinson and Robert Galeta (Minneapolis: University of Minnesota Press, 1989), 216 (emphasis in original).

2   Deleuze, *Cinema 2*, 216.

3   See, e.g., Walter Serner, "Cinema and Visual Pleasure," trans. Don Reneau, and Hermann Duenschmann, "Cinematograph and Crowd Psychology: A Sociopolitical Study," trans. Eric Ames, both in *The Promise of Cinema: German Film Theory 1907–1933*, ed. Anton Kaes, Nicholas Baer, and Michael Cowan (Berkeley: University of California Press, 2016), 41–45 and 256–58; Michael Tratner, *Crowd Scenes: Movies and Mass Politics* (New York: Fordham University Press, 2008).

4   See Elizabeth Alsop, "'The Imaginary Crowd': Neorealism and the Uses of Coralità," *The Velvet Light Trap* 74 (2014): 27–41. Tratner underlines that Hollywood does indeed continue to feature crowds, from *Gone with the Wind* to *Titanic* (*Crowd Scenes*, 3).

the rupture diagnosed by Deleuze continues to reverberate until today.[5] In the 2010s, to be sure, the crowd had a major comeback in cultural theory, sparked by circulating media images of emerging forms of transnational collective activism: Tahrir square, Gezi Park, Occupy. But even as scholars ranging from Judith Butler to Brian Massumi, Jodi Dean, Joshua Clover, Michael Hardt, and Antonio Negri newly set out to theorize the "political potential" of collective assembly, this resurgence of interest in a progressive crowd aesthetics has remained overshadowed by the parallel rise of right-wing claims to embody the people.[6] With an eye to the German anti-immigrant organization Pegida, Butler repeatedly reminds us that a "surging multitude" of publicly assembled bodies would "include lynch mobs, anti-Semitic or racist or fascist congregations."[7] Now in the 2020s, we may think of a new generation of activist movements, prominently including Black Lives Matter, while events such as the Capitol Riot in the U.S. seem to have further cemented the spectral superimposition of the activist people with the fascist mob.

Julian Radlmaier's *Selbstkritik eines bürgerlichen Hundes* (*Self-criticism of a Bourgeois Dog,* 2017) tackles the question of how to cinematically reimagine activist, potentially revolutionary assembly against the backdrop of these concerns. On the plot level, *Selbstkritik* probes the possibilities of worker organization on the "apple plantation OKLAHOMA," located somewhere between contemporary East Germany and Franz Kafka's and Jean-Marie Straub and Danièle Huillet's ambiguously heterotopic America. Radlmaier's film quotes these two intertexts with a poster on a street corner as well as an extradiegetic intertitle culminating in the promise that fascinated Kafka's protagonist: "Jeder ist willkommen!" (All are welcome!).[8] In renaming Kafka's "nature theater" an "apple plantation," to be sure, Radlmaier more clearly introduces "Oklahoma" as a

---

5   Most specifically, see Fatima Naqvi's chapter on choric configurations in Ruth Beckermann's films, as overshadowed by legacies of fascist and sexist violence.

6   Judith Butler, *Notes Towards a Performative Theory of Assembly* (Cambridge, MA: Harvard University Press, 2015), 1. See Brian Massumi, *The Power at the End of the Economy* (Durham, NC: Duke University Press, 2015); Jodi Dean, *Crowds and Party* (London: Verso, 2016); Joshua Clover, *Riot. Strike. Riot: The New Era of Uprisings* (London: Verso, 2016); Michael Hardt and Antonio Negri, *Assembly* (Oxford: Oxford University Press, 2017).

7   Butler, *Notes,* 3, 182–83. Massumi is also aware of this concern about "fascist contagion" (*The Power,* 66).

8   I quote the translation from Franz Kafka, *Amerika: The Missing Person,* trans. Mark Harman (New York: Schocken, 2008), 267. Volker Pantenburg emphasizes the "utopian impulse" associated with Kafka's nature theater as characteristic for Radlmaier's filmmaking more generally. See Volker Pantenburg, "Class Relations: Diagnoses of the Present in the Films of Julian Radlmaier and

location of heightened exploitation.[9] Among the resident crew of precarious harvest workers, a hapless unemployed filmmaker deployed by his social security office—who is called Julian and played by Radlmaier himself—pretends to be doing research for a political film. While he lacks the backbone required for translating his professed communist inclinations into political action, the farm workers nonetheless begin to collectively challenge their exploitation and take over the farm. However, their political assembly remains crisscrossed by bad memories of state-sponsored socialism as well as by fascist fantasies; and it ends quickly when their boss awakes from her state of unconsciousness induced by a pitchfork hitting her forehead. The diegetic filmmaking project turns out to be outwardly more successful: towards the end of *Selbstkritik,* we see Julian on stage for a Q&A at the Venice film festival. Talking about the "decline" of the working class, he defensively quotes Deleuze's formula about the missing people to underscore his belief that the only thing "we can do" is to "keep on making art" because changing reality would "need a miracle," which he does not believe in.

As indicated throughout this section of our volume, *Selbstkritik* can be situated as part of an emerging genre of experimental cinema that has been dubbed the "neue deutsche Diskurskomödie" (New German Discourse Comedy).[10] Although there is no manifesto or full-fledged group, critics have associated Radlmaier's work with that of Irene von Alberti, Susanne Heinrich, and Max Linz. Taking "theory seriously," this recent work shares "an interest in the idea of political cinema . . . in historical and formal terms as well as on the level of contemporary discursive positions," and it develops this interest (in Radlmaier's own words) in a "playful" way, in what amounts to a "respectful rupture" with the Berlin School's "serious" realism.[11] The anti-naturalist aesthetics of these films arguably operates in a partly Brechtian manner to reflexively address and explicitly confront the crisis of neoliberalism. As indicated by the Kafka and Huillet/Straub connections, the films foreground intertextual

---

Max Linz," *New German Critique* 46, no. 3 (138) (2019): 54. Of course, this utopian vector is complicated even in Kafka.

9   As is well known, Kafka established a resonant connection insofar as his protagonist infamously identifies with the descendants of America's slave populations in introducing himself to the theater agents with the "nickname from his last few positions" (Kafka, *Amerika,* 278). This is virtually the only moment of the long hiring conversation that Huillet and Straub retain for their film. Radlmaier refrains from using the N-word.

10   Lars Meyer, "Zu jedem Bett gehört ein Mann," *Zeit Online,* June 22, 2019, https://www.zeit.de/kultur/film/2019-06/das-melancholische-maedchen-film-susanne-heinrich.

11   Pantenburg, "Class Relations," 57; Radlmaier as quoted there, 75. Pantenburg focuses on Linz and Radlmaier, referencing other male directors.

reference to a vast archive that is multimedial in scope while prominently including the postwar new waves as well as longer traditions of socialist cinema.[12] Perhaps out of long-term critical habit, I was initially inclined to read *Selbstkritik*'s theatrical self-reflexivity as primarily effecting deconstructive irony. The filmmaker's on-stage performance in the film seems to echo, and possibly seal, the preceding failure of the apple farm workers to assemble the people from the ashes of a socialist dream perished in the historical realities of fascism and authoritarianism.

However, other possibilities emerge in the film's metaleptic folds and plot twists. During the above-mentioned Venice Q&A, Julian's diegetic audience challenges his resigned conclusion with Lenin quotes and the production of precisely the kind of miracle that the filmmaker on stage does not believe in. Thus it is in response to Julian's interpretation of Deleuze's formula about the missing people that he is transformed into the dog who gives the film its title, and who has been serving as its voice-over narrator all along. The agent of this miracle production seems to be a silent monk who had suddenly appeared on the East German apple farm earlier. Inspired by Roberto Rossellini's film *The Flowers of St. Francis* (1950), he may have escaped from a painting, Fra Angelico's *Apparition of St. Francis at Arles* (1429) that we saw in the Berlin *Gemäldegalerie* in the beginning of the film, where it had provoked derogatory visitor comments about the medieval "communist."[13] In the diegetic film (of which we have seen some), the monk leads Hong and Sancho, the film's holy fool characters, along with Camille, the female lead, on a pilgrimage to Italy after the Oklahoma rebellion has failed, in response to the prophesy that revolution will have occurred by the time of their arrival. Unsurprisingly, this voyage across the Alps ends in disillusionment also—and incarceration for Hong and Sancho. But rather than diegetic Julian's public fatalism, Radlmaier has echoed a statement that his on-screen double made earlier in the film in the tactical context of trying to seduce Camille: then, he characterized the film project as oriented towards "something

---

12 Pantenburg, "Class Relations," 54, 59. Radlmaier himself credits Roberto Rossellini, Jean Renoir, Straub and Huillet, Pier Pasolini, Jean-Luc Godard, and Yasujirō Ozu (see "Director's Statement: Markus Nechleba and Julian Radlmaier Talking about Self-Criticism of a Bourgeois Dog," *Fakturafilm*, accessed December 19, 2022, https://www.fakturafilm.de/dogstatement; and "Fatalismus interessiert mich nicht. Interview with Jakob Hayner," *jungle.world*, June 1, 2017, https://jungle.world/artikel/2017/22/fatalismus-interessiert-mich-nicht). Radlmaier also worked as Werner Schröter's personal assistant. See Pantenburg on the connections to Soviet 1920s cinema that emerge via archaeologies of the leftist history of the Deutsche Film- and Fernsehakademie Berlin ("Class Relations," 59).

13 See Pantenburg, "Class Relations," 69; On Rossellini, see Radlmaier, "Director's Statement."

like a fairytale on the beauty of communist utopia."[14] Despite all of the "eccentricities, obstructions, stupidities, short-circuits, and aberrations," Radlmaier hopes, quoting Marx, "the film might give you the feeling that 'the world has long since possessed the dream of something.'"[15] Critics have resonantly described the film's amalgamation of disillusionment and satire with affirmation and hope: the infusion of "Ernst" (seriousness) and utopian stretches in its mixture of "Agitprop-Theater, Filmessay und burlesker Komödie" (agitprop theatre, film essay, and burlesque comedy), or the "Mut . . . sich nicht ernst zu nehmen und gleichzeitig utopisch zu sein, und von der Revolution zu erzählen" (the courage to not take oneself seriously while being utopian, and telling of revolution).[16]

Cinematic Assemblages—Political Assembly

Taking this amalgamation of modes and political affects seriously, my reading details the ways in which *Selbstkritik*'s complicated aesthetic *assemblage* both playfully reflects on and unfolds a project of political *assembly*. Cinematic worldmaking, I have stressed elsewhere, rarely operates in straightforward political "unison," or as the kind of homogeneous assembly that classical crowd theory feared—and which is a "fantasy," Butler stresses, even outside of art.[17] The Deleuzian notion of assemblage nicely designates the complexity of cinema's aesthetic operations in the collective networks of production and reception: as the process of making multiple connections between heterogeneous but interwoven forces, it captures the multidimensional and multivectoral processes in which cinematic worldmaking entangles form elements, affects, intertexts, technologies, film team and audience associations, and more.[18] But this emphasis on cinematic complexity does not entail that there is any categorical dissonance, tension, or conflict between art and politics. Resonant with the

14   Radlmaier, "Director's Statement." One of Radlmaier's earlier films is indicatively titled, *Ein proletarisches Wintermärchen* (*A Proletarian Winter's Tale*, 2014).

15   Radlmaier, "Director's statement."

16   Bert Rebhandl, "Der Typ sieht ja aus wie von Fassbinder: Julian Radlmaiers Kinofilm," *Frankfurter Allgemeine Zeitung*, June 10, 2017, https://www.faz.net/aktuell/feuilleton/kino/julian-radlmaiers-selbstkritik-eines-buergerlichen-hundes-15054239.html; Andreas Busche, "Früchte der Revolution," *Der Tagesspiegel*, June 10, 2017, https://www.tagesspiegel.de/kultur/fruchte-der-revolution-3839137.html; SWR review (per DVD cover).

17   Butler, *Notes*, 157, 166; see also Claudia Breger, *Making Worlds: Affect and Collectivity in Contemporary European Cinema* (New York: Columbia University Press, 2020).

18   See Jasbir Puar, "Queer Times, Queer Assemblages," *Social Text* 23, nos. 3–4 (84–85) (2005): 121–39.

disappearance of the people from the screen, mainstream postwar discourse on aesthetics and politics has claimed such conflict all-too-often, and all-too-conveniently. Sometimes the (direct or indirect) reference is to Theodor W. Adorno's verdict on "engagierte Kunst" (committed art), sometimes to Jacques Rancière's surprisingly consonant generalization that in modernity's aesthetic regime, art "promises a political accomplishment it cannot satisfy, and thrives on that ambiguity."[19] Radlmaier presents the underlying opposition between art and politics as an occasion for audience laughter when Julian gets scared of the unfolding rebellion and starts to argue for making art *instead* of striking "so that possibility can survive as form."

Camille is not pleased by that opposition, and Radlmaier's montage all but suggests that her frustration facilitates the appearance of the monk in this very moment: an implicit counter-emphasis on artistic possibility re-emerging into the political realm. An inserted detail shot of the *Apparition of St. Francis* painting foregrounds the door that opens onto green space in its background, followed by the monk character running through the frame for the first time. Instead of replaying categorical tensions between art and politics, I argue more generally, we can specify the layered relations that aesthetic works entertain with their surrounding real-life worlds in the "multiplicity of folds in the sensory fabric of the common," as Rancière also (and more helpfully) words it.[20] The political actions that artworks assemble in these folds are less straightforward, heroic, or (single-strike) revolutionary than the defenders of radically activist models of art long wanted to believe. Nonetheless, their layered assemblages may come together—to various degrees—to operate in political "concert."[21] My use of the latter concept draws on Butler's rethinking of assemblies with Hannah Arendt's emphasis on plurality: a crowd on the street—or a film in my adaptation of the concept—can effectively enact political claims even as it moves in more than one direction and speaks in multiple voices, variously "convergent and divergent."[22] The same goes for aesthetic works: In unfolding *Selbstkritik*'s heterogeneous filmic concert, I propose that its assemblage of form elements, affects, intertexts, and other associations comes together to both critique and model—or more modestly indicate and invite—specific acts of political assembly. The title of my chapter pinpoints several elements of this

19   Theodor W. Adorno, *Noten zur Literatur* (Frankfurt am Main: Suhrkamp, 1991), 410; Jacques Rancière, *Dissensus: On Politics and Aesthetics*, ed. and trans. Steven Corcoran (London: Continuum, 2010), 133. Of course, Rancière distances himself from Adorno.

20   Rancière, *Dissensus*, 148.

21   Butler, *Notes*, 157.

22   Butler, *Notes*, 157; see also Hannah Arendt, *The Human Condition* (Chicago: University of Chicago Press, 1958).

argument. "A few takes towards" signals not only the processual, unfinished nature of the undertaking and the crucial idea of trying again in the wake of political disillusionment. It also designates one of *Selbstkritik*'s key framing and editing techniques: as I will show, the film brings "into concert" deliberately incongruous, tableaux-like portrait takes of the individual members of "the people" in the making. Or, of the people in the *dreaming*: no less crucially, the project of such cinematic assembly is framed by an unabashed commitment to fiction, or fabulation, understood not in a simple opposition to the real but as an artistic mode of reimaging real-world conditions.

The People in the Dreaming: Fiction/Fabulation

Let me explain this second point first. Radlmaier has translated several works of Rancière into German and written on Rancière's "Concept of Fiction and Its Significance for a Political Aesthetics of Counter-cinema."[23] In the multiplicity of folds in which art is embedded into surrounding lifeworlds, Rancière insists, fiction is not "the imaginary as opposed to the real."[24] Rather, "it involves the reframing of the 'real'": the real must become fiction, not least for "invention . . . to testify to a reality that evades recognition or conciliation."[25] Radlmaier himself describes the act of "sich der Fiktion bemächtigen" (to take possession of fiction) as a precondition for political filmmaking.[26] While mentioning his "pleasure of fabulating improbable stories," he also characterizes his work as "looking for a short-circuit between something almost documentary and something very playful."[27] For example, he has a miracle-working monk escape from Renaissance art and show up in a contemporary world of precarious harvest workers, in which he can only be made sense of as an undocumented immigrant. Instantly apprehended as a "foreign apple thief," the monk is later abducted by the Italian border police for lack of papers.

Radlmaier's reference to fabulation probably owes to Deleuze (more than Rancière), who evokes postwar cinema's deployment of the "powers of the false" as (in Tavia Nyong'o's words) "an alternative heuristic

---

23   See Pantenburg, "Class Relations," 56.

24   Rancière, *Dissensus*, 141.

25   Rancière, *Dissensus*, 141; Rancière, *The Intervals of Cinema*, trans. John Howe (London: Verso, 2014), 141.

26   Radlmaier, "Fatalismus."

27   Radlmaier, "Director's Statement"; Radlmaier, "The New Wave of Political Satire: An Interview by Tuhin," *The Projection Room*, March 14, 2018, https://theprojectionroomorg.wordpress.com/2018/03/14/julian-radlmaier-inteview/.

for linking . . . the aesthetic and the sociopolitical."[28] In this cinema, Deleuze claims, the "'making up fiction'" and "'story-telling" (*fabulation* in the original French) serve the "invention of . . . the people to come."[29] Nyong'o, who develops the concept of fabulation with Deleuze as well as Saidiya Hartman for the context of Black queer performance, also underlines the ways in which fabulation intimately interweaves fiction with the real: it is less "a matter of inventing tall tales from whole cloth" than a piecemeal "tactical fictionalizing of a world that is, from the point of view of black social life, already false."[30] Of course, Radlmaier's film deploys these tools in a different context, albeit arguably a resonant one: with Achille Mbembe, we might say that the film's imaginative critique of precarious, part undocumented labor targets a contemporary world of necropolitics, in which "the principle of equality" is being undone not least by "the brutality of borders."[31]

In the extradiegetic worlds of contemporary European art cinema and theory, Radlmaier's unabashed embrace of fabulation as a tool of fictionalization as well as storytelling is innovative enough to raise eyebrows. Even Rancière remains ambivalent in this respect: while he acknowledges the constitutive role of narrative for cinema's artistic practices, he characterizes these practices through the notion of the necessarily "thwarted fable."[32] Radlmaier's film playfully indicates the conundrum of articulating an aesthetics of fabulation against the backdrop of prevailing antinarrative sentiment. Early on, the character Julian encounters a malicious critic who frankly declares that his "Schritt ins Narrative" (stepping into narrative) has made his work less radical. But what these malicious critics—and perhaps even less awful ones like Rancière—fail to imagine is that narrative practice might unfold as a layered aesthetic assemblage that is rich enough to afford dedramatizing the opposition of *muthos* (plot) versus *opsis* (the spectacle's sensible effect), which has shaped European aesthetic traditions from Aristotle to the avant-gardes and beyond.[33] In Radlmaier's cinema, fabulation interlinks with "the fundamental capability" of the cinematic image "to give evidence of the equivalence of all human beings," as the director words it with indirect reference to Rancière.[34] Rancière's formula of redistributing "the sensible" in a more

28 Tavia Nyong'o, *Afro-Fabulations: The Queer Drama of Black Life* (New York: New York University Press, 2019), 222n48.

29 Deleuze, *Cinema 2*, 222–23.

30 Nyong'o, *Afro-Fabulations*, 6.

31 Achille Mbembe, *Necropolitics* (Durham, NC: Duke University Press, 2019), 3.

32 Rancière, *Film Fables*, trans. Emiliano Battista (Oxford: Berg, 2006), 11.

33 Rancière, *Film Fables*, 2. On narrative as such an aesthetic assemblage, see Breger, *Making Worlds*.

34 Radlmaier, "Director's Statement."

egalitarian way by framing "a new fabric of common experience" is probably the most well-known element of his discussion of what art *can* do in modernity's aesthetic regime.[35] In the awkward English that Julian deploys to seduce the Canadian Camille, he claims that "the image gets something like a call for communism" if "you manage to capture an individual existence with all its beauty with the camera . . ., like an evidence that the world should be reorganized in a way that respects the beauty and grace of life."

The Image as "A Call to Communism": Portrait Shots in the Comedy Ecology

While Rancière's concept of redistributing the sensible has been taken up widely in both contemporary art and theory, Radlmaier's reiteration of it as a building block for his project of fabulatively reclaiming cinematic assembly comes with a less common twist. He highlights the potential specifically of the comic mode "to establish new sensible or non-sensical relations between conflictual ideas and notions."[36] In mixing the "funny, joyful, and dead serious," he elaborates, the "comic" facilitates intertwining the deconstruction of "ideological sense" with the construction of "something like an 'emancipatory counter-sense.'"[37] But how exactly does the comic mode do this? Scholars have developed widely diverging accounts on its operations: while some recent work emphasizes comicality's potential to create open worlds by way of joyful reparative play in Eve Kosofsky Sedgwick's sense, most twentieth-century accounts rather foreground the aggression and negativity involved, in particular, in the less benign forms of parody and satire, on which *Selbstkritik* certainly draws as well.[38] A closer look is needed at how comicality reshuffles affects in the film's play of fable and form.

To begin with, the film's treatment of its diegetic director Julian's lack of any political backbone seems designed to undermine, if not

---

35 Rancière, *Dissensus*, 141. Rancière qualifies that art accomplishes this by framing "new forms of individuality" rather than "a *we*," as politics does (141–42, Rancière's emphasis). This distinction between aesthetics and politics has never made sense to me—and Radlmaier certainly challenges it.

36 Radlmaier, "Director's Statement."

37 Radlmaier, "Director's Statement."

38 On playful reparation and the creation of open worlds see John Bruns, *Loopholes: Reading Comically* (New Brunswick, NJ: Transaction, 2009), with reference to Sedgwick. Although parody arguably always intertwines homage and critique, it has been characterized primarily through its vectors of "assault." Geoff King, *Film Comedy* (London: Wallflower Press, 2002), 107; see also Linda Hutcheon, *The Politics of Postmodernism* (New York: Routledge, 1989), 101.

A FEW TAKES TOWARD REASSEMBLING (THE DREAM OF) THE PEOPLE ♦ 171

entirely undo the audience sympathy that his awkward, physically halting and stumbling—in short slapstick—romantic quest might have otherwise induced. The trope of Julian's transformation into a dog would then seal the film's satirical verdict through an act of bodily diminution. In revoking Julian's presumed human—or white male—autonomy privileges, the miracle makes him "demütig" (humble). This deployment of the transformation trope arguably reinscribes a conventional human-versus-animal contrast rather than (in Butler's words) "transforming the field of appearance itself" by showcasing every human's vulnerability as a "living creature among creatures."[39] However, we might also note that the film's particular dog is beautiful and acts in a much more dignified way than his human predecessor. Throughout the film, the dog's brief visual appearances against green nature backgrounds function as a sensory attraction for the film audience. A more generous reading might then emphasize the imaginative agency of transformation in the cinematic actor-network—towards a making visible the equivalence of not only human beings?[40] After all, the miracle transfigures an evasive coward into a member of the small human-nonhuman collective who, at the end of the film, works on liberating Hong and Sancho from their jail cells: we see the dog digging. As voice-over narrator, the dog also has significant structural authority, even if the perhaps inescapable association with his laughable human embodiment casts some doubt on his reliability. At the intersection of these divergent indications, how does satirical diminution assemble with more affirmative gestures here and in the film's comical mediation of political assembly more generally?

The visual presentation of the dog notably resonates with *Selbstkritik*'s overall emphasis on presenting "individual subjects" via "monumental, erratic, autonomous" portraits.[41] These portrait shots are deployed throughout the film but in particular in several sequences on the apple farm that first establish the exploitative labor conditions imposed on the harvest workers and later feature their deliberations towards striking and eventually taking over the farm. Along with the main protagonists, these sequences feature a number of nonprofessional actors mostly identified by their real-life first names in close-ups of individuals or pairs. Per the extradiegetic filmmaker's intentions, the portrait shots aim to balance his investigations of the "relation of body and space" in his earlier films.[42]

---

39 Butler, *Notes*, 43.

40 See Bruno Latour, *Reassembling the Social: An Introduction to Actor-Network-Theory* (Oxford: Oxford University Press, 2005), 107; see also Jerome P. Schaefer on a Latourian "film theory of transformations": *An Edgy Realism: Film Theoretical Encounters with Dogma 95, New French Extremity, and the Shaky-Cam Horror Film* (Newcastle upon Tyne: Cambridge Scholars Publishing, 2015), 13.

41 Radlmaier, "Director's Statement."

42 Radlmaier, "Director's Statement."

They also balance *Selbstkritik*'s continued resonant explorations: namely, the film's extreme long shots that might be said to transform the field of vision in line with Butler's reflections on creatureliness by highlighting the embeddedness and vulnerability of human bodies in their environment—Potsdamer Platz at the center of Berlin, the farmland, or the Alps.[43] The portrait shots supplement this emphasis on vulnerability with an emphatic mode of appearance for regular—according to Radlmaier, randomly and thus democratically chosen—people.[44] With a documentary touch that is created precisely by defiance vis-à-vis hegemonic protocols of representational realism, the portrait shots foreground individual workers "not as images to be voyeuristically captured, nor in the name of a cultural provenance that keeps them imprisoned as 'different.'"[45] Rather, they underline how each of these precarious bodies matters, and how they are equipped with agency: a gaze and voice of their own.[46]

In terms of aesthetic genealogy, the static portrait shots emerge out of the postwar new waves. We may think of the tableaux arrangements in Fassbinder's films that *Selbstkritik* evokes not only with a verbal reference to his characters but also with the excessive use of (door/painting/window) framings in the opening museum sequence. And, of course, there is the ongoing engagement with Huillet and Straub's Kafka adaptation *Klassenverhältnisse* (*Class Relations*, 1984), whose long takes of minor characters telling their stories (or arguing their cases), in Rancière's words, present "the performances of autonomous bodies, freed from all narrative servitude."[47] *Selbstkritik*'s portrait shots, to be sure, are less excessive in length than many of these takes and less frozen in terms of character action than many of Fassbinder's tableaux (the blank stare of Julian's social security caseworker constitutes an exception to that rule). As indicated, Radlmaier's portrait shots interweave the powers of spectacle and narrative: the editing preserves their relative autonomy insofar as the shots are not harmonized through continuity editing, eyeline matches, or lighting. At the same time, the film non-congruously assembles the shots—brings them into concert—through their similar framing, "equal in their difference," as well as their participation in the larger scenarios of assembly at the farm.[48]

While thus challenging the absence of the people on screen, the portrait shots are also definitively from the postwar context insofar as earlier

43 Butler, *Notes*, Chapter 4.

44 Radlmaier, in Q&A at summer school on "Visions of Europe: Cinema and Migration in Contemporary Germany" (Rutgers University, September 9, 2022).

45 Mieke Bal, "Lost in Space, Lost in the Library," *Thamyris/Intersecting* 17 (2007): 34; and on the anti-realism also Radlmaier, Q&A.

46 See Butler, *Notes*, 10, 18.

47 Rancière, *Intervals*, 120 (on their cinema more generally).

48 Radlmaier, "Director's Statement."

A Few Takes toward Reassembling (the Dream of) the People ♦ 173

cinema did not need them as a tool of assembling the people. In Jean Renoir's 1936 popular front-inspired comedy *Le Crime de Monsieur Lange* (also acknowledged as an intertext by Radlmaier), analogous sequences of collective deliberation on forming a publishing cooperative after the apparent death of the boss are filmed as busy crowd sequences: "the people" still easily appears as such on screen. Of course, the close-up of the individual within a crowd does have a longer history as well. In assessing the politics of cinematic crowds, scholars have underlined that Soviet as well as Weimar socialist films give more room to the individual in the crowd than Leni Riefenstahl's fascist choreographies; in that sense, leftist representations even then partly constituted the collective from individualities come together.[49] But once the people are missing from the cinema screen, such visual explorations of individuality assume the key function of standing in for the collective or legitimizing its prospective appearance and helping to recuperate it. The technique as such transcends political affiliations today. In variations, the collective is assembled through a focus on individual faces, for example, in Spike Lee's treatment of Black Power crowds in his 2018 *BlacKkKlansman*, in Black Lives Matter documentaries such as *Whose Streets?* (2017, co-directed by Sabaah Folayan and Damon Davis), as well as in Sabine Michel's *Montags in Dresden* (*Merkel Must Go*, 2017), which has received mixed reviews for its failure to distance itself clearly from its right-wing protagonists.[50] What matters for the aesthetic politics of cinematic assembly then is less the deployment of individuality per se than the details of composition and choreography.

As indicated by the contrast between the dog shots and those of diegetic Julian's awkward human body, *Selbstkritik*'s portrait takes often provide a dignifying counterpoint to comedy—or a counterpoint in the spirit of respecting not-always-dignified human bodies.[51] As the heterogeneous, multinational harvest crew assembles for their first shift at the Oklahoma apple farm, for example, the workers are portrayed in a series of medium close-up two shots from a slightly low angle, which capture their skeptical attention as the boss outlines the exploitative work regime. The boss (Johanna Orsini-Rosenberg), whom we see in a long shot framed by the backs of the workers closer to us, is clearly the butt of the joke here with her umbrella held by a quasi-servant, Farmer Motzen, played by Mex

---

49 See, e.g., Christoph Schaub, "Labor-Movement Modernism: Proletarian Collectives between *Kuhle Wampe* and Working-Class Performance Culture," *Modernism/Modernity* 25, no. 2 (2018): 335.

50 I am drawing on Julia Alekseyeva's paper on *Whose Streets?*, delivered at the Society for Cinema and Media Studies 2021 conference here.

51 For a rethinking of the traditional concept of dignity for an anthropocenal humanism premised on "vulnerability and coexistence or belonging with others," see Gerda Roelvink, *Building Dignified Worlds: Geographies of Collective Action* (Minneapolis: University of Minnesota Press, 2016), 147.

Schlüpfer, who is primarily known as an actor at the Volksbühne under Frank Castorf. The dignity counterpoint offered by the crew portraits includes even Zurab, a co-worker who had induced terror in Julian and others in the preceding scene in the men's bedroom: with the sheer force of his imposing physical appearance and habitus, he overrode a majority vote for opening the window denouncing it as "fake democracy." Julian soon calls him a "fascist," and he may have a point for once.[52]

But the portrait shots do not present a simple counterpoint to comedy. Rather, they themselves function in modulated ways, including comedic layers. Depending on shot composition as well as narrative embedding, Radlmaier's portraits can denounce as well as dignify. During the later process of deliberation on taking over the farm, for example, a more extended series of—now single—portrait shots sharply contrasts Zurab with Marina, the co-worker united with him in the earlier two shot (see Figs. 9.1 and 9.2). As Zurab enthusiastically fantasizes about the authoritarian leadership he wants to provide for the new "dictatorship of the proletariat," his portrait is satirized by way of performance (his manner of speaking, wickedly evil smile, and the thick accent inflecting his English) and the back lighting of the shot. Eventually, Marina forcefully tells him to shut up. As she speaks in French and Russian, another worker translates her words into German, providing emphasis to her words through deceleration and repetition. With fierce authority, Marina insists that "our" communism must be "hedonistisch, anarchistisch und demokratistisch" ("hedonistic, anarchist, and democratic")—otherwise she would go home. In this way, the film's comedic vector specifically serves to disempower fascism aesthetically. Such fascism, as *Selbstkritik* indicates through Zurab's character, may lurk in the mixture of Stalinist memory with late capitalist ideology: we have also seen Zurab proclaim himself to embody "the American dream," declaring himself "strong" enough for capitalism, as he holds poor Julian in a headlock. Zurab is played by Georgian poet Zurab Rtveliashvili, one of Radlmaier's long-term collaborators. At moments, the comedy seems to traffic in ethnic clichés that feel perhaps more sensitive as I write in the 2020s, against the backdrop of the war in Ukraine. However, the ethnic tropes are balanced by counter images (e.g., Marina and other down-to-earth Eastern European actor-characters) as well as moments of attention for the processes of racist exclusion, as indicated above regarding the monk. And in

---

52 Zurab seems to be friends with a local whose T-shirt features a German flag icon. To be sure, the film also problematizes the quick, denunciatory use of the fascism label when Julian's (ridiculous) professor reminisces about his activist days and the learning outcome that the workers were "die größten Faschisten" (the greatest fascists).

Figures 9.1 and 9.2. Portrait shots contrasting Marina and Zurab (screen capture; *Selbstkritik*).

any case, comedy renders a verdict that is clear but performs only situational, reversible exclusion from the collective.

Across the film, the portrait shots offer a spectrum of tonal shades between homage and satire, sometimes inviting incongruous audience feelings shifting from moment to moment: there are also echoes of Huillet and Straub's often similarly ambiguous portraits in this respect. Thus, the deliberation sequence also includes portrait shots that facilitate affective slivers of respectful attention to individual experiences amalgamated with ongoing satire, for example when Farmer Motzen—up to this point primarily a comic figure—reports on his disappointment with the socialism he has experienced with sudden emotion in his voice. Another white worker addresses Hong (Kyung-Taek Lie) using a racist epithet before articulating his agreement with him. When this white crew member proceeds to tell a lengthy story about his family's GDR experience, I sense the portrait to be saturated with (quasi-) documentary authenticity, even as it invites less immediate empathy than Farmer Motzen's memory since this speaker talks too fast and in a monotonous, seemingly unemotional voice.

In Conclusion: "People, Hear the Signal"?

The assembly of tonal shades and modulations in the deliberation sequence prepares the following diegetic moment of utopian political assembly. While pathetic diegetic Julian keeps insisting on the realities of global capitalism, the female workers in particular turn the conversation towards a tentative plan for learning "together . . . to organize life." With reference once more to Renoir's comedy *Le Crime de Monsieur Lange*, where the title-giving murder happens when the boss, who had faked his own death, returns in the midst of the collective's drunken celebrations of their success, Radlmaier's film does stage an actual moment of (audio-)visual on-screen assembly. Initially in an extreme long shot, we see the crew's highly theatricalized outdoor feast of fruit and booze, uniting everyone except for Julian (but including Zurab) in drunken, decidedly undignified cheers of "Long live the Revolution." Then, three extended small group portraits capture them collectively singing the Internationale in multilingual concert. In these shots, the singers are physically loosely oriented towards each other in shared joy and (in Zurab's case) fierce determination. Still comically inflected, this moment of musical-political assembly performs barely more than a brief tonal shift towards an affirmative audiovisual fiction of inclusive political collectivity. It provides but a few audiovisual cues for imagining how solidarity might operate politically, and unlike in Renoir's film, the return of the boss in the midst of the feast does not lead to her murder but—for now—squashes the revolution.

However, the moment of collective singing as on-screen assembly also provides an interface with the film's extradiegetic soundtrack. The latter's (more than momentary) instrumental leitmotif recalls the Internationale in situational modulations of tone, varying and imbricating irony and melancholy with political agitation.[53] To be sure, we may want to be cautious in hypothesizing how Radlmaier's cinematic work of assembly will affect extradiegetic audiences. Rancière's reminder apropos the Brechtian "paradigm of critical art" also resonates for Radlmaier's comic inflection: there is no "calculable transmission" between the production of "sensory" form, discursive analysis, and any "political mobilization" following from them.[54] But, as indicated, this does not actually mean that there is "a contradiction" in the logic of political art, or that the heterogeneous elements of a filmic assemblage cannot come together as an effective concert to various degrees.[55] In my own viewing experience, the extradiegetic Internationale soundtrack facilitates a degree of imaginative co-assembly: an affective sharing of the fantasy, even as my own left-wing melancholia makes it difficult to perceive it as potentially more than just fantasy.[56] Still, in cueing my biographical memories of events of collective mobilization sustained by radically egalitarian, internationalist dreams, Radlmaier's aesthetic assembly invites me to activate resilient hope towards reimagining political alternatives in our difficult moment. The concluding resurgence

---

53 With a melancholy inflection, for example, the soundtrack underscores Camille's disillusionment after she separates from Hong and Sancho (unwilling to face capitalist reality) in Italy. At the same time, it keeps her virtually connected with them: with the music continuing, Radlmaier's editing takes us back to them.

54 Rancière, *Dissensus*, 142–43.

55 Rancière, *Dissensus*, 143.

56 See Enzo Traverso: *Left-wing Melancholia: Marxism, History, and Memory* (New York: Columbia University Press, 2021).

of this musical *leitmotif* potentially extends such extradiegetic echoes of assembly beyond the end of Radlmaier's film, after the dog narrator's final words about his ongoing learning process accompanied by footage of the collective digging of a tunnel to liberate the prisoners. (Notably, Hong and Sancho have remained in prison despite their protests that they got there in a film: again, art and life cannot easily be disentangled.)

To conclude, *Selbstkritik* makes a fascinating contribution to contemporary German cinema at the end of neoliberalism in the twofold sense that this volume is exploring. First, the film engages the ways in which the neoliberal regime of exploiting precarious human bodies is becoming ever more noticeably unsustainable. Second, it invites us to think and feel beyond this state of affairs in the face of new fascisms, and after the dissolution of socialist promises in the realities of twentieth-century authoritarianism. I have spelled out this imaginative contribution in the framework of a nuanced rethinking of art's political affordances: if we conceptualize cinema's political promise as that of making revolution, single-handedly, Radlmaier's film clearly fails to deliver. But even as it fails to spell out a fuller image of a different world—or a coherent plan for getting there—the film's multivectoral assemblage of sight and sound, body and intertextual association, memory and fantasy does develop a forceful, if disharmonious, concert of political sights and sounds. In layering the aesthetic powers of documentary and fabulation, comedy and more serious modes of reshuffling the sensible, *Selbstkritik* assembles actions of political verdict—namely, on authoritarian fantasies—with an homage to precarious human actors. At the intersection of unabashed fabulation with the documentary force of portraits assembled in a radically democratic manner, the film clears imaginative ground for reassembling "the people" as a collective of solidarity. In chasing the specters of fascism overshadowing the people with its ongoing modulation of tone as well as its entwined gestures of exclusion and inclusion, might this aesthetic assembly even model some of the tactics we could try towards reclaiming political assembly in our extrafilmic worlds? Such potential translations from aesthetics to politics will need ongoing efforts of imagination—but as Camille knows better than Julian, it won't do to just make art instead of politics.

Bibliography

Adorno, Theodor W. *Noten zur Literatur*. Frankfurt am Main: Suhrkamp, 1991.

Alsop, Elizabeth. "'The Imaginary Crowd': Neorealism and the Uses of Coralità." *The Velvet Light Trap* 74 (2014): 27–41.

Arendt, Hannah. *The Human Condition*. Chicago: University of Chicago Press, 1958.

Bal, Mieke. "Lost in Space, Lost in the Library." *Thamyris/Intersecting* 17 (2007): 23–36.

BlacKkKlansman. Dir. Spike Lee. US: Blumhouse Productions, 2018.

Breger, Claudia. *Making Worlds: Affect and Collectivity in Contemporary European Cinema*. New York: Columbia University Press, 2020.

Bruns, John. *Loopholes: Reading Comically*. New Brunswick, NJ: Transaction, 2009.

Busche, Andreas. "Früchte der Revolution." *Der Tagesspiegel*, June 10, 2017. https://www.tagesspiegel.de/kultur/fruchte-der-revolution-3839137.html.

Butler, Judith. *Notes Towards a Performative Theory of Assembly*. Cambridge, MA: Harvard University Press, 2015.

Clover, Joshua. *Riot. Strike. Riot: The New Era of Uprisings*. London: Verso, 2016.

Le Crime de Monsieur Lange. Dir. Jean Renoir. France: André Halley des Fontaines, 1936.

Dean, Jodi. *Crowds and Party*. London: Verso, 2016.

Deleuze, Gilles. *Cinema 2: The Time-Image*. Translated by Hugh Tomlinson and Robert Galeta. Minneapolis: University of Minnesota Press, 1989.

Duenschmann, Hermann. "Cinematograph and Crowd Psychology: A Sociopolitical Study." Translated by Eric Ames. In *The Promise of Cinema: German Film Theory 1907–1933*, edited by Anton Kaes, Nicholas Baer, and Michael Cowan, 256–58. Berkeley: University of California Press, 2016.

Hardt, Michael, and Antonio Negri. *Assembly*. Oxford: Oxford University Press, 2017.

Hutcheon, Linda. *The Politics of Postmodernism*. New York: Routledge, 1989.

Kafka, Franz. *Amerika: The Missing Person*. Translated by Mark Harman. New York: Schocken, 2008.

King, Geoff. *Film Comedy*. London: Wallflower Press, 2002.

Klassenverhältnisse. Dir. Danielle Huillet and Jean Marie Straub. West Germany: Janus Film und Fernsehen, 1984.

Latour, Bruno. *Reassembling the Social: An Introduction to Actor-Network-Theory*. Oxford: Oxford University Press, 2005.

Massumi, Brian. *The Power at the End of the Economy*. Durham, NC: Duke University Press, 2015.

Mbembe, Achille. *Necropolitics*. Translated by Steven Corcoran. Durham, NC: Duke University Press, 2019.

Meyer, Lars. "Zu jedem Bett gehört ein Mann." *Zeit Online*, June 22, 2019. https://www.zeit.de/kultur/film/2019-06/das-melancholische-maedchen-film-susanne-heinrich.

Montags in Dresden. Dir. Sabine Michel. Germany: solo:film gmbh, 2017.

Nyong'o, Tavia. *Afro-Fabulations. The Queer Drama of Black Life*. New York: New York University Press, 2019.

Pantenburg, Volker. "Class Relations: Diagnoses of the Present in the Films of Julian Radlmaier and Max Linz." *New German Critique* 46, no. 3 (138) (2019): 53–78.

Puar, Jasbir. "Queer Times, Queer Assemblages." *Social Text* 23, nos. 3–4 (84–85) (2005): 121–39.

Radlmaier, Julian. "Director's Statement: Markus Nechleba and Julian Radlmaier talking about Self-criticism of a bourgeois dog." *Fakturafilm.* Accessed December 19, 2022. https://www.fakturafilm.de/dogstate ment. [German version: *Pressemappe* 13–16.]

———. "Fatalismus interessiert mich nicht. Interview with Jakob Hayner." *jungle.world*, June 1, 2017. https://jungle.world/artikel/2017/22/ fatalismus-interessiert-mich-nicht.

———. "The New Wave of Political Satire: An Interview by Tuhin." *The Projection Room*, March 14, 2018. https://theprojectionroomorg. wordpress.com/2018/03/14/julian-radlmaier-inteview/.

———. Q&A at Summer School: Visions of Europe Cinema and Migration in Contemporary Germany (Rutgers University, September 9, 2022).

Rancière, Jacques. *Dissensus: On Politics and Aesthetics.* Edited and translated by Steven Corcoran. London: Continuum, 2010.

———. *Film Fables.* Translated by Emiliano Battista. Oxford: Berg, 2006.

———. *The Intervals of Cinema.* Translated by John Howe. London: Verso, 2014.

Rebhandl, Bert. "Der Typ sieht ja aus wie von Fassbinder: Julian Radlmaiers Kinofilm." *Frankfurter Allgemeine Zeitung*, June 10, 2017. https:// www.faz.net/aktuell/feuilleton/kino/julian-radlmaiers-selbstkritik-eines-buergerlichen-hundes-15054239.html.

Roelvink, Gerda. *Building Dignified Worlds: Geographies of Collective Action.* Minneapolis: University of Minnesota Press, 2016.

Schaefer, Jerome P. *An Edgy Realism: Film Theoretical Encounters with Dogma 95, New French Extremity, and the Shaky-Cam Horror Film.* Newcastle upon Tyne: Cambridge Scholars Publishing, 2015.

Schaub, Christoph. "Labor-Movement Modernism: Proletarian Collectives between *Kuhle Wampe* and Working-Class Performance Culture." *Modernism/Modernity* 25, no. 2 (2018): 327–48.

Selbstkritik eines bürgerlichen Hundes. Dir. Julian Radlmaier. Germany: Faktura Film, 2017.

Serner, Walter. "Cinema and Visual Pleasure." Translated by Don Reneau. In *The Promise of Cinema: German Film Theory 1907–1933*, edited by Anton Kaes, Nicholas Baer, and Michael Cowan, 41–45. Berkeley: University of California Press, 2016.

Tratner, Michael. *Crowd Scenes: Movies and Mass Politics.* New York: Fordham University Press, 2008.

Whose Streets? Dir. Sabaah Folayan and Damon Davis. USA: Magnolia Pictures, 2017.

Part IV

Intimate Connections:
Aesthetics and Politics of
a Cinema of Relations

10: Choric Configurations and the Collective: Ruth Beckermann's Films

Fatima Naqvi

IN THIS RE-POLITICIZED AGE, the collective and its representation has moved to the forefront of our interest. How can the collective be figured in documentary films with aesthetic ambitions? Is there a way for the body politic to emerge without using obvious historical footage of protest movements, parades, processions, or a panoply of talking heads? How might these kinds of films, which tend to wear their politics on their sleeve, represent the group without falling prey to propaganda? Are there new ways of representing the agon of collectives in the public sphere, and, if so, what stylistic means are used?[1] How do the films negotiate the consent of their subjects, that is, what a director chooses to show about the implied community? And, finally, what are the possibilities for new polities—perhaps a kind of rejuvenated chorus of antiquity—to emerge from particular modalities of such documentary filmmaking?

In attempting to answer some of these questions, I take as my case study the films of acclaimed Austrian director Ruth Beckermann. She establishes a documentary mode of choric configurations, one that presses spatial qualities into the service of explicit and implicit collectives. In *Die Geträumten* (The Dreamed Ones, 2016, 89 min.), *Waldheims Walzer* (The Waldheim Waltz, 2018, 93 min.), and *Mutzenbacher* (2022, 100 min.), Beckermann reflects on contemporary socio-sexual, economic, and political mores through the lens of the past. Whether it be the fraught love story between two of the German-speaking world's postwar literary greats, the election of a former SA member as President of the Second Austrian Republic, or the re-publication of the 1906 pornographic novel, *Josephine Mutzenbacher* (2021), all three films represent marginalized or oppositional voices. In this regard, Beckermann uses overdetermined

---

1 For a discussion of the aesthetics and politics of assemblage in narrative fiction film, see Claudia Breger's contribution to this volume, "A Few Takes Towards Reassembling (the Dream of) the People: Julian Radlmaier's *Selbstkritik eines bürgerlichen Hundes* (2017)."

sites to profoundly reflect on the possibility and ephemerality of political collectives that arise out of a sense of historical injustice. She sets *Die Geträumten* in the soon-to-be-defunct inter-war radio broadcast studio *Funkhaus Wien*, she circles the central St. Stephen's Square during Waldheim's election campaign in *Waldheims Walzer*, and she situates an open casting call for *Mutzenbacher* in the now partially razed coffin factory-cum-cultural center *Kulturzentrum F23 Wien-Liesing*. These locales, where readings from the correspondence between Ingeborg Bachmann and Paul Celan, protests against presidential candidate Kurt Waldheim, and conversations about the pedophilic novel *Mutzenbacher* occur, become spatially and temporally porous. The literary and historical past, the present of the filming, and the future discussed by the actors/laypeople are consciously interwoven in these resonant places. The readings from the critical edition of the pornographic novel in particular are theatrically staged in such a way as to allow the concept of consent to enter the vast halls of the cultural center—a concept at the heart of documentary filmmaking and at issue throughout Beckermann's oeuvre.

Before I delve into the particularities of the films, let me briefly outline the concept of the chorus as it has emerged as a new focus in theater studies.[2] Drawing on scholarship by Ulrike Haß, Evelyn Annuß, and Sebastian Kirsch, I argue that a newly energized choric imagination migrates into the domain of documentary film and lies at the heart of Beckermann's undertaking. It is a complex translation from the theatrical realm into that of the moving image. By looking at the chorus in various eras, these scholars have sought to turn away from the individual protagonists that have held our attention for so long. As Haß argues in *Kraftfeld Chor*, the chorus comes from outside the polis and is never quite native to the city-state; it disturbs a Western tradition that is keen on establishing patriarchal lineages and distinct ancestries. Choruses, she writes, "machen uns darauf aufmerksam, dass die Anfänge des europäischen Theaters mit einer Standardisierung jener genealogischen Ordnung einhergingen, die sich unter der Ägide des Mannes etablierte" (make us aware that the beginning of European theater went hand-in-hand with the standardization of the type of genealogical order that was established under the aegis of man).[3] The chorus recalls a moment preceding the displacement of women and girls from tragic conflict. It also stands for a multiplicity at

---

2   In relation to the chorus, see the special issue "Choric Figurations" of *The Germanic Review: Literature, Culture, Theory* 98, no. 2 (2023), in particular the introduction by Evelyn Annuß, Sebastian Kirsch, and myself (137–42) as well as Annuß's article "Alienating Choruses in German-speaking Performing Arts" (158–69). The introduction provides an overview of the development of this subfield, which emerged in theater studies in Germany.

3   Ulrike Haß, *Kraftfeld Chor* (Berlin: Theater der Zeit, 2020), 13.

odds with the singularity of the tragic individual. Inhabiting thresholds, the chorus troubles the clear boundaries marking the theater, the polis, and the community. It divides voices across bodies and bodies across space. It allows plural presents to emerge simultaneously. The chorus re-emerges as a point of interest in moments of crisis, when institutions crumble and the Name of the Father no longer holds absolute authority. It is worth keeping in mind that the chorus represents a multiplicity, not a majority; it responds to a transhuman and otherwise ecological environment. It carries traces of the ritualistic and cultic into secularizing processes.[4] To think about such choric configurations in documentary film—for we are not always dealing with a particular chorus, but often with a constellation of bodies and voices in tandem—means being attuned to the textures of sounds emanating from material bodies in space; the complicated presence of mediating technology; the dispersal of power relations; and the existence of thresholds. Such an attunement lends itself to a better understanding of the current historical moment, where a sense of urgency emerges from the multiple present tenses conjured up within the theatrical tradition.

Given the proximity between theater and Beckermann's recent documentary endeavors, it stands to reason that the director uses a variety of choric configurations. She draws on an imagined community of listeners produced by media technology or through acoustically produced temporal simultaneity and spatial contiguity—aspects I delve into below.[5] Beckermann's technique shares certain similarities with choral strategies utilized in Italian neo-realism, where a "spectrum of collaborative vocal activity" instigates what Elizabeth Alsop describes as an "overbestowing" of speech on marginalized groups.[6] I agree with Alsop that this should be seen "less as a naturalistic technique than as a theatrical and often polemical one—a device used by directors not to reflect an existing social group so much as to project or enact an imaginary one." She draws attention to *coralità*'s constructed nature, producing a sonic "impression of collectivity in excess of diegetic reality."[7] In a related vein, Olivia Landry has shown how a "theatricality bleed" occurs as a result of "mediatic effects of liveness" in the films of the Berlin School.[8] This assertion could also be made for Beckermann's work since 2016. Expanding on this mediated theatricality bleed, the Austrian director's films conjure up the chorus in

---

4   For a summary see Haß, *Kraftfeld Chor*, 7–35.

5   Elizabeth Alsop, "The Imaginary Crowd: Neorealism and the Uses of Coralità," *The Velvet Light Trap* 74 (2014), 27–41.

6   Alsop, "Imaginary," 29.

7   Alsop, "Imaginary," 31.

8   Olivia Landry, *Movement and Performance in Berlin School Cinema* (Bloomington: Indiana University Press, 2018), 7, 11, 62.

various forms, calling to mind Alsop's "spectrum of collaborative vocal activity."[9] For Beckermann, a choral configuration may be evoked on the part of an imagined audience soldered together through socio-political concerns, on the part of an oppositional group seeking political clout, or in the service of providing a feminist perspective on sexuality. For instance, in *Die Geträumten* an imagined community of radio listeners-cum-film viewers "tune" into and thus witness the persistent failures of post-war Austrian-Jewish life as it unfolds in the intimate relationship between Ingeborg Bachmann and Paul Celan. For *Waldheims Walzer*, a small group of activists (including the director herself) oppose the election of Kurt Waldheim as president; they emerge as a marginalized but persistent chorus in interstitial spaces, addressing viewers' retrospective sense of injustice and democratic frustration. Finally, in *Mutzenbacher*, a literal chorus of straight and queer men demonstrate the politics of chorality in its subversive and—more importantly—in its problematic aspects. On the one hand, they drain the pornographic and pedophilic literary source of its sexually demeaning semantics; on the other, they literally inundate and drown out the director's own critical voice, which questions the gender trouble adumbrated in the novel.

Beckermann herself became known for a deeply committed kind of filmmaking beholden first to leftist political activism and then to exploring a "Jewish Vienneseness or a Viennese Jewishness" entangled with the city of Vienna, as the writer-director Georg Stefan Troller states.[10] Beckermann's early films *Arena besetzt* (Arena Squatted, 1977), *Auf amol a Streik* (Suddenly, A Strike, 1978), and *Der Hammer steht auf der Wies'n da draußen* (The Steel Hammer Out There on the Grass, 1981) look at cultural politics, workers' rights, and labor strikes against the backdrop of declining industrial production. These low budget films from the late 1970s and early 1980s are concerned with chronicling and protesting the burgeoning moments of socio-economic liberalization in Austria's welfare state. Beginning with *Wien retour* (Return to Vienna, 1983), her films turn to the obscured, exiled, overwritten, or eradicated Jewish past in Vienna itself (*Die papierene Brücke*/Paper Bridge, 1987; *homemad[e]*, 2001), Jewish attachment to the idea of Israel (*Nach Jerusalem*/Towards Jerusalem, 1990), people on the move in *Ein flüchtiger Zug nach dem Orient* (*A Fleeting Passage to the Orient*, 1999), and *Those Who Go Those Who Stay* (2013). Singularly important in the Austrian public sphere is her *Jenseits des Krieges* (East of War, 1996), where she captures visitors' ambivalent reactions to an exhibition about atrocities committed by the

9   Alsop, "Imaginary," 29.
10   See Georg Stefan Troller's illuminating foreword in the first book devoted to her oeuvre: "Filme machen in Wien," in *Ruth Beckermann*, ed. Alexander Horwath and Michael Omasta (Vienna: Synema, 2016), 5.

German Wehrmacht in World War II. In her work, Beckermann succeeds in unsettling territorial certainties and ideas of nativity. *Nach Jerusalem* or her essay film on the United States, *American Passages* (2011), are particularly pertinent examples. In these later films, borders, boundedness, and belonging are constantly undermined. Beckermann queries the frameworks defining these terms, and she also perceptibly shifts definitions. Her interviewees are always privy to a here-and-now that is shot through with the elsewhere of another historical moment and often another place. This spatio-temporal oscillation characterizes her most recent films, which bring in variations of the chorus to think about collectives and their strengths—as well as their gender issues.

Die Geträumten (2016)

In her acclaimed film *Die Geträumten*,[11] Beckermann stages a reading from the letters between Carinthian-born writer Ingeborg Bachmann and Paul Celan, who hailed from the Bukowina (formerly a part of Austria-Hungary). For the duration of the nearly ninety-minute film, the two actors, Anja Plaschg and Laurence Rupp, move into and out of the recording studio, read into microphones, and prepare for the audio recordings by studying their excerpts from the recently published Bachmann and Celan correspondence. Between sessions, Plaschg—a musician known as Soap & Skin—and Rupp—erstwhile actor at the Wiener Burgtheater and the Berliner Ensemble—chat, flirt, and dissect the writers' complicated relationship. *Die Geträumten* takes place in the soon-to-be-defunct interwar Funkhaus Wien; as part of the city's economic liberalization program, the radio journalists for the Austrian Broadcasting Corporation are largely being moved to Vienna's periphery and the historically landmarked building partially privatized.[12] Beckermann uses the building to reflect on literature's contemporary purchase for intergenerational memory—by extension asking about the mediating function of technology in that very transfer. The ephemeral site, where the passages from Bachmann and Celan are read, becomes

11 Among other awards, it won Best Feature Film at the Diagonale Film Festival in 2016. A full list of awards can be found at ruthbeckermann.com, accessed August 2, 2022, https://www.ruthbeckermann.com/en/films/filmlist/the-dreamed-ones/.

12 The sale caused a great deal of controversy, including protests by well-known actors such as Karl Markovics. See "Herr Markovics, ist Radio noch zeitgemäß?," March 23, 2016, https://www.meinbezirk.at/wieden/c-lokales/herr-markovics-ist-radio-noch-zeitgemaess_a1673671. After the protests, a part of the building remained with the ORF. See "ORF verkauft nur das halbe Funkhaus," June 14, 2016, https://kurier.at/kultur/orf-funkhaus-verkauf-an-vorarlberger-investorf-funkhaus/204.378.748.

porous, allowing the interweaving of various historical moments. The past within the literature, the historical moment of writing, the present of the filming, and the future adumbrated by the actors (who also double as interviewees for the director) meld as the camera drifts off into nooks of this complicated building.[13] The Funkhaus was built in 1935–1939 during the Austrian corporate state and completed with the *Anschluß*, using plans by architects Clemens Holzmeister, Hermann Aichinger, and Heinrich Schmid. Since the regime recognized the benefit of the radio for propaganda purposes, this building was still utilized during the Austrian corporate state for radio transmissions under the RAVAG, the Radio Verkehrs AG, as Andreas Suttner has shown.[14] Interestingly enough, the film at no point shows the famous Holzmeister-façade in the Argentinierstraße from the outside, with its characteristic monumental proportions. Rather, the film focuses on one of the sound stages: Studio 3, with paintings by Hilda Jesser. Jesser's large-scale, apolitical cycle, portraying lovers and groups gathered in wetland meadows, sets the enigmatic tone for the film's opening, where the camera zeroes in on abstract details of the paintings. Jesser, mentioned only in the closing credits, had a career that spanned the Wiener Werkstätte in the interwar period, the Austrian corporate state, as well as the Nazi and postwar periods (when she was professor at the Kunstgewerbeschule, which became the Hochschule für angewandte Kunst).[15] However, her political views remain a cipher in the paintings, which do not conform to a recognizable strain of modernism. The wall paintings suggest the timelessness thematized in some "moderately" modern art during the interwar period.[16] The compositions home in on small social units, the lyricism of the landscape, and lack any signs of modernity.[17] They neither clearly reveal the influence of her illustrious teachers and colleagues (Oskar Strnad, Josef Hoffmann, Anton Hanak, Dagobert Peche), nor do they

13 On the temporal interweaving see Alice Leroy, "Celan, Bachmann, Beckermann: Korrespondenz der Geträumten," in *Ruth Beckermann*, ed. Horwath and Omasta, 113.

14 Andreas Suttner, *Das schwarze Wien: Bautätigkeit im Ständestaat 1934–38* (Wien: Böhlau, 2017), 182.

15 For insight into her work, see "Hilda Jessers Wandmalereien im Wiener Funkhaus," July 1, 2022, https://oe1.orf.at/artikel/694531/Hilda-Jessers-Wandmalereien-im-Wiener-Funkhaus.

16 See Veronika Pfolz's essay in a catalogue accompanying a special exhibition of the Vienna Museum from October 20, 2005, to January 29, 2006, "'Zur Ergänzung und Steigerung seines Werkes'—Zwei Mitarbeiterinnen von Erich Boltenstern," in *Moderat Modern: Erich Boltenstern und die Baukultur nach 1945*, ed. Judith Eiblmayr and Iris Meder (Salzburg: Verlag Anton Pustet, 2005), 113–19.

17 Conversation with Veronika Pfolz, Vienna, June 30, 2023.

evince corporatist monumentality. Fantastic realism, which emerged in Austria after 1945, is foreign to them. Due to their harmlessness, Anne-Kathrin Rossberg speculates, the National Socialists allowed Jesser to complete the murals in 1939 although she had been forced into early retirement after the *Anschluß* (her teaching did not conform to National Socialist tenets).[18]

The credit sequence, relaying the basic outlines of the relationship between Celan and Bachmann in lapidary statements, utilizes close-ups of Jesser's paintings to convey a sense of uncharted waters and unbounded emotion. To the sound of mournful music, unfurling intertitles transmit the sparse data of the writers' ancestry: Celan was the son of Jews who died in a Ukrainian concentration camp, while Bachmann was the daughter of an NSDAP-member who returned from the war but did not discuss his past. The time and place of their first meeting, Vienna in 1948, as well as their unequal footing are also mentioned. She was still an unknown poet, he already a celebrated figure. The camera lingers on the bluish-gray shapes from one of Jesser's paintings to conjure up a map, with what appears to be a land mass set off against water. Jesser's murals—evoking longing, togetherness, and loneliness simultaneously—thus stand in a metaphorical relationship to the later readings from the Bachmann–Celan correspondence, which expresses similar feelings on the part of both writers. As the explanatory titles unfold piecemeal, diagonal lines between the sentences suggest divisions as well as potential connections. Against continuity, the slashes intimate impending breaks. What might be bridges could become chasms, and the dreamed ones could dissolve ("Die/ GETRÄUMTEN"). A black screen divides these suggestive credits from what follows. Over and over, the film's editing performs the divisions at which the opening hints.

The entire film that follows draws on the interpellative structure of the radio address. In the beginning, we are reminded of radio broadcasts with their disembodied appeals to an invisible mass of listeners. In the first sequence after the credits, we see Plaschg's three-quarter profile in close-up in front of a black microphone, while Rupp's voice from off-screen intones the following lines from Celan's poem "In Ägypten" (In Egypt), the poem with which Celan dedicates a book on Matisse to Bachmann on the occasion of her twenty-second birthday: "Du sollst zum Aug der Fremden sagen: Sei das Wasser! / Du sollst, die du im Wasser weißt, im Aug der Fremden suchen. / Du sollst sie rufen aus dem Wasser: Ruth! Noemi! Mirjam" (Thou shalt say to the strange woman's eye: Be the water! / Thou shalt seek in the stranger's eye those whom thou knowest

---

18 See the essay by Anne-Kathrin Rossberg, curator for the Museum of Applied Art (MAK), "Hilda Jesser—Meisterin der Wandgestaltung," June 30, 2022, https://blog.mak.at/hilda-jesser/.

190 ♦ Fatima Naqvi

to be in the water. / Thou shalt call them from the water: Ruth! Noemi! Miriam!).[19] The poem's formal structure catches our attention, with its imperatives (*be*), commandments (*thou shalt*), appellatives (*Ruth! Noemi! Miriam!*), and appeal to contiguity (the prepositions "next," "besides"). It is an ethical injunction as well as a love poem, an appeal to others and the self, an entreaty for a side-by-side, neighborly mode of existence *and* a fusion of perspectives. "In Ägypten" addresses both the second-person listener in the form of the "you," as well as the lyrical I engaged in a dialogue with itself. Rupp's forceful voice invokes a nascent love while recalling lost Jewish ones. The poem calls forth the present moment of the budding relationship, all the while remembering an irrevocably lost past that must not be forgotten. The camera registers the changes in Plaschg's mien, as she first looks on solemnly while listening to Rupp and then breaks into a smile with Celan's humorous dedication, which tempers the poem's solemnity: "Der peinlich Genauen . . . Der peinlich Ungenaue" (To the scrupulously precise one . . . from the embarrassingly imprecise one).[20] Like Plaschg, we primarily become listeners in this segment, attuned to the acoustic register; Rupp's warm voice from off-screen beseeches, cajoles, and romances, all at once.

The reading is jarringly interrupted when a radio technician enters to check the sound. The whole history of the Funkhaus building is evoked when the lights go on; we are torn out of the intimacy of the two actors reading the correspondence. We have also been led to lose ourselves as viewers, with eyeline matches within the close-up shot sequence suggesting an increasing closeness between Plaschg and Rupp. It is as if we were witnessing their theatrical transformation into Bachmann and Celan. We just got a sense of the intensity of the unfolding relationship between the young Bachmann and the somewhat older Celan, who arrived in Vienna in the immediate postwar period *en route* to Paris, only to have this expectation of revealed interiority and embodied affection dashed.[21] Entering the studio, the radio technician reminds the startled actors as well as the viewers of the conditions underpinning the scenario: intimacy and authenticity are mediated effects in film and radio. They stimulate and simulate the sensation of being close-up, nearby, in the vicinity. Adjusting microphones and setting the signal sources, the technician recalls the technological conditions enabling every sigh or lighting of a cigarette to be captured and conveyed, which we heard over the music in the opening

19 Quotations from Ingeborg Bachmann and Paul Celan, *Herzzeit: Briefwechsel* (Frankfurt am Main: Suhrkamp, 2008), 7. All translations taken from the official subtitles of Beckermann's films (here *Die Geträumten*, 0:00:01–0:03:03).

20 Bachmann and Celan, *Herzzeit*, 7.

21 On the role of the voice in this film, see Christa Blümlinger, "Studien zur Bodenlosigkeit," in *Ruth Beckermann*, ed. Horwath and Omasta, 59.

credit sequence. Furthermore, we are led to reflect on the building itself, as we move out of the proximity of the facial close-up into the long shot, taking in the ORF-sound stage with the full Jesser paintings. We think about the relationship of part to whole, of excerpt to entire work. We also cannot help but ponder the conditions that helped make possible the National Socialist take-over, the historical backdrop for Celan's and Bachmann's life stories. We viewers surveying the Funkhaus via Beckermann's film necessarily think of fascism's reliance on propaganda transmitted via the ubiquitous German radio receivers or *Volksempfänger*, which sought to create an imagined Nazi community. In this manner, the location in what became the Reichssender Wien radio station also implies an earlier "chorus," which colluded with the Nazis in a sonic sphere of total acquiescence.

As Evelyn Annuß has shown, the National Socialists utilized the changing media landscape of the 1930s to stage and steer affective politics. The acoustic media generated an atmosphere in which elements of liveness created the sensation of belonging to a larger, obedient whole. In radio broadcasts or *Thingspiele*, the audience was made to feel and participate via the co-presence of a chorus; it suggested a fusion with a disembodied Führer voice in a vertical relationship based on blind loyalty and submission.[22] While Annuß analyzes specific theatrical mass stagings utilizing choric figurations, the auditory aspect is worth stressing—this was employed at the same time in radio broadcasts to create a sense of the *Volk* in the absence of a visible body.[23] "Das vor 1933 verstaatlichte und damit von der NS-Diktatur umstandslos okkupierbare Radio und die zeitgenössische Optimierung der Lautsprechertechnik nämlich ermöglichen erst den Versuch," Annuß writes, "die dauerbeschallten Massen durch chorische Praktiken nicht nur miteinander in Verbindung zu bringen, sondern an eine vermeintlich allgegenwärtige Führerfigur anzudocken"[24] (Radio, which was state-controlled before 1933 and thus easily occupied by the Nazi dictatorship, and the contemporary optimization of loudspeaker technology first make possible the attempt to connect the masses, acoustically irradiated as they were, with a supposedly omnipresent Führer figure). Citing the National Socialist sound designer Werner Pleister, Annuß argues that appeals to the Führer and the use of choruses were complexly fused in practice, to make it seem like there was always already a supportive community for Nazi ideology. In the process, the

---

22 See Evelyn Annuß, "Affekt und Gefolgschaft," in *Following: Medien der Gefolgschaft und Prozesse des Folgens; Ein kulturwissenschaftliches Kompendium*, ed. Anne Ganzert, Philip Hauser, and Isabell Otto (Berlin: de Gruyter, forthcoming 2023), 2.

23 Annuß, "Affekt," 3–4.

24 Annuß, "Affekt," 5.

public became a follower of the mediatized and mediated voice of the Führer. The chorus, understood as an affective political tool to elicit fealty and subservience, was further shaped by architectonic constraints in the theaters. Special staircases, for example, broke down spatial boundaries between audience and chorus, and the framing of mass choruses below a centralized leader enacted and modeled appropriate audience responses.[25] Later propagandistic experiments with mass "superornaments" in stadiums departed from the need for staged leaders or representative figures, instead relying on the corporeal, quasi-contagious element of the chorus. The chorus, in these permutations, triggers affects in the followers that we associate with a right-wing mindset.[26]

The dark history of the radio and its imbrications with power are always implicit within *Die Geträumten*, as are the enduring socio-political and technological conditions of the post-1945 period, when the postwar Austrian Broadcasting Corporation (ORF) took over the function of the RAVAG and its subsequent incarnation as the Reichssender Wien. In Plaschg and Rupp's readings, we hear the relationship between Celan and Bachmann undergo various stresses such as financial troubles, new lovers, and misunderstandings in communication. However, most importantly we are privy to the element of anti-Semitism in the FRG and the Second Austrian Republic.[27] Celan bemoans an anti-Semitic review of his poems by Günter Blöcker, turning it into a litmus test for Bachmann's relationship to him. The film's implicit choric configuration points to the Nazi majority of radio listeners and the silent post-1945 majority, which accepts the continuities with National Socialism and inadvertently expresses itself in the negative review. Plaschg and Rupp, the two readers of Bachmann and Celan's increasingly hurt letters, are also no longer shown in any relationship to one another within the film itself. They occupy separate spaces in the Funkhaus, and the editing does not allow for eyeline matches. *Die Geträumten* breaks off with two intertitles recounting Celan's suicide in the Seine and Bachmann's death by fire a few years later. In the coda,

25 See Annuß, "Affekt," 3: "Durch Führeranrufung und Chorpraxis wären die Massen gewissermaßen zur Einheit verbacken. Das Publikum wird hier zunächst als Anhängsel einer mediatisierten Stimme begriffen, das sich von dieser gewissermaßen erweckt . . . erst zur Volksgemeinschaft formt."

26 Annuß's fine-grained reading of the chorus in National Socialist propaganda makes the same affective politics legible in contemporary alt-right social media groups ("Affekt," 12–14).

27 An interesting scene takes place on the steps outside the Funkhaus, where Plaschg and Rupp discuss the light down on her arm (she ironically calls it "rassig" or "hot blooded," while he jokes about his hairless, "un-masculine" arm) and her lower-arm tattoo. The tattoo, of an alchemical cube signifying the material universe, arises from an act of volition. Of course, it conjures up the memory of other lower-arm tattoos that were not.

immediately after the closing intertitles have disappeared, Plaschg whisperingly reads an excerpt from Bachmann's novel *Malina*. Smoking heavily, she murmurs the passage, in which the first-person narrator recounts her lover's death by drowning. Plaschg, sitting at a table, ends the fairy tale excerpt as if reading to herself: "Ich habe ihn mehr geliebt als mein Leben" (I loved him more than my own life). The black studio microphone, which is otherwise ubiquitous in the reading scenes, has disappeared in this segment. The collective that could have been converted into a new kind of polity via public postwar ORF broadcasts from the Funkhaus has receded. It would have been a collective in the name of absolute love and in the service of commemoration, the kind that Celan's poem "In Ägypten" envisioned and for which the two oeuvres stand. The potential radio collective disappears, the film implies. *Die Geträumten* ends with the solitary televisual spectator to Bachmann's tragic epitaph, witnessing in the mass medial manner that the moving image today encourages, located somewhere beyond a sonic shared space.

Waldheims Walzer (2018)

In this film, the chorus emerges in the form of a small protest group during the election of former SA member Kurt Waldheim as president of Austria in 1986 despite obfuscations of his past as an SA officer in Yugoslavia and Greece. The chorus materializes from the conflict between the two sides, in the form of video footage and the director's voice-over narration versus the many Waldheim interviews and his supporters' statements. The medial conditions for representation, the ability to form a collective via sound, and the architectonic requirements for political protest are continually (re)negotiated throughout the film. *Waldheims Walzer* explicitly uses a quotation from Abraham Lincoln as its epigraph: "You can fool some of the people all of the time, and all of the people some of the time, but you can not fool all of the people all of the time." In an era of fake news and populist manipulation, the film posits the emergence of present-day collectives that can mine the past for oppositional material.[28] Beckermann thematizes her archaeological search in the analogue world of VHS tapes and radio broadcasts to show how enlightenment plays a kind of "long game" and to make apparent how much easier it is to be filming all the time in the era of the smartphone. The continuities to the present time of narration are made explicit in the images of crosses and presidents that still grace Austrian classrooms to this day. "Maybe it is no coincidence that the old footage [from the protests] just happened

28   Karin Schiefer discusses this with the director in her December 2017 interview, "I see the Waldheim affair as a conflict of generations," July 1, 2023, https://www.austrianfilms.com/interview/ruth_beckermann/the_waldheim_waltz_EN.

194 ♦ FATIMA NAQVI

to turn up now," she muses on the soundtrack, as her multi-layered film becomes an extended reflection on communal memory and media technology, collective failure and emergent counterpublics.

In Beckermann's own grainy documentary footage, with which the film begins, we first see a conglomeration of like-minded folk in a miniscule protest march in spring 1986. Unfurling banners with anti-Waldheim slogans, they make their way from the central Kärntner Straße into the main Viennese square, with St. Stephen's Cathedral in the backdrop. The handheld video footage shows the protesters carrying placards, which the police quickly requisition. The film returns to crowds throughout its hundred-minute duration, presenting the protesters as a marginal group articulating uncomfortable truths for the majority. For instance, when the police try to stop the demonstrators from reaching the site of Waldheim's last campaign speech on St. Stephen's Square, they are boxed in between a police cordon and angry bystanders. The marchers begin to chant "Waldheim: Nein!" Their "no" signals a powerful response to the police's stubborn refusal to let them pass. Via their shouts, the motley protesters mark themselves as a coherent group—which their actual deliberations in cafés, where they cannot really agree on a strategy, belie. The unprofessional footage, zooming in on cursing protesters and their adversaries, on gestures such as clapping, smiling, or frowning, creates an alternative film view, in conjunction with the director's smooth explanatory voice-over. In contrast to the professionally edited television interviews, her camera work offers a sort of Klugian counter-narrative. However, her willfully amateurish footage unfolds a story to give a sense of the emergent Austrian collective, interspersed as it is with American, (state-sanctioned) Austrian, British, and French news segments via careful editing. The strength of Beckermann's resolutely subjective camera angles ultimately enables one viewpoint—that of the dissenters—to prevail. Via her film, Waldheim's presidential victory turns into an abject post-election failure. The jazz soundtrack used for the opening and closing credits, together with the epigraph and closing credit about Waldheim's international ostracization after his election, underline that her film is *not* an adaptive, mythologizing, circular waltz.

Beckermann, discussing her growing awareness of the political situation in spring 1986, intercuts her own footage of the candidate with newsreels of Waldheim's UN and SA careers and his campaign, as well as the growing American opposition to Waldheim's election. Her own videos tend to drift to the margins, utilizing jumpy camerawork and occasionally elliptical visuals (many of the speakers are only recognizable to Austrians of a certain age). In a steady voice, to give one example, Beckermann comments on Waldheim's hands during his stump speeches, which gesture as if he wanted to embrace the Austrian people and "envelope" ("umschlingen") his "Volk," as she puts it; her camera hones in on his hands and his mid-section. The entire choreography of the film oscillates between these two poles: the charismatic leader, seeking to shape his listeners into a homogeneous, pro-Christian, anti-Semitic mass, and the scraggly group of artists, writers, and activists opposing him and the Austrian People Party's diatribes against the World Jewish Congress and its chairman, Israel Singer. The chorus of nay-sayers are compelling in their gritty testimony; the moral poverty of the People's Party, working with smear campaigns and anti-Semitic innuendo, is more than abundant. The film shows how hard it is to galvanize popular opinion against Waldheim, since the ORF-broadcasting station gave Waldheim a platform from which to mount his defense, namely that he—like the vast majority of Austrians during World War II—only did his "duty" ("Pflicht") and remained "decent" and "respectable" ("anständig"). To undercut Austrian public television's media dominance, the director utilizes footage from critical US, British, and French news reports about Waldheim's obfuscations. Beckermann recounts that the ORF did not send any investigative journalists to Thessaloniki, where a huge segment of the Jewish population was deported while SA officer Waldheim was stationed on the outskirts of the city during the Nazi occupation.

As a chorus commenting on the action, her "little group" ("Grüppchen") begins to grow, organizing protests and recording their actions. This includes holding up critical placards probing Waldheim's memory lapses behind a panel of expert witnesses that exonerate Waldheim. It also involves unveiling a wooden horse in public to symbolize the tongue-in-cheek remark made by the Socialist Party chairman, Fred Sinowatz: "Wir nehmen zur Kenntnis, dass er [Waldheim] nicht bei der SA war, sondern nur sein Pferd bei der SA gewesen ist" (We acknowledge that he [Waldheim] was never a member of the SA, and that only his horse was).[29] Especially with the footage showing the expert panel, Beckermann formulates the director's dilemma: in her voice-over, she states that the question was always whether to demonstrate or to document, a question that had to be answered anew repeatedly. In this case, she belonged to the protesters so that someone else had to document the proceedings. One can be of the chorus of protesters, emerging from the margins to briefly occupy the metaphorical and literal center, or apart from it; occupying both positions at the same time is impossible. In Beckermann's view, the documentarian needs to re-evaluate the work of filming as *a part of* and *apart from* the emerging collective at all times. This dilemma, allowing only an either/or answer, is undermined by the film itself; the choral configuration can encompass dis- and reintegration.

---

29 Sculptor Alfred Hrdlicka, who appears briefly in the footage, designed the horse. We also see a series of public figures like Doron Rabinovici and later members of the Republican Club speaking out against Waldheim.

Mutzenbacher (2022)

Arraying a wide variety of well-known artists, journalists, curators, and mixing these with actors at a casting call in a Viennese cultural center, Beckermann turns the novel *Josefine Mutzenbacher* into a meditation on the political potential of her aesthetically complex documentaries. Beckermann again draws on a published literary source, translating it into a provocative reflection on contemporary sexual mores and socio-aesthetic predilections by way of the specific site, a former coffin factory. In *Mutzenbacher*, she uses the Kulturzentrum F23 Wien-Liesing to profoundly reflect on literature's contemporary purchase for gender relations and intergenerational relationships—by extension asking about the mediating function of film in that very transfer. Like the Funkhaus, the Kulturzentrum F23, where readings from an anonymous author rumored to be Felix Salten take place, enables the interweaving of various historical moments within the conversations.[30] Intertitles announce the backdrop for the casting call, seeking "männliche Mitwirkende zwischen 16 und 99 Jahren" (male participants between the ages of 16 and 99 years) on April 25, 2021. The film partakes of a larger societal interest in the non-normative sexual history of Vienna, evidenced by the publication of a critical edition of *Josefine Mutzenbacher oder Die Geschichte einer wienerischen Dirne von ihr selbst erzählt* (Josefine Mutzenbacher or the Story of a Viennese Prostitute Told by Herself) with the prestigious publishing house Sonderzahl in 2021 and the mounting of an exhibition titled *Sex in Wien: Lust. Kontrolle. Ungehorsam* (Sex in Vienna: Lust, Control, Disobedience) at the *Wien Museum* on the Karlsplatz with corresponding catalogue in 2017.[31] The intertitles and credit sequence, utilizing the same heart-shaped curlicue found in the new edition of Mutzenbacher, suggest that the film is an extension of the fictional novel and a kind of quasi-documentary, somewhere between fact and fiction.[32]

---

30 About the unlikelihood of Salten being the author, see Clemens Ruthner's afterword to the critical edition, "Die nackte Kehrseite der Wiener Jahrhundertwende: Handreichungen für eine Mutzenbacher-Lektüre," in Anonymous, *Josefine Mutzenbacher oder Die Geschichte einer wienerischen Dirne von ihr selbst erzählt*, ed. Clemens Ruthner, Melanie Strasser, and Matthias Schmidt (Vienna: Sonderzahl, 2021), 379–402, esp. 385.

31 See Anonymous, *Josefine Mutzenbacher*, ed. Ruthner, Strasser, and Schmidt, and Andreas Brunner, ed., *Sex in Wien: Lust. Kontrolle. Ungehorsam* (Vienna: Metroverlag, 2016). See also the edited volume to accompany a conference organized in conjunction with the publication of *Josefine Mutzenbacher*, with the title *Die Mutzenbacher: Lektüren und Kontexte eines Skandalromans*, ed. Clemens Ruthner and Matthias Schmidt (Vienna: Sonderzahl, 2019). On the novel's turbulent history see Ruthner's afterword to *Josefine Mutzenbacher*, 382–84.

32 The intertitles are similar to the experimental intertitles from *Die Geträumten*, giving a sense of the complexity of the source material and its changing

The aesthetic potential of Beckermann's film mode to thematize competing claims to moral truth in sex becomes evident in her dialogues and in her use of choric interludes. Seating a few men on a pink sofa reminiscent of the boudoir within the cavernous hall, Beckermann poses questions from off-screen, evidently across from them but not visible to us. By starting with the novel, where the men read the first-person female perspective on sexual acts between all age groups (between adults, adults and the narrating child, narrating child and other children) in each of the film's vignettes, she uses the text itself to segue into a consideration of broader issues. She asks her subjects about *Mutzenbacher*'s legendary aura, the role of sexuality and gender in the cited passages, contemporary sexual relations among men, women, and children. All interviewees agree that childhood sexuality exists, that relations between the genders have become more fraught since the 1960s, and that sexual adventurousness is constrained today because of the widespread consumption of online pornography. Most, but not all, find that the *Mutzenbacher* text engages in verbal seduction. Especially noticeable is how the younger generation often discusses consent during the sexual act, clearly departing from the cavalier and occasionally chauvinistic attitudes of the older generation (although there are prominent exceptions to this generalization in the film).

The chorus enters explicitly as a culmination of Beckermann's prior experiments with such configurations. Interrupting the many interviews and staged readings from the novel, the director symmetrically arranges a large group of men vis-à-vis the camera four times. This group chants various words from the book (see Fig. 10.1). As in a theater production, the men are arrayed in rows within one of the derelict factory halls of the cultural center. At first, they intone what are normally terms of endearment. The men's faces and torsos are shown, and the editing focuses on single faces within the larger crowd, while they all whisper the same words in a repetitive loop. The susurration is hardly sweet; the Viennese diminutive "-erl" at the end of the expressions ("Schatzerl," "Mauserl," "Herzerl") and the sibilants convey a sense of menace. The second time the chorus appears, led by Beckermann's off-screen voice, they replay a sexual encounter between the protagonist nicknamed Pepi, a neighborhood boy called Alois, and his nursemaid Klementine.[33] Now halfway through the film, the chorus chants a series of Viennese dialectal words for coitus.[34] The chorus in this three-minute-long sequence is incredibly ambivalent.

---

cultural importance over time, as well as the novel's controversial status as both salacious pedophilia/pornography and high-brow eroticism.

33 See *Josefine Mutzenbacher*, 55.

34 The chorus, having literally taken the stage in minutes 25:20 and in 48:00, appears with another sentence from this episode "Schluss mit Genuss" (finish with relish) at 1:08:55 and finally falls silent at 1:36:25.

On the one hand, the choric speaking updates the text, endowing its verbal seduction (barrage?) with a sense of presentism and liveness. The choric staging estranges the vulgarity and renders the words funny. For the viewers, semantic satiation occurs, where the words lose their meaning through repetition. On the other hand, the chorus creates a sense of masculinized menace: the group physically fills the screen, arranged as a military phalanx. When the director's voice comes from off-screen, she slips up. Trying to control the staging, she does not succeed. One of the actors wrests control from her with his dominant voice and towering physical presence in the front row; then her dramaturg enters the discussion to regroup and reorganize the proceedings from off-screen. Finally, she has to ask the group to redo the sequence, since it does not conform to her wishes: we hear her injunction to stop. In a film in which individual actors have articulated what they would or would not do for the director and that they trust her not to breach personal borders, this comes across as quite ironic. She has respected their boundaries, but have they respected hers? It seems that the chorus' purpose is to hold this very concept of consent up for examination and to ask what happens when men appear *en masse*.[35]

The chorus falls silent at the film's end, when it appears a fourth time. A boom operator passes in front of the group, another reminder of the medial conditions underpinning the film's supposed immediacy and of sound's importance in creating a collective. *Mutzenbacher* has shown the diversity of opinion regarding the representation of sex and its practice in individual interviews. Efforts to shape something like a coherent whole out of the one hundred male actors fail in the choric configuration. While the potential of physical violence—when men appropriate women's speaking positions—does not manifest itself in these choric interludes, it remains latent. Where has the female narrator Pepi gone in all of this?, we viewers might ask ourselves of both the child narrator and the self-reflective grown-up narrator who concludes the novel. "Thank you," Beckermann's voice says, rounding off the proceedings. We end with another coda, where Austrian author Robert Schindel sadly reads the closing lines of *Mutzenbacher* as if to himself, like Anja Plaschg at the close of *Die Geträumten*. Schindel intones the adult Pepi's reflections in a melancholy manner: "Die Männer tun alle dasselbe. Sie liegen oben, wir liegen unten. Sie stoßen und wir werden gestoßen. Das ist der ganze Unterschied" (All men do the same. They lie on top, we lie on the bottom. They pound us, and we get pounded. That is the whole difference). We viewers are left to ponder the "whole difference" that relies on the

---

35 This has been an on-going concern of Beckermann's as evidenced by her exposé entitled "Die Flaneurin," in *Ruth Beckermann*, ed. Horwath and Omasta, 60–65.

Figure 10.1. *Mutzenbacher* (dir. Ruth Beckermann, 2022)
© Ruth Beckenmann Filmproduktion.

tension between the whole—the heterogeneous yet masculine chorus—and the parts—the individual interviewees, the female director.

Clearly, gendered bodies arranged symmetrically and speaking in unison are politically and affectively charged. It does not take much for their collective articulation to tilt from good to bad, and it does not take much for their words to be evacuated of meaning and even emanate menace. In contrast to Ulrike Haß's book *Kraftfeld Chor*, which sees the chorus as an ethical minoritarian presence, a marginal yet rejuvenating power, a non-genealogical manner of being-together in works from Aeschylus to Beckett and Jelinek, Beckermann is keen to conjure up a spectrum of choric configurations that run the gamut from good to bad. The chorus, Beckermann demonstrates, can become a force recalcitrant to manipulation *or* a force of manipulation within the shortest of time spans. It migrates from the theatrical tradition into filmic space as a potential community of witnesses; as a disruption to the smooth functioning of state power and its politics of representation; as the literal embodiment of groupspeak (even if not groupthink). Then it comes from a feigned place of powerlessness to reassert its dominance. With Hans-Thies Lehmann, we might say that its "additive language causes the *impression of a chorus*" without truly being one or that it is a "purloined voice," where the "unadulterated particularity" of Pepi is dispersed uncannily across male-identified bodies.[36] With its inherent corporeality and sonority, the

36 See the discussion in Hans-Thies Lehmann, especially of the German enfant terrible Einar Schleef in *Postdramatic Theatre*, trans. Karen Jürs-Munby (New York: Routledge, 2006), 97, 129–31; quotes here from 128, 129.

chorus is an iridescent and ambiguous figure, which moves from the center of acclaimed German postdramatic theater to the center of an aesthetically ambitious documentary film practice like Ruth Beckermann's.[37] It remains to be seen how and whether she configures further choric alternatives in her works to come.

Bibliography

Alsop, Elizabeth. "The Imaginary Crowd: Neorealism and the Uses of Coralità." *The Velvet Light Trap* 74 (2014): 27–41.

Anonymous. *Josefine Mutzenbacher oder Die Geschichte einer wienerischen Dirne von ihr selbst erzählt.* Edited by Clemens Ruthner, Melanie Strasser, and Matthias Schmidt. Vienna: Sonderzahl, 2021.

Annuß, Evelyn. "Affekt und Gefolgschaft." In *Following: Medien der Gefolgschaft und Prozesse des Folgens; Ein kulturwissenschaftliches Kompendium,* edited by Anne Ganzert, Philip Hauser, and Isabell Otto, n.p. Berlin: de Gruyter, forthcoming 2023.

Bachmann, Ingeborg, and Paul Celan. *Herzzeit: Briefwechsel.* Frankfurt am Main: Suhrkamp, 2008.

Beckermann, Ruth. "Die Flaneurin: Exposé zu einem Film." In *Ruth Beckermann,* edited by Alexander Horwath and Michael Omasta, 60–65. Vienna: Synema, 2016.

———. *Die Geträumten.* Ruth Beckermann Produktion, 2016. DVD. 89 minutes. Vienna: Hoanzl, 2017.

———. *Josephine Mutzenbacher.* Ruth Beckermann Produktion, 2022. DVD. 100 minutes. Vienna: Hoanzl, 2023.

———. *Waldheims Walzer.* Ruth Beckermann Produktion, 2018. 93 minutes. Vienna: Hoanzl, 2020.

Blümlinger, Christa. "Studien zur Bodenlosigkeit." In *Ruth Beckermann,* edited by Alexander Horwath and Michael Omasta, 60–66. Vienna: Synema, 2016.

Brunner, Andreas, ed. *Sex in Wien: Lust. Kontrolle. Ungehorsam.* Vienna: Metroverlag, 2016.

Haß, Ulrike. *Kraftfeld Chor.* Berlin: Theater der Zeit, 2020.

Horwath, Alexander, and Michael Omasta, eds. *Ruth Beckermann.* Vienna: Synema, 2016.

Landry, Olivia. *Movement and Performance in Berlin School Cinema.* Bloomington: Indiana University Press, 2018.

Lehmann, Hans-Thies. *Postdramatic Theatre.* Translated by Karen Jürs-Munby. New York: Routledge, 2006.

---

37 On the elements of postdramatic theater see Lehmann, *Postdramatic Theatre,* 68–106.

Leroy, Alice. "Celan, Bachmann, Beckermann: Korrespondenz der Geträumten." In *Ruth Beckermann*, edited by Alexander Horwath and Michael Omasta. 108–15. Vienna: Synema, 2016.

Rebhandl, Bert. "Das ewige Thema. 'Judenkind, Flüchtlingskind, Wirtschaftswunderkind': Die Identifikationen von Ruth Beckermann." In *Ruth Beckermann*, edited by Alexander Horwath and Michael Omasta. 7–33. Vienna: Synema, 2016.

Ruthner, Clemens. "Die nackte Kehrseite der Wiener Jahrhundertwende: Handreichungen für eine Mutzenbacher-Lektüre." In Anonymous, *Josephine Mutzenbacher oder Die Geschichte einer wienerischen Dirne von ihr selbst erzählt*. Edited by Clemens Ruthner, Melanie Strasser, and Matthias Schmidt, 379–402. Vienna: Sonderzahl, 2021.

Ruthner, Clemens, and Matthias Schmidt, ed. *Die Mutzenbacher: Lektüren und Kontexte eines Skandalromans*. Vienna: Sonderzahl, 2019.

Troller, Georg Stefan. "Filme machen in Wien." In *Ruth Beckermann*, edited by Alexander Horwath and Michael Omasta, 5–6. Vienna: Synema, 2016.

11: Aerial Aesthetics, Queer Intimacy, and the Politics of Repose in the Cinema of Nils Bökamp and Monika Treut

Ervin Malakaj

Q UEER GERMAN CINEMA in the aftermath of the 1960s and 70s cultural revolutions espoused what Alice A. Kuzniar describes as a cinematic "counterpolitics," variously deployed against what today might be called cisheterocapitalist violence burdening queer life.[1] Queer filmmakers of this era practiced a type of political cinema that turned to the documentation of structural violence against queer people and the expression of various forms of queer life in order to challenge dominant narratives about how to be in the world. On the basis of interviews with Stefanie Jordan, Bärbel Neubauer, and Matthias Müller, among others, Kuzniar established how the work of these filmmakers pursued a type of transformative spectatorship. Their queer cinematic practices position viewers to "reframe [their] desires and transform [themselves]."[2] Kuzniar turns to Jörg Fockele to expound this claim. Fockele, expressing a dislike of queer feel-good romances with a low threshold for political transformation, calls for a cinema featuring "outrageously queer characters who do totally abnormal things and make the audience wonder."[3] Such cinematic techniques of excess would stimulate among viewers reflection about their investment in the *status quo* and prompt them to consider other ways of being in the world.

Nils Bökamp's *You & I* (2014) and Monika Treut's *Von Mädchen und Pferden* (*Of Girls and Horses*, 2014) might at first sight appear to be restrained rearticulations of the earlier counterpolitical queer German cinema. The aesthetic-political principle underpinning their films is indeed less characterized by queer suffering and audience provocation than by rest and repose. The queer characters in these films turn away from their daily lives in the city to embrace the countryside, where they overcome

---

1 Alice A. Kuzniar, *The Queer German Cinema* (Stanford, CA: Stanford University Press, 2000), 258.
2 Kuzniar, *Queer German Cinema*, 264.
3 Kuzniar, *Queer German Cinema*, 264.

obstacles that burden queer relations. This is not to say, however, that Bökamp's and Treut's films are devoid of political transformation. Rather, they turn to a different configuration of political commitment than that familiar to the queer German cinema of the postwar generations. Favoring relational bonds that emerge from an opting out of normative rhythms of daily life, Bökamp and Treut pursue a cinematic mediation tactic that acknowledges queer struggle while also generating new strategies to overcome the burdens endemic to queer life under neoliberalism. The liberatory potential of their cinema then urgently speaks to queer life in the 2010s and 20s, which continues to be differentially burdened by the demands of the interplay between privatization and global capitalist production depending on intersectional struggles attendant to life for various queer subgroups.

You & I and *Von Mädchen und Pferden* indeed implicate viewers in a collective struggle for a better world. They do so through an aerial aesthetic unfolding along the mediation of natural landscapes and countryside soundscapes. The cinematographic and narrative procedures of their films subdue character development through a pronounced interest in human–human and human–nature relations. These are not, however, practices advancing an uncritical neo-*Heimatfilm* celebration of the German countryside, which fosters belonging. Both films indeed reject ethnonationalist enthusiasm for "German" cultural history. Instead, Bökamp and Treut pursue different politics with their cinema of repose. The cinematography foregrounding the landscapes and a soundtrack highlighting the gentle soundscapes of the countryside in their films frame figures variously "catching a breath" from the nonnurturing life they lead at home (in the city). The rhythm of such mediation practices attunes viewers to the characters' repose. It indeed stages moments in which viewers can breathe with the characters on screen. This collective breathing forms an intimate and messy bond between viewers and characters. Ultimately, as this chapter argues, this collective experience becomes a technology to apprehend the capacities of collective being in the world as a means to repudiate neoliberal structures of precarity that lay claim on characters' and viewers' lives.

Breathing as Strategy to Overcome Neoliberalism

Bökamp's and Treut's work is positioned in a broader cinematic tradition, which served as an important site for analyses about the conditions of life under neoliberalism. As Hester Baer admirably demonstrates, German filmmakers from the 1970s onward have variously turned their attention to the effects of the privatization and individualization of the planetary capitalist suprastructure. Through an analysis of films ranging from the 1970s to the early 2010s, Baer attends to individual "self-optimization, personal responsibility, and an entrepreneurial attitude" as means to apprehend neoliberalism's claim on individual lives.[4] Part of this method pertains to affect. Germany's cinema of neoliberalism archives the structures of feeling bad, which Ann Cvetkovich has described as the affective attunement to "the current state of political economy" under neoliberalism.[5] In this vein, Baer turns to the work of Lauren Berlant in order to expound how individualized and privatized struggles in global economies are based on a dangerous dynamic—namely, cruel optimism. This dynamic produces population-wide attachments to a liberalized self-realization discourse: in order to reach a good life, individuals have to work hard and keep trying (no matter the cost). As a structure of feeling under neoliberalism, cruel optimism thereby sponsors a gradual wearing down of populations.[6] In Baer's assessment, the German cinema of neoliberalism articulates cruel optimism's effects cinematographically.

While *You & I* and *Von Mädchen und Pferden* certainly index neoliberalism's burdens on queer life, the films are more than cultural depositories for the negative affect affiliated with life under neoliberalism. Isabell Lorey's work is an important point of departure in expounding this claim. For Lorey, neoliberalism's wearing down of populations has amplified precarization of life on a global scale. Importantly, precarization is "not an exception" but is indeed "the rule" under the neoliberal world order.[7] Here, contemporary economic and political systems do not provide the means by which populations can feel secure in the world. Rather, their operations are best characterized through an investment in managing and, indeed, administering insecurity among the most vulnerable.[8] Extensive labor in the form of competition for few resources effects a type of slow wearing down of populations actively demoralized by never-ending vulnerability. In Lorey's assessment, however, the sets of interlocking vectors of power burdening populations are not too vast to tackle. Their power is certainly severe enough to embolden the profit-driven state eager to extract value from populations. But "exodus and constituting"— i.e., a capacity to opt out at strategic points and regroup toward different potentialities—emerge as two strategies for the precarious to resist the biopolitical force of the state of insecurity.[9]

---

4   Hester Baer, *German Cinema in the Age of Neoliberalism* (Amsterdam: Amsterdam University Press, 2021), 12.

5   Ann Cvetkovich, *Depression: A Public Feeling* (Durham, NC: Duke University Press, 2012), 11.

6   Lauren Berlant, *Cruel Optimism* (Durham, NC: Duke University Press, 2011).

7   Isabell Lorey, *State of Insecurity*, trans. Aileen Derieg (London: Verso, 2015), 1.

8   Lorey, *State of Insecurity*, 51.

9   Lorey, *State of Insecurity*, 99.

Life suppressed is not affiliated with restriction of activity alone. Because the governability structures of neoliberalism dictate that life is a site for value extraction, Lorey notes that the precarization of populations facilitates the development of "new forms of living and new social relationships."[10] In this regard, those facing precarity are constantly accommodating the vicissitudes of unpredictable situations. The state, too, asks populations to regroup constantly, which is one of the characteristics of precarious life. However, at the site of contingency, populations asked to "re-constitute" themselves on the basis of the ongoing struggle to cope under the pressure of the state might also be able to embrace the moment of rupture: "in dealing with contingency, the possibility arises at the same time of being able to leave and start something new."[11] In the context of precarization, this means rejecting the individuation machine of neoliberalism. By turning to collectivity and relationality in the face of extreme pressure to optimize the body for extraction (a process that goes hand in hand with individuation), the precariat has a way to resist state governmentality.[12] Resistance here is less organized around large-scale events announcing revolutionary breakage from the state than as emerging from daily practices and experiences.

It is precisely the power of "everyday practices of resistance" theorized by Lorey that Bökamp's and Treut's films evoke through their aerial and respiratory aesthetic practices of repose. Maria Stehle and Beverly Weber have discussed what they describe as precarious intimacies along similar lines. Moments of intimacy in European cinema about forced displacement are both an indictment of European neoliberal border politics suppressing life and "a politically sustaining force."[13] Bökamp and Treut do not comment on the condition of forced displacement as such. But they do turn to quotidian practices such as breathing and the intimacy they afford in order to stimulate some sustenance to move through life while passively indicting the dominant world orders suppressing it.

In this regard, their turn to breath is not a straightforward renunciation of threat in favor of life. The filmmakers instead variously attend to what Jean-Thomas Tremblay's discussion of breathing has shown to be "evidence of vulnerability to violence" as well as "a resource for living" through crises.[14] Breathing means vitality. It is a driving force for life. But the planetary cluster of oppressive forces ranging from the vicissitudes of

10 Lorey, *State of Insecurity*, 104.
11 Lorey, *State of Insecurity*, 105.
12 Lorey, *State of Insecurity*, 111.
13 Maria Stehle and Beverly Weber, *Precarious Intimacies: The Politics of Touch in Contemporary Western European Cinema* (Evanston, IL: Northwestern University Press, 2020), 5.
14 Jean-Thomas Tremblay, *Breathing Aesthetics* (Durham, NC: Duke University Press, 2022), 8.

settler-colonial capitalism to its neoliberal iterations regularly quells life by suppressing breathing. Here, respiratory struggles are not evenly distributed but rather disproportionately affect those whose lives have been structurally and historically suppressed or taken on the basis of lived experience as informed by class, race, gender, and disability. In this regard, Tremblay attends to breathing as "an existential phenomenon or shared activity."[15] But the "uneven distribution of risk" affiliated with breathing under racializing, disabling, and otherwise hostile iterations of capitalism "renders unconvincing any conception of the breather as a universal subject."[16] As a differentially fragile process, then, breathing reminds each breather that even subtle pressures on breath have the capacity to suppress or end life and that this fragility is felt differently from person to person, community to community.

For Tremblay, media have been a venue in which the drama between vitality and death affiliated with breathing finds potent expression. Works of art that embrace breathing aesthetics do so in order to study the contours of threat that register not on the scale of a planetary event but within the intimacy of everyday life. Here, Tremblay offers "respiratory spectatorship" as an analytic category through which to identify and examine the media engagement procedures inherent in breathing aesthetics.[17] Respiratory spectatorship positions audiences to apprehend the fragility of breath and thereby remind them that breathing *is* vitality. Moreover, the recourse to the mechanisms of breath at the core of breathing aesthetics orients spectators. Such mediation even patterns their own breath. These rhythms attune viewers to the forces of life that might make living at times of crises bearable.

The intimate nature of cinematic breathing will be vital for the analysis of Treut's and Bökamp's films. Such cinematic intimacy gains in potency because, as Davina Quinlivan has shown, breathing "has the potential to shape our viewing experience."[18] Quinlivan turns to the example of Darth Vader in *Star Wars*, where the quality of breath indexes a character fragility important for the overall understanding of the film's narrative trajectory. Drawing on the scholarship of Vivian Sobchack and Laura U. Marks, whose work is vital in a line of inquiry pertaining to spectatorial intimacy in the engagement with media, Quinlivan posits that breathing in cinema attunes viewers to the delicate nature of the human body. In so doing, the cinematic mediation of breath prompts viewers to

---

15 Tremblay, *Breathing Aesthetics*, 13.
16 Tremblay, *Breathing Aesthetics*, 13.
17 Tremblay, *Breathing Aesthetics*, 59.
18 Davina Quinlivan, *The Place of Breath in Cinema* (Edinburgh: Edinburgh University Press, 2014), 6.

examine their own existence and reflect on their own mortality.[19] This is certainly the case in Bökamp's and Treut's films. Beyond this, however, their films also encourage a collectivity among characters and viewers through breathing that suspends the division between fiction and reality. It is within this moment of suspension that their politics of dreaming beyond neoliberalism become legible.

Journeying the Uckermark: Aesthetics of Repose in *You & I*

Nils Bökamp's *You & I* (2014) relays the events of a break its main characters take from their daily lives. Jonas (Eric Klotzsch), a photographer living in Berlin, plans a trip through the Uckermark, a region northeast of Berlin in the German state Brandenburg bordering Poland. In the aftermath of a breakup with his girlfriend, Jonas pursues the countryside trip to get away and gather material for a new photography project. Philip (George Taylor), a London-based former roommate and coworker, accompanies him and serves as a model. Initially, their relationship to one another is ambiguous. Flirtatious stares, nude swimming, and extensive excitement to be in one another's presence temper any idea that Jonas's prior investment in a heterosexual relationship casts him as straight. On their drive through the countryside, they pick up Boris (Michal Grabowski), a Polish hiker familiar with the region. Initially, Jonas appreciates Boris's knowledge of the terrain and invites him to join them on their trip. Philip's initial reservation about a third party interrupting the reunion between him and his old friend expires as soon as Boris makes advances on Philip. Following a sexual encounter between Boris and Philip, Jonas starts to feel left out and finally gives in to his desires for his longtime friend: the two kiss. In the aftermath of the kiss, they ask Boris to leave their party. The final scenes show Jonas and Philip assemble the photographs Jonas took during their trip for an exhibition. As they curate the exhibition, Jonas and Philip reminisce about their time travelling the Uckermark.

Even though the plot of *You & I* announces a dramatic tension, in particular with regard to Boris's status in the relational triangle, the film's narrative procedures and cinematography draw audience attention in another direction. Subdued dialogue, limited exposition, and slow plot progression temper character development in favor of a cinematic aesthetic that foregrounds the countryside. In this regard, it might be

19 See Vivian Sobchack, *The Address of the Eye: A Phenomenology of Film Experience* (Princeton, NJ: Princeton University Press, 1992); and Laura U. Marks, *Touch: Sensuous Theory and Multisensory Media* (Minneapolis: University of Minnesota Press, 2002).

tempting to read *You & I* as an example of the gay road movie genre with which it shares some qualities. Featuring an escape from city life with an emphasis on the close proximity to nature that the countryside affords, and usually affiliated with anti-queer relational burdens queer characters encounter on the countryside, the gay road movie, according to Ben Walters, "allows for the continual reinvention and rediscovery of the self."[20] Robert Lang's scholarship notes that this self-discovery component of the queer road movie ultimately imagines relational structures that reach beyond received heterosexual kinship models.[21] But *You & I* rejects a character development that would help viewers satisfactorily apprehend such a transformation through self-discovery. Jonas and Philip are together in the end, but what underpins that relation remains unaddressed. The film then pursues other interests. These interests are also not nestled in the anti-urbanism espoused by Scott Herring or related studies focusing on rural queer experience. Herring seeks to center the lives of rural queers and the systems of knowledge about the world they embrace, which have long stayed in the shadow of the sexual cultures of metropoles of the world.[22] *You & I* focuses on the title characters without any screen time for rural queers. Instead, the film's underinvestment in characterization actively draws viewers' attention to the settings the characters traverse and the sighs of relief variously foregrounded through cinematography.

Much of the film's "lightness" indeed stems from a cinematography foregrounding the terrains of the Uckermark and the characters' banter, play, and excitement the setting affords. Take, for instance, the sequence after Jonas and Philip leave Berlin. They find their way to a country road in the middle of the Uckermarck. The two characters are trying to make sense of the road and how to move on to their next location. Philip starts climbing on top of the van to get a better look at the area. Once on top, he looks ahead, his mouth is slightly open, and his brows slightly furrowed as a result of the physical activity that got him there. He breathes as the sunlight and the task at hand motivate a squint. Standing on top of the van, Philip notes they can get "there" (which remains unspecified) by taking a set of roads to which he points. Jonas joins him on top of the

20   Ben Walters, "Stranger Danger: Why Gay Characters and the Countryside Don't Mix," *Guardian*, February 20, 2014, https://www.theguardian.com/film/2014/feb/20/stranger-by-the-lake-films-gay-characters-tom-at-the-farm.

21   Robert Lang, "*My Own Private Idaho* and the New Queer Road Movies," in *The Road Movie Book*, ed. Steven Cohan and Ina Rae Hark (London: Routledge, 1997), 345–46.

22   Scott Herring, *Another Country: Queer Anti-Urbanism* (New York: New York University Press, 2010), 4. See also, Mary L. Gray, *Out in the Country: Youth, Media, and Queer Visibility in Rural America* (New York: New York University Press, 2009).

van, likewise preoccupied with the breathing that attends the activity. A medium shot of Philip pointing cuts to a close-up of the back of his and Jonas's heads with a small portion of the frame revealing a meadow. A cut to a low-angle long shot featuring the two characters on the van is accompanied by a transition in sound: their dialogue becomes no longer audible. Instead, the scene foregrounds the chirping of birds and buzzing of insects, alongside the rustling of the grass and the trees animated by wind. A gradually intensifying musical score accompanies the sounds of nature, which collectively serve as a sound bridge to a long shot of the van driving up a road. The camera is not stationary. Rather, a gentle destabilization of the shot afforded by a handheld camera aligns with the out-of-focus yet visibly moving grass leaves swinging in front of it as the van slowly makes its way across the horizon. This is a moment of calmness facilitated by the setting as well as by the sounds and cinematography. The characters are not lost in nature but rather give themselves over to the area and its qualities that soothe the senses. Their progressively stabilizing breath atop the van becomes the stuff of repose afforded by the moment apprehending their relation to the setting: their squints and furrowed brows transform into smiles. At the same time, the gentleness of the wind-filled horizon caresses the disposition of viewers apprehending the sequencing of these shots.

The next sequence features the two by a campfire conversing about Philip's disenchantment with life in London. An argument with a male figure, presumably his father, helped Philip decide to leave and visit Jonas. His family wants Philip to pursue a professional life as a real estate broker. For Philip the proposed path not only feels wrong but suppresses what he otherwise might describe as his vitality. Here, the neoliberal forces dictating life patterns (embodied in a familial figure exerting pressure to follow a particular professional path) seek to orient Philip. Sara Ahmed has termed such social forces "lines that direct us," articulating the disciplinary function of familial lineage policing by members of the familial network.[23] Philip rejects those lines and their enforcers by pursuing the trip with Jonas, who ultimately invites Philip to live with him in Berlin. In this regard, the off-the-road tracks the van follows in the previous scene embody a queer path which leads the characters away from the social infrastructures that burden them. Notably, Philip does not develop a new professional plan in the conversation by the campfire. Rather, the two make a sort of vacation pact with one another whereby an unspecific gesture assuages the anxieties of facing an uncertain future. Consequently, Jonas's invitation is less future-oriented than it serves the moment the two share, the apex of which is a comforting gesture from one person to the next.

---

23 Sara Ahmed, *Queer Phenomenology: Orientations, Objects, Others* (Durham, NC: Duke University Press, 2006), 16.

In this regard, the scene by the campfire extends the aesthetics of repose foregrounded through the cinematography of nature, its sounds, and the wind in the previous sequence. Jonas's promise grows out of the experience on this journey, the shared bond unfolding in a space far away from their daily lives. Here, in the midst of the Uckermark, both characters indulge in a sigh of relief conditioned by moments that afford them a disconnect from the routines of life long enough to serve as a form of intimacy between the two that reaches beyond but still stands in relation to whatever sexual or relational desires underpin their communion. This intimacy provides some sustenance to live in the aftermath of what for Philip and Jonas are life-suppressing relations. This sustenance begins with the trip itself (an opting out gesture) and regenerates with each breath they share amidst the natural landscape and countryside soundscape. Their relation to one another is conditioned by the liveliness, vitality, and activity made possible by the "room to breathe," unrestricted by the dramatic arc of life suppressed governing relations back home. This does not mean that the characters completely escape the sociability structures of neoliberalism as manifest in received relationship and life trajectories. Rather, the time away affords them a means to opt out of them temporarily to be in relation with one another and let that shared experience guide them from one moment to the next.

By denying a clear insight into characters' futures all the while calling audience attention to them, the film intensifies its earlier prompts for viewers to take a stock of what else patterns the moments of repose. Here, the sounds of the wind, the chirping of birds, the crackling of the fire, and other aerial, scent-oriented, and audial evidence of the archive collectively evoking the atmosphere of the countryside come to the fore. This character embeddedness in the countryside sensorium affects audiences. The mediated nature of the scents, sounds, and textures of, say, the grass on which the two sit or the feel of the water of the lake in which they swim, call for a sensual viewing experience. In this regard, engaging with the film's aerial aesthetics might prompt viewers to take a deep breath with characters apprehending the natural terrains of the Uckermark. The scene sequencing certainly produces a rhythm that transitions characters out of their daily lives into new terrains in which they have to negotiate new relational dynamics. Viewing *You & I* then also means giving oneself over to this rhythm, which again means breathing with the characters. The film may be positioned alongside films such as *Neubau* (Newbuild, 2020) and *Sturmland* (*Land of Storms*, 2014), which similarly turn to countryside aesthetics for repose.[24] Unlike those films, *You & I* (as well

---

24 See Kyle Frackman, "Slow Aesthetics, Fraught Intimacy, and Queer Time in the German Queer New Wave: *Sturmland* and *Neubau*," *Monatshefte* 114, no. 3 (2022): 448–69.

as *Von Mädchen und Pferden*), decidedly suppress character development and the prominence of a narrative arc structured around antiqueer conflict in order to foreground the aesthetics of repose as emanating from the countryside.

The breathing aesthetics of *You & I* are messy. Even as they embrace repose in order to demonstrate what other relations can emerge if characters opt out of the structures that fail to nurture them, they do not valorize the characters. The film's opening already announces Jonas's imperfections. His girlfriend, Julia, is only audible via the voice messages she leaves on the answering machine. Jonas's relational tentativeness as expressed in casual hookups over a long-term relationship she seeks all but hurts her. The fact that his tentativeness is an expression of his possibly repressed queerness that only flourishes in the time-space of the trip does not satisfactorily mitigate the fact that he mistreats her. Moreover, the abruptness with which Philip and Jonas cast Boris out of the relational triangle is discomforting. The rejection devastates Boris, who feels cheated of what could have been lasting relational physicality and communality.

The photography exhibit based on the images Jonas took during the trip, which Jonas and Philip collaboratively stage at the end of the film, proves instructive here. Boris features prominently in the exhibition. Philip and Jonas affix a large portrait of him with his name spelled out in large letters underneath the photograph. The portrait and other photographs from the trip frame the entire space. The two are shown seated next to each other in a medium shot at the end within this space, perhaps nostalgically thinking back to their time in the Uckermark. Even without access to their thoughts and emotions, or without attempts to decipher them from their gestures and expressions, the photographs tether the characters to the past experience their mediation indexes. The white bodies of two men together at the end possibly prefigure a homonormal life trajectory for the two, which hardly is the stuff of reaching beyond neoliberalism.[25] The film's transformative politics then most certainly do not reside in this ending. Instead, they reside in the experience of the countryside. More precisely, they reside in the shared breath that afforded the characters the means to momentarily break from trajectories that burden them and imagine other relations as made possible through shared breathing. The photography exhibition then undermines the film's ending in pointing back to a time of liberation from the normative trajectories of the type of life unfolding at the end. The time in the Uckermarck, which also includes moments such as that of Philip and Boris urinating

---

25 See Lisa Duggan, "The New Homonormativity: The Sexual Politics of Neoliberalism," *Materializing Democracy: Toward a Revitalized Cultural Politics*, ed. Russ Castronovo and Dana D. Nelson (Durham, NC: Duke University Press, 2002), 175–94.

on and thus decrying the ruin of Hermann Göring's residence Carinhall and any latent iterations of the ideologies of this time period, provides the casual renegotiation of relations that bear great potential. Over the course of the film, this potential gets lost in the iteration of the life the two characters pursue at the end. But their memory is enshrined in the photographs and offers the characters some guidance as they move forward. In so doing, they provide the same reminder for viewers that mediation might be the stuff of liberation.

Aerial Aesthetics and the Politics of Breathing in *Von Mädchen und Pferden*

Treut emerged from and shaped the contours of queer German cinema with films such as *Verführung: Die grausame Frau* (*Seduction: The Cruel Woman*, 1985), which she co-directed with Elfi Mikesch, and *Die Jungfrauenmaschine* (*Virgin Machine*, 1988).[26] These films, as well as others on which she worked throughout the 1990s, unabashedly explore lesbian desire, trans embodiment, and BDSM sexual and relational practices variously aligned with the counterpolitical cinematic aesthetic Kuzniar describes. *Von Mädchen und Pferden* then at the very least marks a departure from Treut's earlier work. Through its investment in spectatorial repose as conditioned by a version of the breathing aesthetics discussed in Bökamp's film, *Von Mädchen und Pferden* pursues a type of politics of opting out aligned with Lorey's theory of resistance to neoliberalism. Shared breath in the film emerges as a main strategy to reach beyond it.

In comparison to *You & I*, *Von Mädchen und Pferden* pursues a slightly more robust character development through what Heidi Schlipphacke has described as a mediation strategy that "traces the temporality of lesbian desire."[27] The sixteen-year-old Alex (Ceci Chuh) arrives at a North-German horse farm for an internship. Under the supervision of the horse trainer Nina (Vanida Karun), Alex tends to farm animals and helps out as needed. Her adoptive mother hopes that the work on the farm would help provide Alex with the structure she lacks at home, where she is said to have used and sold drugs. The farm becomes for Alex a last chance to find a better way to relate to the world. But the experience is far from a

---

26 Gerd Gemünden, Alice Kuzniar, and Klaus Phillips, "From *Taboo Parlor* to Porn and Passing: An Interview with Monika Treut," *Film Quarterly* 50, no. 3 (1997): 2. See also, Leanne Dawson and Monika Treut, "Same, Same but Different: Filmmakers and Hikers on the Globe and Create Globalization from Below," *Studies in European Cinema* 11, no. 3 (2015): 155–69.

27 Heidi Schlipphacke, "Lesbian Desire and the Jump Cut in Monika Treut's *Von Mädchen und Pferden*," *The Germanic Review* 97, no. 4 (2022): 366.

disciplining force that serves to conscript Alex back into the neoliberal order from which she failed out. When the teenage Kathy (Alissa Wilms) arrives for her summer vacation at the same farm, Alex quickly transitions from being suspicious of to being enamored by Kathy's kindness. The two bond as a result of a number of shared adventures. By the end of the film, Alex and Kathy even scheme how the two can stay together beyond their time at the farm. The teenage lesbian relationship kindled through their work with horses points to a hopeful, collective, interdependent, and lesbian-affirmative future for the two.

In a reflection about the making of *Von Mädchen und Pferden*, Monika Treut confesses that with the film she indulged in her own "teenage fascination with horses."[28] Acknowledging what might appear to be a cliché trope in a film where dikes literally surround the main setting of the farm as a tongue-in-cheek acknowledgement about the playfulness of the mediation techniques, she also treats the genre's affordances seriously. "I wanted to get away from the noise of city life, away from computer screens and the overflow of information back to experiencing the communication with animals, with horses."[29] Such a turn to the countryside is captured through various cinematographic practices that give detailed access to the natural sensorium of the setting through close-ups and extreme long shots. Take, for instance, the scene in which Nina takes Kathy on a ride through the area surrounding the farm. The shot begins with an over-the-shoulder shot of Alex, who stands out of focus in the foreground as Nina and Kathy are shown in an extreme long shot riding away (see Fig. 11.1). The sequence of shots that follows features the two riding through the area, foregrounding the sounds of the galloping horses, the wind, their laughter, and other sounds of nature. One long shot from the sequence features another paved road. They enter from screen right. The lower segment of the frame features long grass and bushes while the top segment shows sheep. As Nina and Kathy cut through the image, riding their horses, the bleating of the sheep is audible. This bleating almost harmonizes with the sound of the wind hitting the blades of the grass to form the soundscape the two characters (and, by extension, the audience) experience. A few shots later, the two stop by the Rickelsbüller Koog for the first lines of dialogue in the sequence. In a long shot showing the two in the foreground and the koog in the background, Nina relays to Kathy the area's history. The koog, located near the Danish border, is a

---

28 Treut evokes the idea that the material for the film draws on a longstanding trope of lesbian and girl culture linked to equestrianism. Monika Treut, "Director Monika Treut Talks about Making 'Of Girls and Horses,'" *IndieWire*, June 25, 2015, https://www.indiewire.com/2015/06/director-monika-treut-talks-about-making-of-girls-and-horses-215024/.

29 Treut, "Director Monika Treut Talks."

northernmost point of Germany. The dikes that engulf the water structure are a nature reserve today. The area owes its name to a village, which was flooded in 1615 and still lies beneath the water. Nina notes that this community, which once occupied this area, is gone, but that its haunted memory survives. Allegedly, the Rickelsbüll town church bells ring regularly at night if one listens closely. Kathy inquires whether Nina has ever heard the bells. Nina responds humorously that she believes she imagined hearing them. As the silence between the two permeates the scene, it is as though both characters attune to the setting and attempt to discern any possible sound the mentioned bells could make. Instead, what comes to the fore is the sound of the landscape again: birds, the blades of the grass, the wind, and their horses.

If the farm is remote from the city in that it takes Alex an additional car ride from the bus stop at which she was waiting for Nina to pick her up, then Rickelsbüll is even further removed. Through its haunting absence, Rickelsbüll is then also a remoteness only accessible through attunement. Listening to its sounds could pull one back in time, as it were, a gesture further intensified by its isolated location. As the characters apprehend the spectacle of the koog, viewers follow suit. They are embedded within the mediated sensorium of the location. When Nina's story prompts Kathy (and her) to listen in again, viewers align with the request. As Nina and Kathy stare out over the koog listening, they breathe the air made palpable to audiences through the sounds of the setting. As they relish the moment and take a breath apprehending the spectacle, so too do viewers sutured into the sensorium of the landscape serialized throughout the sequence. The story of the bell might be a mournful image of a venue long gone, but Nina's account of it also affords a break from the rhythms of daily life the characters face at home. In so doing, the repose of the moment extends to viewers as well.

The farm's appeal indeed revolves around the fact that it is a venue affording characters access to specified rhythms. Tending to the farmland, its animals, and the relational structures there gives those conscripted into its dynamic a sense of a community dependent on collectivity and careful human-non-human relations rather than individuality. This becomes clearly legible in the manner in which Alex comes to relate to the farm. Her pouty willfulness in the beginning betrays a set of resentments she nurtures about much of the hostility to which she was exposed at home. Over the course of her stay at the farm, she experiences and comes to appreciate a new rhythm. Alex's first lesson in dressage is a case in point. In a sequence at a horse stable at the farm, Nina instructs Alex on the dynamic of working with horses. The crux of the lesson pertains to what Nina calls body language. Instead of forcefully yanking the horse, which is disturbing and possibly violent, Nina instructs Alex to gently guide the horse by means of a controlled pull

Figure 11.1. Alex looks on as Nina and Kathy ride off a paved road into the meadow toward the Rickelsbüller Koog in *Von Mädchen und Pferden* (dir. Monika Treut, 2014).

forceful enough to suggest which direction she wants the horse to move but not too forceful to upset the horse. When Alex tries walking with a horse for the first time, Nina notes that the energy between her and the horse is palpable for the horse. And one way to get the horse to stop is to decelerate energy by relaxing one's body and by taking a deep breath. In this scene, Alex learns how to communicate with horses through gentle body language previously unfamiliar to her. In a follow-up scene Alex is shown on the horse, riding it with her eyes closed and guiding the horse entirely through her body language.

On the farm, the characters access different ways of being, moving, thinking, communicating, and caring. This does not mean that the setting is somehow purely an escapist fantasy in which the troubles of the broader world do not register. On the contrary, the film reminds viewers about the political realities governing German life under neoliberalism. Critics have discussed the scenes in which Nina listens to a radio broadcast. For instance, Sonja M. Schulz views the news report about Angela Merkel's now famed insistence on an "Alternativlosigkeit" (state without alternative) for Germany during the time of the European debt crisis of 2009 as the material realities of a world in trouble seeping into the idyll of the farm.[30] Schultz likewise notes that Nina's antidepressants—hidden

---

30 The slogan harkens back to Margaret Thatcher's austerity politics as UK prime minister. Sonja M. Schultz, "Von Mädchen und Pferden—Kritik," *critic.de*, November 20, 2014, https://www.critic.de/film/von-maedchen-und-pferden-6840/.

in a small box in her room on the farm—signal the troubles about which viewers receive no additional information but which point to challenges. Moreover, viewers receive access through close-ups to Alex's struggles, which register in cutting scars on her arms. Merkel's political austerity discourse advocating individual responsibility and capital growth through hard work meets its consequences as inscribed in the worn-down body-minds of Nina and Alex.

Even if the film shows Nina in a seemingly happy relationship with her girlfriend in Hamburg, life there is not nurturing on its own. She is instead drawn to the farm and the experiences it affords. The rhythms of working with horses and the community there position her differently in the world than she is in the city. She lets go of her life at home when she is "up north" and leans into the experiences conditioned by the setting. As viewers trace the sensorium of the countryside alongside an alternative manner by which to relate to the environment through sense (e.g., Alex's dressage lesson), they come to share the repose from the daily life at home that the characters feel. Viewers relish in the vast landscapes the characters traverse, share in on their adventure, and gradually attune to the opting out of normative rhythms by pursuing the experience at the farm. This attunement takes place via recourse to cinematography and narrative, but also through the experiential spectatorship elicited by the film's formal strategies. The extensive shots of characters traversing nature or sequences mainly featuring horses in the field prompt a soothing spectatorial engagement whereby the dramatic arc of the plot (as was the case with *You & I*) becomes secondary to the cinematography relaying the countryside sensorium. Seeing nature, hearing animals, and observing the wind move grass elicit a deep breath from viewers enamored by the experience of apprehending the elongated spectacle of repose mediated through film. We breathe with the characters, savoring the moment of rupture from our daily lives that the film permits us to experience.

This does not mean we breathe the same air as the fictional characters do in the film. Rather, it means that our breathing might synchronize with the rhythms of life mediated on screen. As the characters make their way through one experience to another, embracing the soothing rhythm of life on the farm as an antidote to what transpires in the city, viewers likewise engage in an intimate alignment with a break. Here, breathing is not an event akin to large-scale political phenomena such as the financial crisis cited in the radio broadcast. Turning to breathing as the quintessence of living and attuning to its patterns instead becomes a manner of opting out via recourse to quotidian experience. In this regard, it is important that *Von Mädchen und Pferden* ends with a sequence in which Nina, Alex, and Kathy are cast as interdependent. Nina helps Kathy and Alex climb a horse to take a ride together. Kathy offers Alex a job opportunity in Berlin to help out with her horse. Kathy and Alex smile as Nina answers her girlfriend's call by noting the beauty of the vast seaside, insisting the latter must join the group the next time they are in the area. As a result, Nina's call implies long-term connections. The multiple interconnected bonds among the characters are thus not only undeniably affirmative in that the cross-generational lesbian support structure nurtures lesbian relationality, but also evidence a communality that provides the characters some sustenance to move forward and not feel alone in their struggles.

Like *You & I*, *Von Mädchen und Pferden* announces a return to life structures outside of the time-space of the farm and its natural surroundings. This return compromises the transformative potential of the ending in that the normative orders endemic to life "at home" might undo what the experience of collective breathing helped bring about. But as was the case with *You & I*, *Von Mädchen und Pferden* calls attention to the powerful potential of the cinematic mediation of breath as a means to enact quotidian resistance to neoliberalism. It prompts viewers to study people and their differentiated lives and imagine better ways to be in community with one another.

Bibliography

Ahmed, Sara. *Queer Phenomenology: Orientations, Objects, Others*. Durham, NC: Duke University Press, 2006.

Baer, Hester. *German Cinema in the Age of Neoliberalism*. Amsterdam: Amsterdam University Press, 2021.

Berlant, Lauren. *Cruel Optimism*. Durham, NC: Duke University Press, 2011.

Cvetkovich, Ann. *Depression: A Public Feeling*. Durham, NC: Duke University Press, 2012.

Dawson, Leanne, and Monika Treut. "Same, Same but Different: Filmmakers and Hikers on the Globe and Create Globalization from Below." *Studies in European Cinema* 11, no. 3 (2015): 155–69.

Duggan, Lisa. "The New Homonormativity: The Sexual Politics of Neoliberalism." In *Materializing Democracy: Toward a Revitalized Cultural Politics*, edited by Russ Castronovo and Dana D. Nelson, 175–94. Durham, NC: Duke University Press, 2002.

Frackman, Kyle. "Slow Aesthetics, Fraught Intimacy, and Queer Time in the German Queer New Wave: *Sturmland* and *Neubau*." *Monatshefte* 114, no. 3 (2022): 448–69.

Gemünden, Gerd, Alice Kuzniar, and Klaus Phillips. "From *Taboo Parlor* to Porn and Passing: An Interview with Monika Treut." *Film Quarterly* 50, no. 3 (1997): 2–12.

Gray, Mary L. *Out in the Country: Youth, Media, and Queer Visibility in Rural America*. New York: New York University Press, 2009.

Herring, Scott. *Another Country: Queer Anti-Urbanism*. New York: New York University Press, 2010.

Kuzniar, Alice A. *The Queer German Cinema*. Stanford, CA: Stanford University Press, 2000.

Lang, Robert. "*My Own Private Idaho* and the New Queer Road Movies." In *The Road Movie Book*, edited by Steven Cohan and Ina Rae Hark, 330–48. London: Routledge, 1997.

Lorey, Isabell. *State of Insecurity*. Translated by Aileen Derieg. London: Verso, 2015.

Marks, Laura U. *Touch: Sensuous Theory and Multisensory Media*. Minneapolis: University of Minnesota Press, 2002.

Quinlivan, Davina. *The Place of Breath in Cinema*. Edinburgh: Edinburgh University Press, 2014.

Schlipphacke, Heidi. "Lesbian Desire and the Jump Cut in Monika Treut's *Von Mädchen und Pferden*." *The Germanic Review* 97, no. 4 (2022): 359–74.

Schultz, Sonja M. "Von Mädchen und Pferden—Kritik." *critic.de*, November 20, 2014. https://www.critic.de/film/von-maedchen-und-pferden-6840/.

Sobchack, Vivian. *The Address of the Eye: A Phenomenology of Film Experience*. Princeton, NJ: Princeton University Press, 1992.

Stehle, Maria, and Beverly Weber. *Precarious Intimacies: The Politics of Touch in Contemporary Western European Cinema*. Evanston, IL: Northwestern University Press, 2020.

Tremblay, Jean-Thomas. *Breathing Aesthetics*. Durham, NC: Duke University Press, 2022.

Treut, Monika. "Director Monika Treut Talks about Making 'Of Girls and Horses.'" *IndieWire*, June 25, 2015. https://www.indiewire.com/2015/06/director-monika-treut-talks-about-making-of-girls-and-horses-215024/.

Walters, Ben. "Stranger Danger: Why Gay Characters and the Countryside Don't Mix." *Guardian*, February 20, 2014. https://www.theguardian.com/film/2014/feb/20/stranger-by-the-lake-films-gay-characters-tom-at-the-farm.

12: Between Observational Detachment and Affective Attachment: The Posthumanist Pedagogy of *Herr Bachmann und seine Klasse* (2021)

Angelica Fenner

AS A GENRE, the education documentary has gained mainstream status at film festivals and on streaming platforms over the past twenty years. Disparate in style and aesthetics, and lacking a common set of formal and narrative conventions, feature-length films such as *To Be and To Have* (France, 2002), *Boys of Baraka* (US, 2005), *Please Vote for Me* (China, 2007), *Girl Rising* (US, 2013), *Our People Will Be Healed* (Canada, 2017), and docu-series such as *Harrow: A Very British School* (UK, 2013) are instead thematically bound by their common object of study: primary school education and its relationship to the production of social and political subjectivity. Institutions around the world are struggling to determine what core skills and values will best equip their pupils to keep pace with the massive socio-economic and political changes afoot in the twenty-first century. Education documentaries have focalized these transformations in the context of specific settings, attending to the ways in which localized human agents who inhabit the roles of student, educator, or administrator define possibilities for social relation.

In settler nations such as Canada, the United States, and Australia, as well as in European nations undergoing multicultural transformations, one of the central stakes in curriculum and pedagogy derives from what Charles Taylor has called "the politics of recognition." The demand for recognition is predicated upon, in his words, "the supposed links between recognition and identity, where this latter term designates something like a person's understanding of who they are, of their fundamental defining characteristics as a human being."[1] Identity, in turn, is presupposed to be partially shaped by (mis)recognition, such that individuals and groups may alternately thrive or suffer damage through the enabling or

---

1 Charles Taylor, *Multiculturalism: Examining the Politics of Recognition*, ed. Amy Gutmann (Princeton, NJ: Princeton University Press, 1994), 25.

distorting images projected back upon them. Indeed, "Nonrecognition or misrecognition," Taylor maintains, "can inflict harm, can be a form of oppression, imprisoning someone in a false, distorted, and reduced mode of being."[2] Within a liberal democracy, the political recognition of cultural particularity of all members of the society is also congruent with a certain form of universalism that regards respect for diverse cultures as ultimately also serving the basic interest of society at large. Whether referencing groups or individuals, the politics of recognition have navigated between legitimizing differences of identity through the latter's claim to something close to ontological status, and alternately, advancing claims to performativity and elective choice. While the former is vulnerable to anti-essentialist critique, the latter may risk valorizing the autonomous subject at the price of acknowledging a common good that binds members of society and shapes our practices and values. Filmmakers have reached for the camera to investigate schools that are navigating these twenty-first century transitions, casting an attentive gaze upon teacher–student dynamics, pedagogical innovation, and strategic infrastructural transformations that may factor into students' individual successes and failures. Such stories, although generally one-off projects in the career of a director, can be quite compelling. Their circumstantial specificity belies a wider, almost universal fascination among spectators, triggering personal recollections of the vulnerabilities of childhood and youth that were made memorable for all the right or wrong reasons during classroom encounters with peers and teachers.

Rethinking Political Agency

Yet a blind spot that remains in existing debates around multiculturalism originates from this singular focus on resolving cultural differences, which privileges the social life and well-being of the human animal over other ontologies while also presuming the former to be determined independently of the latter. The posthuman turn in political and cultural theory has challenged this anthropocentrism, one also grounded in an understanding of individuated human agency as driving the terms of subjectivity, political action, and community. The innovative German documentary, *Herr Bachmann und seine Klasse* (Mr. Bachmann and His Class), which premiered at the 2020 Berlinale and secured that year's Silver Bear, brings into focus the contours of an alternative vision for political agency in contemporary Germany—a vision that has precipitated lively debate in the public sphere. The adjective "hopeful" appears to be the most consistently evoked descriptor among reviewers across disparate media platforms, who lauded the film's capacity to bring into detailed focus the

2   Taylor, *Multiculturalism*, 25.

extraordinary range of relationalities that a multicultural classroom can navigate when differences are bridged through recognition also of commonalities. Drawing from discourses of new materialism, including the conceptual terrain of actor-network theory, I shall argue that the film's overall audiovisual montage within an uncompromising running time of 217 minutes exemplifies a form of "tentacular thinking" that subtly reconceives difference and the social beyond the frame of what Donna Haraway refers to as "human only histories" to encompass a network of evolving nature-cultural relations.[3]

Shot over a period of six months at the Georg Büchner Gesamtschule (elementary school) in the small industrial city of Stadtallendorf, not far from Marburg, Hessen, the film tracks a critical juncture both for a sixth-grade class and for their primary teacher, Dieter Bachmann. The latter was scheduled to retire at the close of that school year in 2017, at which time the students were also to confront their options for the next level of schooling. These twin timelines enable a degree of narrative conjuncture in a documentary otherwise shot and structured in observational format to let images and interactions speak for themselves and capture microdynamics among students and teacher. The project has been compared by numerous reviewers to US documentarian Frederick Wiseman's approach as memorialized in *High School* (1968), an approach motivated less by a pre-conceived thesis than by one that emerges from the extended experience of shooting and then reviewing the resulting footage itself.[4] As Wiseman himself maintains of his so-called "reality fictions": "My work as editor, like that of the writer of a fiction film, is to try to figure out what is going on in the sequence I am watching on the editing machine. What is the significance of the words people use, the relevance of tone or changes of tone, pauses, interruptions, verbal associations, the movement of eyes, hands, and legs."[5] Yet where Wiseman's films aim to be "about institutions and the people who represent them, as well as those the institutions are supposed to serve,"[6] Reinhold Vorschneider's cinematography and director Maria Speth's ensuing editing of over two hundred hours of footage across a three-year period conspire to subtly

---

3   Donna Haraway, *Staying with the Trouble: Making Kin in the Chthulucene* (Durham, NC: Duke University Press, 2016), 30–31.

4   For example, Christian Blauvelt, "Frederick Wiseman-Inspired Doc is one of the Year's Most Hopeful Movies," *IndieWire*, March 21, 2021, https://www.indiewire.com/criticism/movies/mr-bachmann-and-his-class-review-1234620484/; A. O. Scott, "Learning from the Best," *New York Times*, February 20, 2021, https://www.nytimes.com/2022/02/20/movies/mr-bachmann-and-his-class-review.html.

5   Barry Keith Grant, ed., *Five Films by Frederick Wiseman* (Berkeley: University of California Press, 2006), xi.

6   Grant, *Five Films*, 3.

enable new posthumanist understandings of sociality to become visible and palpable.

The film's intervention gains further significance through the cultural diversity of the students at Georg Büchner Gesamtschule, who hail from twelve different countries, and Stadtallendorf's distinctive history of both industrial labor and diversity. An area with roughly 21,500 inhabitants, it acquired city rights only in 1960 and was previously known simply as Allendorf, the site of a secret munitions center during World War II, one of the largest in all of Europe. In two separate facilities together encompassing about six kilometers camouflaged by forest, the armament firms WASAG (Westfälisch-Anhaltische Sprengstoff Aktien-Gesellschaft; or Westphalian and Anhalt Explosives Limited) and DAG (Deutsche Angestellten-Gewerkschaft; or German Independent Trade Union) manufactured munitions and explosives throughout the war without detection. Forced labor was drawn both from German and foreign populations, including prisoners of war and concentration camp inmates, housed in barracks in the surrounding area. The industrial site was also one of the most environmentally contaminated in Germany following the war, with the excavation of 154 tons of chemicals, including three tons of TNT, declared complete in 2006. Today, the small city is home to thriving factories of a different nature, including Ferrero (confectionary), Fritz Winter (engine foundry), and Hoppe (lock manufacture), among others. Bare life has been superseded by a diversity of populations seeking employment, including newer arrivals from across eastern and southern Europe, some of whose children feature in Dieter Bachmann's class. In this layering of the human, inhuman, and nonhuman across the last century, the soil and plant life also underwent transformations, from being the repository of chemical degradation to ensuing environmental rehabilitation.

Stadtallendorf as Assemblage

Speth's film title privileges Herr Bachmann and his students as key nodes in the network that is Stadtallendorf, understood as at once a city, historical legacy, and geographical milieu. In turn, film editing enacts a "reassembling of the social" by embedding the teaching and learning taking place inside the Gesamtschule within a larger framework of human laboring, nonhuman activities, and machinic processes traversing the city's built spaces and surrounding landscapes.[7] In this, it draws pointers from an earlier non-narrative city-film, *Berlin, Symphonie einer Großstadt* (*Berlin, Symphony of a City*, dir. Walter Ruttmann, 1927),

---

7   Bruno Latour, *Reassembling the Social: An Introduction to Actor-Network-Theory* (Oxford: Oxford University Press, 2007).

which casts a similarly ethnographic gaze upon the waxing and waning flows of movement across its vast urban topography, employing montage to bind a highly diversified population of urban dwellers, human and creaturely, with the industrial technologies that drive production and commerce in the metropolis. Ruttmann's theme of "the city awakens" is echoed in *Herr Bachmann*'s opening sequence with glimpses of the dawn of a new day in Stadtallendorf. The initial shot of a dark street at night pierced only by rows of streetlamps replicates the "black box" of theatrical screenings. As a motorcycle approaches, the whine of its motor amplifies along with the light of its headlamp, before receding in volume as the unseen driver's left blinker signals a turn out of the frame. Match cutting to a full moon draws parallels between natural and artificial illumination before returning to the street, where more cars pass and banter is dimly audible among shadowy human figures purposefully crossing the street. Despite increasing traffic volume, a rhythmic thumping reminiscent of a heartbeat emanates from the depths of the darkness, suggestive of the broader scale of (in)human industrial activity already, or still, in progress nearby, even before dawn. There is a cut to a dark store front whose interior lights flicker on moments later, revealing rows of bread and other baked goods behind the glass window, followed by an interior view of hands shaping bread dough into the circular "simit" typically sold in Turkish bakeries. The reverse shot of the dark-haired baker assembling these on a cookie sheet is overlaid by the sound bridge of a muezzin's call to prayer, anticipating the ensuing exterior view of a mosque silhouetted against the pre-dawn sky, its lit interior evidence of morning rituals in progress.

When this montage of establishing shots shifts to the interior of a moving bus, the spectator adopts the mobilized gaze of a traveler just behind the bus driver, surveying the terrain visible beyond the windshield. An arrowed street sign points the way to DAG, whose industrial chimneys are visible on the shadowy horizon while a woman's pre-recorded voice elegantly announces "Nächster Halt: Stadtallendorf, Moldorstrasse" (Next Stop: Stadtallendorf, Moldor Street). A stream of small bodies in colorful jackets and parkas lumbering in the darkness become recognizable as children queuing up at the bus stop. A reverse shot on the face of a child seated inside registers her recognition of peers audible off-screen as they clamber into the bus. Daylight is fast approaching by the time the bus deposits its passengers at the school to disembark and join the stream of young people trudging up the slope toward the entrance amid a cacophony of chatter.

In microcosm, the opening sequence maps the coordinates of the film's worldmaking: children and adults alike are on the move to take up their designated places in the larger constellation of social relations, interconnected through their roles as parent, child, student, teacher, and sundry occupations by means of which adults featured in the film earn their living and strive daily to shape better opportunities for their children. They do so in a region whose topography—forests, fields, and built environments alike—are not merely backdrop, they are the material support and substance permeating this human activity and enabling and inspiring it in dynamic intra-action. German society, this film will assert in affirmative terms, is a palimpsest on which past triumph and tribulation have been inscribed, and from which suffering and succor alike have been drawn and continue to be renegotiated. Stadtallendorf is an ecosystem and Herr Bachmann's classroom is one terrain on which its human inhabitants assemble anew with each waking day, converging along paths both well-traveled and renegotiated amid a wider cast of nonhuman actants.

Performativity and the Classroom

This performativity is disclosed as the film's enunciative terms when students shuffle quietly into an empty classroom, flipping the upturned chairs from rows of desks onto the floor to take their usual seats. A man's voice off-screen announces that because Ilknur (one of his "home room" students) spoke, everyone should exit and do a retake of their entry into the classroom. Reassuring them that it is a good opportunity to practice, the voice calls out "Second Try," as on a film set, and they trudge back into the room in complete silence. Once all are seated, he encourages the sleepy entourage to lay their heads on their desks and rest a few minutes longer while someone leaves the room to retrieve Stefi, the one missing student. This suspension of action functions like the pause just prior to a curtain rising on a theatrical performance, with a reverse shot introducing Dieter Bachmann presiding over the scene from his desk at the front of the classroom. If his toque, hoodie, and jeans appear indistinguishable from the attire of some of his adolescent students, the ensuing hours of screentime will reveal how the man with the gray, scruffy beard and gravelly voice nonetheless elicits the respect of those under his tutelage through his strikingly jovial and unflappable demeanor.

The ensuing film title projected in white text on black screen makes explicit that we have just encountered the heart of the film's observational project: Mr. Bachmann and his class. Bachmann's teaching philosophy, indeed, what I would suggest is also the film's worldview, now comes into closer focus as the viewer is catapulted *in medias res*, as it were, with a discussion that locates us in what Bruno Latour terms "the parliament of things," a world in which the dichotomy of subject and object, whose axes also include nature and society, is overturned. In this parliament it is acknowledged that the humanism deemed distinctive of modernity is actually predicated upon false classificatory assumptions, for "we have never been modern," politically or culturally.[8] Instead, we continually sociologize phenomena such that humans and nonhumans alike shift between recognition as subjects—e.g., actants—to objects attributed the status of "mere" matter, perhaps significant to the extent that this matter acquires use-value.

The class lesson revolves around a fictional story of seemingly universal significance: unrequited desire and affection, including the ways in which people—and, it would seem in this case, nonhuman things, too—strive to solicit attention from those that remain indifferent to their supplications. It is a story that, in the course of the lesson, gains relevance for the politics of recognition in a multicultural society and for addressing class and social differences, as well as processes of reification under late capitalism. The actants in the story, however, are not people but an electric guitar and a table. According to Bachmann's recounting of the tale in dialogue with the students, when the table hears the amazing sounds that this new guitar is able to produce, it twirls on one leg and seeks in every way possible to gain the attention of the shiny black instrument, so alluring when compared to the old and battered red guitar perched nearby. A glimpse of a guitar in the film frame's depth of field and the neck of another visible in the foreground renders unclear whether this plot derives from a published story whose protagonists merely happen to coincide with the ubiquitous contents of the classroom, or was collectively improvised by the class, or is even the result of Bachmann's own inspired authorship. Regardless, in the ensuing hours of the film, guitars will prove significant actants within Bachmann's classroom.

As the lesson continues, Bachmann repeatedly verifies students' comprehension of key vocabulary, since many are navigating German as a second language. When he prompts one student, Ayman, to elaborate the nature of the table's frustrated desire, this leads to his disclosure of confusion between the homonyms "Frust" und "Frost." Language, too, is a place of stumbling, if not over literal roadblocks, then figurative ones that dislocate their interlocutors within a semantic field of crossed signals, mixed messages, and false friends. Another student suggests that the table is discouraged because the guitar does not "see" him or acknowledge his presence. The connection to the invisibilization of social minorities and newer arrivals in German society could not be clearer: as a result of their lagging capacity to master the discourse by which they must represent themselves and are viewed by others—also exemplified in Ayman's fractured comprehension—they lose traction in language and, by extension, fail to gain a foothold socially and economically.

8   Bruno Latour, *We Have Never Been Modern* (Cambridge, MA: Harvard University Press, 1993), 6.

What begins as a harmless story of desire between nonhuman objects also transforms through its collective interpretation into an object lesson of another sort, one addressing gendered libidinal economies in the age of late capitalism. As a provocation, Bachmann speculates how the table might best overcome its frustration. Suppose it hit the jackpot and won the lottery and could now buy the guitar anything the latter desired? Ayman responds by projecting a masculine identity ("der Tisch," after all), speculating that now that the table has the means, "he" will surely succeed in winning "her" ("die Gitarre") attention and they will meet at night in the empty classroom. But, he adds, maybe she will only exploit him for his money. Spinning the story further, Bachmann asks, what could the table buy her that might impress her next? Lucia suggests flowers, but Bachmann points out that these might not be especially useful to a guitar, unless drawn decoratively on its side as adornment. And while she might enjoy those on the first day, what of thereafter, when these presents are no longer enough to hold her attention? Two boys then propose respectively an amplifier and strings, inspiring Bachmann to embellish further by suggesting "so richtig AC/DC brutalo Saiten . . . die schreien richtig wenn man die spielt" (real, brutal AC/DC strings . . . that really wail when played).

While the boys fidget almost unceasingly during this particular lesson, the girls are nonplussed and seem to grasp more effectively the conceptual terrain and overarching moral of the story, congruent with a common understanding that language development in girls tends to advance more quickly than in boys. When Bachmann asks the class what one can glean from this tale, Lucia volunteers: "Die Gitarre beutet ihn aus. Das ist auch verständlich, das kommt auch in mehreren Beziehungen vor" (The guitar is exploiting the table. That makes sense and happens in a lot of relationships); while Karoline beside her slowly and thoughtfully adds, "dass die Geschichte wirklich fast wie im wahren Leben ist. Dass manche Leute nicht ersthaft über etwas nachdenken, sondern sich bestechen lassen" (This is a story truly drawn from real life. Some people don't think things through, and instead they let themselves be manipulated). Bringing the discussion to a close, Bachmann adds: "Ja, für Schönheit, Geld, Aussehen. Ich könnt's nicht besser sagen" (That's right: by beauty, money, appearances. I couldn't have said it any better). In essence, the discussion has illuminated a tale of cruel optimism, a condition Lauren Berlant first memorialized by defining it as "when something you desire is actually an obstacle to your flourishing."[9] It is pertinent to students on the threshold of making important choices about their future educational or vocational training, which entails reconciling their own desires

---

9   Lauren Berlant, *Cruel Optimism* (Durham, NC: Duke University Press, 2011), 1.

and aspirations with the pressures and expectations of their parents and a wider social circle, as well as pragmatic consideration for their abilities and available resources.

Musical Mediations

During the classroom break, the spectator is privy to an over-the-shoulder close-up of Tim's lined notebook, in which he has just completed a drawing of a red table with a white guitar draped over it, enacting a monstrous coupling or merging of indeterminate desiring "quasi-objects," in Latour's formulation, whose agential status in this instance is acquired through human fantasy that undoes the partition of subject/object.[10] Tim's idle doodling confirms a quintessential quality evidenced in the ensuing hours of footage: namely, that the guitar as musical instrument comprises a significant component of Dieter Bachmann's pedagogy. He is clearly a passionate musician for whom playing is so engrained that it would be reductive to attribute to it the status of mere hobby or one form of expressivity among others. The guitar has become central to how he apprehends the world, a veritable sensory organ mediating his engagement with the students. In this, Bachmann embodies Latour's hybrid. Playing the guitar and singing lyrics that conjure fragments of narrativized desire, he communicates snippets of knowledge while establishing relational ties with and among his pupils by modulating their affects.

In a later conversation with the sculpture teacher, he notes that, in his experience, when students observe someone following their passion, it also inspires their own. At the same time, Bachmann says: "Wenn ich die Gitarre nehme, und was kompliziertes spiele, das animiert die gar nicht. Es geht hier wie bei jedem Lernenden auch darum, dass jeder den eigenen Weg findet" (If I reach for my guitar to play something really complicated, that doesn't animate them at all. It's ultimately about each person finding their own path forward). Having come of age in the immediate wake of '68, Bachmann's classroom persona is one of deconstructing authority while nonetheless upholding structures and boundaries that can productively guide students forward in accordance with both their desires and their abilities. He explains that he had studied sociology in the 1970s and then was not sure what to do with his degree, so he undertook teacher training to qualify for the state exams, primarily to gain a secure income with which to support his two children. He resisted school as an institution for a long time, even up to the present, thinking he really did not belong there. He did not want to fall into the common trap of trying to hold the students' attention just in order to preserve his own authority.

10 Latour, *We Have Never Been Modern*, 10–11.

We can frame this anti-authoritarian stance, one that troubles traditional demarcations in the teacher–pupil dynamic, as a deconstruction of agency overall, such that "action is overtaken . . . it is dislocated. . . . is borrowed, distributed, suggested, influenced, dominated, betrayed, translated."[11] This also entails redefinition of what learning is and how it is animated. Bachmann continues: "Irgendwann habe ich gespürt, dass die Dressur, die ich da täglich auch machen muss, nur noch etwa zehn Prozent der Arbeit ist, und der Rest schon irgendwie sinnvoll ist" (At some point, I realized that a regimented focus on the curriculum that I was tasked to inculcate is really only about ten percent of the job and everything in between ends up being meaningful in its own way). At stake, it seems, is a pedagogy that modulates between instrumental reason, entailing mastering discrete rules (of grammar, math, etc.) toward purposeful ends, and what one could summate as "play" (e.g., juggling, playing musical instruments, drawing, also casual banter and socializing). The latter, Bachmann has concluded, is more central to his pupils' developmental advancement than one might expect—in his estimation, 90 percent of the job. Play, as we know, can certainly entail rules and entrainment of motor skills, but there also remains space for imagination and improvisation that engage the right hemisphere of the brain. These require being present to the moment and also co-present to others in coordinated action, both initiating and responding. In this regard, play is inherently relational, emphasizing prehension, that is, interactions that entails perception but not necessarily cognition.

We witness this most vividly in scenes of music making, which flow seamlessly into or from curricular activities. In one example, Bachmann has been guiding the class through a literary lesson about Till Eulenspiegel, the Lower Saxon protagonist of a collection of picaresque tales first assembled as a sixteenth-century chapbook and redacted and condensed in sundry formats over the centuries. The stories recount the predominantly scatological puns and pranks this trickster plays, which expose hypocrisies, vice, greed, and foolishness in the townspeople he encounters. They achieve this by rethinking the relationship between signifier, signified, and referent, to bring forth the material (and corporeal) foundation underpinning social discourse. As J. W. Goethe observed, "alle Hauptspässe des Buches beruhen darauf, dass alle Menschen figürlich sprechen und Eulenspiegel es eigentlich nimmt" (all the chief jests of the book depend on this: that everybody speaks figuratively and Eulenspiegel takes it literally).[12] As such, the choice of text seems of an accord with the

---

11   Latour, *Reassembling the Social*, 43, 46.
12   Quoted in Paul Oppenheimer, trans. and ed., *Till Eulenspiegel: His Adventures* (Oxford: Oxford University Press, 1995), xxii.

students' overall initiation into the polysemy of language, which especially confounds—but also intrigues—many second-language learners.

When Bachmann also tells the class that he feels especially drawn to this literary figure and his special relationship to children, we may surmise that he identifies with Eulenspiegel's rebel status. He then offers to play a song he was inspired to compose about Eulenspiegel, inviting Ilknur to the keyboard and Stefi to backup vocals. As they run through the opening chord progression, the tone in the room palpably shifts from one of focused textual analysis, primarily teacher-centered, to one of sensorial attunement in which students begin to physically assemble themselves in whatever way inspiration overtakes them. A series of cutaways reveal Cengizhan juggling tennis balls in rhythm with the strumming guitar, while Hassan has taken his place at the drum set and waits attentively for the opening lead-in to Bachmann's lyrics. Raimundo sits with a Djembe, Jaime beside him plucks at a bass guitar, and Ferhan stands at the sideboard with a hot water kettle in hand while distributing tea leaves into a collection of mugs. The musical remediation of the Eulenspiegel legend functions not unlike a Greek chorus; students each in their own way continue integrating its content at sensorial and affective levels.

As sound art, music lacks the concrete and fixed contours associated with a sculpture or a painting framed on the wall; temporally based, its emanations surround players and listeners as long as the performance lasts, implicating them in a collective experience. In the words of musicologist Antoine Hennion, music "must surge into existence or, rather, it is made to surge into existence and, for this to happen, work is needed on the part of the musicians as well as the audience."[13] In performance, the composition, improvisation, or even just a simple chord progression is made "to surge anew as its transmitted elements are reactivated and its score is brought back to life."[14] Its performativity originates in "what the audience—and also the artist—do in order to make the work surge within them."[15] There is thus still "learning" taking place in Bachmann's classroom during this musical remediation, but there is an individual corporeal dimension to this "doing" among both those listening and those performing: "There can only be music if the audience (which can be constituted of an individual or a group) tune into it with their bodies, interests and emotions. And there can only be a performance if a reciprocal

13 Antoine Hennion, "Playing, Performing, Listening: Making Music—or Making Music Art?," trans. Margaret Rigaud-Drayton, in *Popular Music Matters*, ed. Lee Marshall, Dave Laing, and Simon Frith (New York: Routledge, 2016), 166.
14 Hennion, "Playing, Performing, Listening," 167.
15 Hennion, "Playing, Performing, Listening," 170.

movement is established, as each grasps—or takes hold of—the other."[16] In this, a musical piece—here, Bachmann's simple lyrics rendered in a melodic form guided by chord progression—then becomes a relation, "that is, 'a work in progress' which does not exist until those who perceive it have appropriated it, relived it, and made it their own. This notion also emphasises the role of the body, although this time the focus is on the body of the listeners."[17]

As such, music can be understood as "a heterogeneous tissue," something at once human, material, corporeal, and collective that "hangs together."[18] Effectively, music is mediation: in its immediacy and nonlinearity of unforeseeable effects on players and listeners alike it "has come to be theorised as a non-organic and non-linear constellation of mediations, or an assemblage," one entangled with technologies, things, and material practices.[19] Bachmann's implementation of music unsettles inherited boundaries between otherwise differentiated or "purified" domains traditionally defining classroom learning. It disrupts teacher-directed hierarchies to enable a degree of lateral interaction among the students and teacher, although Bachmann often takes on lead vocals or lead guitar in the footage included. For the most part, players follow standard chord progressions and otherwise improvise without reading sheet music, instead attuned to one another through ongoing auditory cues and exchanges of glances, nods of the head, and other gestures.

Neoliberalism and Affective Labor

Bachmann has become skilled in implementing his guitar, and music more generally, to channel affects in circumstances where they threaten to impede communication, as when students are insecure or cannot adequately express themselves in German. In one notable instance, the guitar participates in a provisional assemblage helping Stefi and her father past an awkward moment in a key parent–teacher consultation, one at which the teacher is supposed to elaborate on the student's performance and potentials and explore both the parent's and the student's vision for future training. Bachmann tells Stefi's father, a burly man in a leather jacket who works as a baker, that Stefi will be ready for the Realschule in the next year. The father turns to his daughter and asks her in Bulgarian to explain his hesitations about this, which appear to be grounded in a

16 Hennion, "Playing, Performing, Listening," 167–68.
17 Hennion, "Playing, Performing, Listening," 171.
18 Antoine Hennion, "From ANT to Pragmatism: A Journey with Bruno Latour at the CSI," *New Literary History* 47, no. 2 (2016): 292.
19 Georgina Born and Andrew Barry, "Music, Mediation Theories and Actor Network Theory," *Contemporary Music Review* 37, nos. 5–6 (2018): 448.

concern that her language skills are not sufficient. Stefi instead explains to her teacher that they need to stay in Germany for gainful employment because there is "keine Chance" (no chance) of economic progress in Bulgaria. When Bachmann directly asks Stefi what she would like to eventually do with her life, she begins to assert that she would like to sing and become a doctor. Her father's body language in the two-shot betrays his disbelief at this aspiration, shaking his head and emphatically repeating "no chance" to her in Bulgarian and then to Bachmann in German. The teacher deftly bypasses the father's pessimism, asserting "am liebsten möchte sie Sängerin werden" (she'd love to become a singer), which elicits another frustrated "keine Chance" from her father. One might speculate that his pessimism is conditioned by wanting to protect his daughter from the cruel optimism that may very well have defined his own "relation of attachment to compromised conditions of possibility" back in Bulgaria or upon arrival in Germany, predicated upon fantasies of "the good life" Berlant maintains have traditionally encompassed "upward mobility, job security, political and social equality, and livable, durable intimacy."[20]

Yet when Bachmann reaches for his guitar and begins to strum a few chords, inviting Stefi to sing along, her father laughs and leans back in his chair, easing off with his negative prognosis. He remarks something in Bulgarian to Stefi, who translates for Bachmann: "Mein Vater hat gesagt, dass Sie ein guter . . ." (My father says you is a good, eh . . .), and while searching for the right words seizes upon the phrase, "emotionaler Lehrer ist" (emotional teacher). However clumsy, the descriptor gets at the heart of Bachmann's skill in putting students (and parents) at ease through the mediations of music. His music enables relation, while reversing the direction of agency—the musical instrument "works," it makes things happen, it transforms users and listeners to forge relations that would not otherwise exist. Bachmann also flips the guitar to serve as darbuka and begins to tap a Middle Eastern rhythm while encouraging Stefi to sing a Turkish song she apparently sang previously in class. Her father visibly squirms in his seat, his face beaming with pride at his daughter's voice even as he struggles to maintain the serious comportment he probably feels the meeting should occasion, and perhaps self-conscious of the watchful gaze of the documentary camera. Although Bachmann cannot resolve for Stefi and her father the decisions she confronts, he draws on the guitar as an affordance that can modulate affective attachments where they threaten to impede communication, for example, when students (and here, parents) cannot adequately articulate their desires in their non-native language and, by extension, claim agency in relation with others. In this instance, the recourse to music lends Stefi a voice with which to

20 Berlant, *Cruel Optimism*, 24, 3.

Figure 12.1. Modulating affective attachments through musical mediation in Maria Speth's *Herr Bachmann und seine Klasse* (2021).

gain recognition in the eyes of her father, and perhaps win his confidence in her capacity to eventually thrive in this new culture.

What Bachmann does in the classroom can be framed as "affective labor," but given the multiple ways that term has been implemented in the critique of neoliberalism, its significance in this instance begs clarification. The term generally identifies the increasingly immaterial nature of labor under post-Fordism, in which the service sector—be it call centers, flight attendants, food service, or healthcare—has expanded to accommodate a Toyotist model of industrial production calibrated to shifting markets. This has entailed management of the collection and flow of consumer information (e.g., the attention economy) and the affects of those whose consumer practices drive demand. Of course, Fordist production is still very much with us, having spread to redefine the earlier agricultural model with the same efficiency, technology, and waged labor. Indeed, in industrialized nations all of society has become a factory, including the education sector tasked not only to disseminate knowledge but also to cultivate citizens able to manage their own affects and presumably those of others as well.

Speth's film makes these equivalencies clear through its editing while also bringing a different twist to our understanding of affective labor. For example, the Christmas party, in which students perform for visiting parents and siblings, is immediately followed by an abrupt parallel edit to the cacophony of automated machinery in the Fritz Winter foundry running noisily and overseen by workers in blue coveralls. The startling cut renders these institutions in Stadtallendorf not merely adjacent to one another but interconnected—students in the school are the offspring of the workers in the plant, and both operations forge a larger network of "flattened ontologies" encompassing production both of "goods" and of social subjects, entangled in ways that level (or diminish) the hierarchies between industrial laborers and teachers, between students and teachers, between children and their parents, and indeed, between things and humans, and nonhuman and human actants.[21] The scenes of automated production in the plant also exemplify "the creativity of nonhuman entities and processes" paralleling that of students performing music at the Christmas party.[22] At stake, then, is less a reification of people and things than a dynamic assemblage, in which the "object" is understood as "a knot of relations, as a tissue of associations and links that test each other and are more or less resistant, this object in turn transforms the collectives that take hold of it."[23]

As a schoolteacher, Bachmann indisputably participates in what Michael Hardt defines as "the production and reproduction of affects, in those networks of culture and communication," where "collective subjectivities and sociality are produced."[24] While these are certainly prone to exploitation by capital, and by the state as an arm of capital, Bachmann's labors may more properly be understood as what feminist theory and anthropology refer to as "kin work," the labor invested in rearing and nurturing children, whether in immediate family or throughout the community. When he jokingly remarks to Hassan during class, "Du weißt, ich hab' dich ja schon adoptiert" (You know I've already adopted you), this underscores Bachmann's importance as figure of identification for especially the more vulnerable male students, including Aydan and Cengizhan, seeking approbation from a member of the target culture and a foothold in this new society. That Bachmann's affection thereby participates more in the economy of the gift than that of capital is exemplified by the new guitar that Hassan receives as a birthday gift at a class retreat toward the close of the school year. If affection is "instrumentalized" here, it is in the literal sense, vividly exemplified in the scene of students seated around an evening bonfire. Bachmann is playing Hassan's new guitar, or rather fingering the frets with his left hand while Hassan seated to his right strums the strings with his right hand. Their coordination of movements to produce harmonious sounds literalizes the way in which the instrument has mediated, indeed, produced their filial relationship as much it has the (acoustic) circulation of affects in the classroom.

The guitar is again framed as actant the following week, when Bachmann learns that Hassan has brought his new guitar to school. The teacher exhorts his student to just leave the new one at home saying:

21 Manuel DeLanda, *Intensive Science and Virtual Philosophy* (London: Continuum, 2002), 47.

22 Georgina Born, "On Nonhuman Sound—Sound as Relation" in *Sound Objects*, ed. James Steintrager and Rey Chow (Durham, NC: Duke University Press, 2019), 190.

23 Hennion, "From ANT to Pragmatism," 293.

24 Michael Hardt, "Affective Labor," *boundary 2* 26, no. 2 (1999): 96.

"Die neue Gitarre hat mit mir gesprochen und erklärt, dass sie nie wieder in die Schule will" (The new guitar had a chat with me and told me she never wants to return to the school). His words recall both the "die alte, zerdepperte Gitarre" (the old, battered guitar) and the shiny new one that were central protagonists of the cautionary tale discussed in the first classroom scene, but they also offer a different twist. Certainly, Hassan's attachment to guitar playing, like all attachments according to Berlant, is fundamentally optimistic "if we describe optimism as the force that moves you out of yourself and into the world in order to bring you closer to that satisfying *something* that you cannot generate on your own but sense in the wake of a person, a way of life, an object, project, concept, or scene."[25] It becomes cruel when "the very pleasures of being inside a relation have become sustaining regardless of the content of the relation, such that a person or world finds itself bound to a situation of profound threat that is, at the same time, profoundly confirming."[26] Bachmann's words to Hassan seek to forestall precisely this vicious cycle to which his pupil could otherwise succumb. The retiring teacher may himself identify with the older guitar, ceding in retirement ground to a younger generation coming of age and staking a claim in the new society emerging in Germany. As such, it is important that Hassan not grow too attached to his current relationship with Bachmann, metonymized by the older guitar, and instead go forth with the gifted one to forge future attachments that "surge" anew.

Bachmann's altruism, like that of other teachers witnessed in Georg Büchner Gesamtschule's classrooms, exceeds the connotations of instrumentalized affective labor under late capitalism to become a labor of love and of "biopower from below."[27] What Speth's documentary thus offers are utopian glimpses into the potentials for enacting belonging in society as multi-sited and dispersed across activities whose valorization is not wed exclusively to their commodity value. Whether (wage) laboring, learning, playing music, consuming a meal, resting, or being, the gerund verb form underscores the ongoing transformation of ontologies and relations within the entangled networks encompassing the Georg Büchner Gesamtschule and Stadtallendorf as a whole. Capturing Mr. Bachmann's classroom on film serves not solely to memorialize these transformative pedagogies but also to extend their reach, inspiring present and future audiences across Germany and around the world.

---

25 Berlant, *Cruel Optimism*, 2.
26 Berlant, *Cruel Optimism*, 2.
27 Hardt, "Affective Labor," 100.

Bibliography

Berlant, Lauren. *Cruel Optimism*. Durham, NC: Duke University Press, 2011.

Blauvelt, Christian. "Frederick Wiseman-Inspired Doc is one of the Year's Most Hopeful Movies." *IndieWire*, March 21, 2021. https://www.indiewire.com/criticism/movies/mrbachmann-and-his-class-review-1234620484/

Born, Georgina. "On Nonhuman Sound—Sound as Relation." In *Sound Objects*, edited by James Steintrager and Rey Chow, 185–207. Durham, NC: Duke University Press, 2019.

Born, Georgina, and Andrew Barry. "Music, Mediation Theories and Actor Network Theory." *Contemporary Music Review* 37, nos. 5–6 (2018): 443–87.

DeLanda, Manuel. *Intensive Science and Virtual Philosophy*. London: Continuum, 2002.

Grant, Barry Keith. *Five Films by Frederick Wiseman*. Berkeley: University of California Press, 2006.

Guttmann, Amy. "Introduction." In *Multiculturalism: Examining the Politics of Recognition*, edited by Amy Guttmann, 3–24. Princeton, NJ: Princeton University Press, 1994.

Haraway, Donna. *Staying with the Trouble: Making Kin in the Chthulucene*. Durham, NC: Duke University Press, 2016.

Hardt, Michael. "Affective Labor." *boundary 2* 26, no. 2 (1999): 89–100.

Hennion, Antoine. "From ANT to Pragmatism: A Journey with Bruno Latour at the CSI." *New Literary History* 47, no. 2 (2016): 289–308.

———. "Playing, Performing, Listening: Making Music—or Making Music Act?" Translated by Margaret Rigaud-Drayton. In *Popular Music Matters*, edited by Lee Marshall, Dave Laing, and Simon Frith, 165–79. New York: Routledge, 2016.

Latour, Bruno. *Reassembling the Social: An Introduction to Actor-Network-Theory*. Oxford: Oxford University Press, 2007.

———. *We Have Never Been Modern*. Cambridge: Harvard University Press, 1993.

Oppenheimer, Paul, trans. and ed. *Till Eulenspiegel: His Adventures*. Oxford: Oxford University Press, 1995.

Scott, A. O., "Learning from the Best." *New York Times*, February 20, 2021. https://www.nytimes.com/2022/02/20/movies/mr-bachmann-and-his-class-review.html.

Taylor, Charles. *Multiculturalism: Examining the Politics of Recognition*. Edited by Amy Gutmann. Princeton, NJ: Princeton University, 1994.

Contributors

HESTER BAER is Professor of German and Cinema and Media studies at the University of Maryland, where she also serves as a core faculty member in the comparative literature program and an affiliate in the Harriet Tubman Department of Women, Gender, and Sexuality Studies. Baer is the author of *German Cinema in the Age of Neoliberalism* (Amsterdam University Press, 2021). Her monograph on West Germany's first feminist film, Ula Stöckl's *The Cat Has Nine Lives* (1968), appeared in the series German Film Classics (Camden House, 2022). Her co-edited volume *Babylon Berlin, German Visual Spectacle, and Global Media Culture* is forthcoming (Bloomsbury, 2024). Baer currently serves as co-editor of the *German Quarterly.*

CLAUDIA BREGER is the Villard Professor of German and Comparative Literature at Columbia University, New York. Her scholarship focuses on modern and contemporary culture, with emphases on film, performance, literature, and literary and cultural theory, as well as the intersections of gender, sexuality, and race in a transnational framework. Her more recent book publications include *An Aesthetics of Narrative Performance: Transnational Theater, Literature and Film in Contemporary Germany* (Ohio State University Press, 2012) and *Making Worlds: Affect and Collectivity in Contemporary European Cinema* (Columbia University Press, 2020).

ANGELICA FENNER is Associate Professor of German and Cinema Studies at the University of Toronto. Her scholarship on feature and documentary film engages intersectional feminism, affect and material culture, and the environmental humanities. She is author of *Race Under Reconstruction in German Cinema* (University of Toronto Press, 2011) and co-editor of *The Autobiographical Turn in German Documentary and Experimental Film* (Camden, 2014), as well of special issues of *Transit* (2014), *Camera Obscura* (2018), *and Feminist German Studies* (2022).

RANDALL HALLE is the Klaus W. Jonas Professor of German Film and Cultural Studies at the University of Pittsburgh. He directs the European Studies Center/EU Center of Excellence and the Critical European Culture Studies PhD program. His essays have appeared in journals

238 ♦ Notes on the Contributors

such as *EuropeNow, Screen, The International Journal of Cultural Policy, New German Critique, Camera Obscura, German Quarterly*, and *Film-Philosophy*. He is the author of, among others, *German Film after Germany: Toward a Transnational Aesthetic* (University of Illinois Press, 2008), *The Europeanization of Cinema: Interzones and Imaginative Communities* (University of Illinois Press, 2014), and *Visual Alterity: Seeing Difference in Cinema* (University of Illinois Press, 2021).

Lutz Koepnick is the Max Kade Foundation Chair in German Studies and Professor of Cinema and Media Arts at Vanderbilt University. He has published widely on film, media theory, and visual culture. His most recent monographs include *On Slowness: Toward An Aesthetic of the Contemporary* (Columbia University Press, 2014), *The Long Take: Art, Cinema and the Wondrous* (University of Minnesota Press, 2017), *Michael Bay: World Cinema in the Age of Populism* (University of Illinois Press, 2018), and *Resonant Matter: Sound, Art, and the Promise of Hospitality* (Bloomsbury, 2021).

Angelos Koutsourakis is Associate Professor in Film and Cultural Studies at the University of Leeds. He is author of *Rethinking Brechtian Film Theory and Cinema* (Edinburgh University Press, 2018), and of *Politics as Form in Lars von Trier: A Post-Brechtian Reading* (Bloomsbury, 2013). He has also co-edited *Cinema of Crisis: Film and Contemporary Europe* (Edinburgh University Press, 2020) and *The Cinema of Theo Angelopoulos* (Edinburgh University Press, 2015).

Olivia Landry is Associate Professor of German at Virginia Commonwealth University. She is author of *Movement and Performance in Berlin School Cinema* (Indiana University Press, 2019), *Theatre of Anger: Radical Transnational Performance in Contemporary Berlin* (University of Toronto Press, 2020), and the *A Decolonizing Ear: Documentary Film Disrupts the Archive* (University of Toronto Press, 2022).

Richard Langston is Professor of German at the University of North Carolina, Chapel Hill. His research crisscrosses twentieth- and twenty-first-century German literature, film, television and the visual and performing arts. His recent books include *Difference and Orientation: An Alexander Kluge Reader* (Cornell University Press, 2019), *Dark Matter: A Guide to Alexander Kluge & Oskar Negt* (Verso Books, 2020), and *The Patriot* (Camden House, 2021).

Priscilla Layne is Professor of German and Adjunct Associate Professor of African and Afro-American Studies at the University of North Carolina, Chapel Hill. She is author of *White Rebels in Black: German*

Appropriation of Black Popular Culture (University of Michigan Press, 2018) and co-editor of the volume *Minority Discourses in Germany since 1990* (Berghahn, 2022).

ERVIN MALAKAJ is Associate Professor of German Studies, affiliate faculty in the graduate programs in Film Studies, and affiliate faculty in the Centre for European Studies at the University of British Columbia. His scholarship and teaching interests lie in nineteenth-century literary cultures, German film studies, queer studies, and critical approaches to the university. He is the author of *Anders als die Andern* (McGill-Queen's University Press, 2023), and co-editor of *Slapstick: An Interdisciplinary Companion* (De Gruyter, 2021) as well as *Market Strategies and German Literature in the Long Nineteenth Century* (De Gruyter, 2020).

GOZDE NAIBOGLU is Lecturer in Film Studies in the Department of History of Art and Film at The University of Leicester. Her research focuses on contemporary European cinema with an emphasis on German and Turkish German cinemas, film theory and philosophy. She is author of numerous articles and the monograph *Post-Unification Turkish German Cinema: Work, Globalisation and Politics Beyond Representation* (Palgrave Macmillan, 2018).

FATIMA NAQVI is Elias W. Leavenworth Professor of German and Film and Media Studies at Yale University; she is currently the chair of FMS. Her recent books include *How We Learn Where We Live: Thomas Bernhard, Architecture, and Bildung* (Northwestern University Press, 2016), *The White Ribbon* (Camden House, 2020), the co-edited volume *Michael Haneke: Interviews* (University of Mississippi Press, 2020), and *The Insulted Landscape: Postwar German Culture 1960–1995* (Königshausen und Neumann, 2021). She is currently working on a book on the topic of "Fremdschämen."

Index

Abdulwahed, Khaled, 5, 8, 83, 96
abjection, 5, 61, 85, 87, 88–89, 91, 95–98; abjecting apparatus, 83, 85–91; "cinema of abjection" (Elsaesser), 60; juridico-political, 8, 115
actants (human and nonhuman), 224, 225, 233
activism, 5, 61 163, 186; feminist, 143, 146–47
Actor-Network Theory, 171, 221
Adorno, Theodor W., 130, 167; and Horkheimer, 122, 128, 129, 137
Adorno, Theodor W., works by: *Dialectics of Enlightenment* (with Max Horkheimer), 122
aesthetics, 5, 167, 169, 170n35, 177, 219; of abjection, 51, 61; anti-naturalist, 164; of breathing (aerial), 206, 210–12; citational, 9, 152; of the crowd, 163; feminist, 145, 151–53; forensic aesthetics, 79; political, 7, 11, 162; pop, 152, 155; of repose, 210. *See also* breath
affect, 6, 10, 53, 63, 123, 167, 233; affective attachments, 231; affective attunement, 204; affective labor, 230, 232, 234; affectless acting, 25–26; collective, 91; negative, 51, 64, 204; political, 166, 191–92; studies, 5
Again, 8, 70, 74, 76, 81
agency, 43, 152, 157, 171–72, 228, 231; political, 220
ahumanism, 62, 63
Akın, Fatih, 52–61, 70–73, 77; filmography, 50–51
Alberti, Irene von, 122–23, 144–45, 146n6, 148, 151–52, 155–56, 164
Alzakout, Amel, 83–84, 86, 89–90, 93, 95, 97–98

anachronism, 7, 15, 22, 47
Anderson, Benedict, 87. *See also* community
antifascist novel, 7, 15, 19, 29
anti-Semitism, 192
archaeology, 93, 132, 135
archive, 9, 77–78, 105, 114, 134, 165, 210; archival newsreel, 105, 133, 194; "archive effect" (Baron), 113; "archive of noise" (Doane), 113; digital, 135; film archives, 138
Arendt, Hannah, 69, 80–81, 167
art cinema, 4, 70, 127, 169
assemblage, 22, 53, 167, 176–77, 222, 230, 233; aesthetic, 169; Deleuze on, 166
assembly, 163, 172, 176–77; cinematic, 168, 170, 173; political, 164, 166, 167, 171, 175. *See also* crowd
asylum, 15, 69, 97; asylum seekers, 17, 40–42, 44, 115
attachment, 11, 34, 44, 204, 231, 234
attunement, 185, 204, 214, 216, 229
Aus dem Nichts, 7–8, 50–55, 58–62, 64, 70–72, 77, 81
Austria, 6, 183, 187, 189, 193
authoritarianism, 1, 7, 165
autobiographical turn, 9, 95

Bachmann, Ingeborg, 184, 186–87, 189–93
Bataille, Georgé, 17, 19, 163n5
Beckermann, Ruth, 10, 183–88, 193–200
Benjamin, Walter, 21, 27, 28, 128
Berardi, Franco "Bifo," 51; on futurability, 51, 61
Berlant, Lauren, 38, 44–45, 47, 204, 226, 231, 234

242 ♦ INDEX

Berlant, Lauren, works by: *Cruel Optimism*, 39
Berlin, 37, 39, 46–48, 83, 90, 97, 98, 129, 133, 151–52; West Berlin, 147
Berlin Alexanderplatz (Qurbani), 7, 32, 35, 42, 46n22; as novel (Döblin), 7, 32–34, 36, 39, 40n18, 41–45, 48; as series (Fassbinder), 33–34, 40n18, 43
Berlin School, 4, 7, 9, 133, 145, 152, 155n31, 164, 185
Berlinale, 91, 126, 220
Blackness, 34; anti-Blackness, 48, 63
Blutsauger (*Bloodsuckers*), 1, 3, 122–23
Bökamp, Nils, 202–3, 205–7, 212
Bonitzer, Pascal, 104, 106, 108–10
borders, 8, 15, 22–23, 36, 47, 70, 84–89, 92, 169; as apparatus, 85, 90–91, 93, 95, 97, 98; border politics, 205; European border zone, 8, 87, 89, 90, 94
breath, 11, 203, 206, 212, 214, 216–17; breathing, 10, 88, 205–7, 209–10, 216; collective breathing, 203, 217
Brecht, Bertolt, 19, 122, 128–30, 136–37; Brechtianism, 16, 124, 164, 176
Brexit, 87
Brown, Wendy, 2
Brückner, Jutta, 10, 148
Butler, Judith, 163, 166–67, 171–72

capitalism, 1, 2, 6, 127–28; global, 175; late, 149, 154, 225–26, 234; neoliberal, 7; settler-colonial, 206
care, 6, 103; self-care, 130, 136
catharsis, 57–59, 142
Celan, Paul, 184, 186, 187, 189–93
Chion, Michel, 104, 109–10
chorus, 10, 183–87, 191–93, 195, 197–99; Greek, 229
cinefeminism, 144–45, 147–50, 152, 159; definition of (Rich), 146. *See also* feminism

cinematography, 73, 203, 207–10, 216
citizenship, 7, 19, 21, 34, 42, 48, 145; universal (Tamás), 16, 23, 27
class, 16–17, 33–34, 145, 206, 225; creative, 151; working, 7, 164
climate catastrophe, 2
collectivity, 3, 5, 6, 10, 11, 145, 205, 207; the collective, 173, 177; collective action, 3, 116; collective experience, 203, 229; political, 176
color, 11, 25, 55, 153, 155
comedy, 10, 166, 173–75, 177; comic mode, 170; ecology, 170; humor, 123, 137; political, 1. *See also* New German Discourse Comedy
communication, 69, 89, 106, 192, 213, 230–31, 233
communism, 1, 170, 174
community, 6, 10, 18, 87–88, 183, 191, 199, 206, 216–17, 220; civic, 16; communal memory, 194; European community, 85, 89; imaginative, 89, 98, 185–86; Nazi, 191; non-community, 87; sense of, 124, 214
consent, 184, 197–98
contemporaneity, 134, 138; the contemporary, 70, 105, 123, 128–29, 134; "the ethos of" (Rabinow), 136–37; present times, 27, 34, 124, 126, 143
corporeality, 199
counter-publics, 138
countryside, 11, 202–3, 207–8, 210–11, 213, 216
COVID-19 pandemic, 2, 87
crisis, 2, 5, 35n12, 73, 164, 185; debt, 215–16; as standstill, 3. *See also* refugee crisis
critique, 19, 29, 33, 85, 102, 131, 134, 136, 145–46, 149, 167, 169, 220; of neoliberalism, 152, 232; political, 25, 151, 157–58
crowd, 103, 162–63, 167, 173, 194, 197; proletarian, 1; theory of, 166

INDEX ◆ 243

Das melancholische Mädchen (*Aren't You Happy?*), 9, 122, 142–45, 148–55, 157
dehumanization, 45
Deleuze, Gilles, 10, 124n11, 128, 162–65, 168–69; Deleuzian sense, 61, 166
democracy, 2, 27, 132, 220; "fake democracy" (Radlmaier), 174
Der lange Sommer der Theorie (*The Long Summer of Theory*), 10, 122, 144–46, 148, 151–52, 155–57, 159
Derrida, Jacques, 96–97, 112
DFFB (German Film and Television Academy in Berlin), 9, 126, 134–36
Die Geträumten (*The Dreamed Ones*), 10, 183–84, 186–90, 192–93, 198
digital culture, 154, 156
disability, 7, 33, 130, 206
discourse theater, 9, 121–22. *See also* Pollesch, René
Doane, Mary Ann, 104, 108, 110, 113. *See also* voice-over
Documenta, 69, 70, 77–78, 90
documentary, 8, 9, 10, 92, 95, 103–10, 114–16, 134, 145, 151, 185, 221, 235; camera, 231; education, 219; experimental, 85; filmmaking, 102, 183–84, 200; footage, 194; force, 177; observational, 11; quasi, 196; realism, 76, 134n54; studies, 114; voice, 116
Duggan, Lisa, 1

editing, 73, 91–92, 172, 176, 189, 192, 194, 197, 221–22, 232; process, 42; techniques, 168
essay film, 5, 187; essay filmmaker, 93
ethnonationalism, 32; ethnonationalist enthusiasm, 203
EUROMED, 89
European Union (EU), 86–87
evidence, 52–53, 57, 69, 76–82, 93, 95, 110, 70, 205; audial, 210; forensic, 8, 71–73, 76, 80

"exclusionary incorporation" (Partridge), 35

fabulation, 10, 168–69, 177
fairy tale, 21, 166, 193
fantasy, 3, 38, 47, 63, 176–78, 215, 227; Butler on, 166
far right, 17–19, 51, 55; far-right terrorism, 53–54, 57
fascism, 1–3, 11, 15, 22, 24–27, 128, 162, 165, 174, 177, 191; neo-fascism, 7, 15; new fascism, 7, 177; postfascism, 15–19, 23–24; Tamás on, 26
Fassbinder, Rainer Werner, 33–34, 40, 42–43, 51, 126, 131, 137, 172
federal film subsidies, 127, 131
feminism, 5, 145, 151, 153, 155, 157; popular feminism, 150, 154; post, 149, 155, 157–59; second wave, 149, 159
fiction, 70–71, 81, 114, 125, 168–69, 176, 196, 207; auto-, 149; fictional tropes, 53; narrative, 130: "reality fictions" (Wiseman), 221
film archaeology, 93, 135
flows, 6, 16, 24, 223, 232
Forensic Architecture (FA), 8, 52–53n10, 70–72, 77, 83, 85, 90–95
forensic turn, 85, 92–93; definition of, 92
Fortress Europe, 18, 22, 26–27, 34, 87
French Resistance, 27
Frontex, 85, 90, 93–94
Funkhaus Wien, 184, 187, 191–93, 196; history of, 188, 190

gender, 35, 121, 145, 147–50, 152–55, 186–87, 197; as category, 16, 34, 43, 143, 145, 158, 206; quota, 147, 159; relations, 136, 196; theory, 121
genre, 3–7, 10, 36, 121, 164, 213, 219; road movie, 208
German Cinema Book, The, 6

244 ♦ INDEX

German Cinema in the Age of Neoliberalism (Baer), 4
Germany, 4, 6, 33, 43, 45, 47, 50–51, 53–54, 69–70, 72–74, 85, 97, 134, 154; East, 76, 148, 163; postwar, 42; as setting, 1, 32, 35–37, 48, 214; Weimar, 34n5; West, 32, 103, 127, 143, 148, 156
globalization, 6, 47
Godard, Jean-Luc, 125, 131, 137, 165n12
good life, 4, 7, 38, 47, 156, 204, 231
Greece, 22, 54–55, 73, 83, 91, 193
grief, 54–58, 111
Grierson, John, 104, 106

Hanau, 52
happiness, 34, 39, 46, 48, 145
Haraway, Donna, 122, 221
Hartman, Saidiya, 63, 169
Harvey, David, 3
Heinrich, Susanne, 122, 142, 144–45, 148–49, 150–54, 157, 164
Herr Bachmann und seine Klasse (*Mr. Bachmann and His Class*), 11, 220–22
heterotopia, 124, 133, 137
hope, 22, 29, 39, 47, 96, 98, 166, 176; hopefulness, 213, 220
Huber, Wolfgang, 102, 104–5, 107–8, 110–12, 115

Ich will mich nicht künstlich aufregen (*Asta Upset*), 9, 122–24, 126–27, 129–31, 133–34, 173–78
illiberalism, 18
index, 34; crisis of the indexical, 73; indexical proof, 72; indexical signs, 72; indexical truth-telling, 8; photographical indexicality, 79–80; restoration of the indexical, 74
installation, 3, 5, 70, 74–75, 78, 81, 91, 93, 138
intersectionality, 34
intimacy, 6, 10–11, 38, 151, 190, 205–6, 210; Berlant on, 231

Jewish European culture, 21

juridico-political regime, 86, 88, 93

Kafka, Franz, 19, 20–21, 28, 163–64, 172; Kafkaesque, 25
Kaurismäki, Aki, 22
Kluge, Alexander, 132–33, 137–38
Kristeva, Julia, 8, 87–88
Kroske, Gerd, 102–8, 110–15

Lampedusa, 83
language, 17, 37, 77, 154, 225, 229; additive, 199; artificial, 121; body, 214–15, 231; legal, 90
Latour, Bruno, 11, 224, 227
Le Crime de Monsieur Lange, 173
Linz, Max, 9, 122–24, 126–38, 144, 164
liveness, 185, 191, 198
Lorey, Isabell, 204–5, 212

machinic voice, 105, 109, 111
Marx, Karl, 2, 28n28, 122, 130, 166; Marxism, 2, 6n8, 9, 25, 102, 130–31, 136; neo-Marxism, 3
Marx, Karl, works by: *Das Kapital*, 1, 112, 122
masculinity, 33, 35, 40–41, 43–44, 46
Mbembe, Achille, 34, 169
media technology, 93, 103, 114, 185, 187, 191
mediation, 108, 114, 171, 203, 206, 211–13, 217, 230–32. *See also* remediation
Mediterranean Sea, 20, 36–37, 83–86, 89–90
melancholy, 127, 138, 149, 176; left-wing, 29, 176
memory, 53, 174, 177, 212, 214; intergenerational, 187
migration, 5–7, 16, 18, 22, 37–38, 59, 83n1, 84, 91; mass, 81; politics, 33, 69, 73
militancy, 5, 103
Moria, 18
mourning, 29, 127, 138
multiculturalism, 219–21, 225; multicultural society, 225

Murder of Halit Yozgat, The, 8, 70, 77–81
museum, 90–91, 93, 129, 138, 172, 196; white cube, 127
music, 43, 112, 154, 189–90, 227–31, 233–34; leitmotif, 177
Mutzenbacher, 10, 183–84, 186, 196–98

"narrative prosthesis" (Mitchell and Schneider), 33, 46
National Socialist Underground (NSU), 7–8, 50–51, 71, 74; NSU trial, 50–52, 56, 71
nationalist turn, 2
Nazism, 10; National Socialism, 192; neo-Nazis, 50n1
negativity, 50–51, 61–64, 170; negative affect, 51, 64, 204; negative futurability, 80, 51, 61, 64
neoliberal subject, 122; and self-optimization, 151–52, 203; wearing down of, 204
neoliberalism, 1–2, 11, 19, 61, 135–38, 150–51, 159, 203–4, 207, 210, 215, 217, 232; crisis of, 164; critique of, 1, 146, 152; end of, 2, 177, 211; structures of, 205, 210
network, 11, 56, 222, 232–34; actor-, 171, 221; collective, 166; far-right, 55, 57; participatory, 77
Neun Leben hat die Katze (*The Cat Has Nine Lives*), 152
New German Cinema, 4, 9, 127, 131, 133
New German Critique, 4
New German Discourse Comedy, 5, 9, 10–11, 124; definition of, 121, 129, 144, 164
new materialism, 221
new waves, 165, 172
Nyong'o, Tavia, 168–69

Oberhausen Manifesto, 126, 129, 132–33
Ottinger, Ulrike, 25, 149, 154

pedagogy, 92, 94, 219, 227–28; posthuman, 11
people, 163, 168, 173; as concept, 10, 177; the missing, 162, 164–65, 167, 173. *See also* Volk
performativity, 220, 224, 229
pessimism, 8, 48, 62, 231; Afropessimism, 62–63; politics of, 50, 61–62; radical, 7, 51
Petzold, Christian, 7, 15, 19, 22, 24–31
Pfeifer, Mario, 8, 70, 74–76
phenomenology, 5; of the refugee, 76
play, 170, 228; playfulness, 1, 168, 213
pluralism, 80; anti-pluralism, 26
political violence, 2, 7, 17, 53, 61
politics, 4, 7, 10, 35, 60, 70, 81, 103, 115–16, 124, 136, 166–67, 177, 183, 207, 212; activist, 5; aesthetic, 173; affective, 192n26; affirmative, 61; anti-, 19; border, 205; cultural, 186; equality, 148; gender, 153, 155; of hate, 6; identity, 26, 69; mainstream, 15–16, 22; migration, 33, 69; necro, 169; of negativity, 62; of pessimism, 50, 61–62; of the present, 144; queer, 63; radical, 11, 114, 116; of recognition (Taylor), 219–20, 225; of refusal, 8; of repose, 203; of representation, 156, 159, 199; of resistance, 29
Pollesch, René, 9, 121–22, 128–30
Pong Film, 85
portrait shots, 171–76
postdramatic theater, 200
postfascism, 15–19, 23–24
posthumanism, 222
post-truth, 8, 69–71, 73, 77, 79, 81–82, 92
praxis, 125, 130, 134; aesthetic, 129, 133, 137; cinematic, 133; feminist filmmaking, 143; political, 123–24
precarization, 4, 204–5
Pro Quote Film, 10, 144, 147
Purple Sea, 8–9, 83, 85, 89, 91, 95–96, 98

246 ♦ INDEX

queer German cinema, 11, 202–3,
212; queer intimacy, 202
Qurbani, Burhan, 7, 32–37, 39–44,
46–48

Rabinow, Paul, 9, 123, 125, 133, 136
racism, 45, 52, 58, 77, 127; anti-
Black, 33; as category, 5, 91, 132
radio, 94, 127, 184, 186–93
Radlmaier, Julian, 1–3, 10, 122, 162–
70, 172, 176
Rancière, Jacques, 124, 167–70
Red Army Faction (RAF), 53, 102,
115
refugee crisis, 7, 15, 19, 22, 84
relation, 5, 11, 23, 38, 84, 87–88, 90,
98, 123, 135, 137–38, 145; gender
relations, 136; labor relations,
121; power relations, 102; social
relations, 112
remediation, 107, 114, 143–46, 149–
50, 153–55, 158–59, 229
repose, 202–3, 205, 209, 212, 214,
216; aesthetics of, 210–11
resistance, 3, 5–7, 62, 205, 212;
antifascist, 26, 28; political, 29;
queer, 63; quotidian, 217
revenge, 8, 54–55, 57–58, 61, 71, 74
revolution, 97, 125, 165–66, 176–77,
202; counter-revolution, 16

Said, Edward, 76
Sander, Helke, 10, 148–49, 153–54
Scheffner, Philip, 4, 93
Schlingensief, Christoph, 129–31,
133, 137
Seghers, Anna, 7, 15, 19–24, 26–29
Selbstkritik eines bürgerlichen Hundes
(Self-Criticism of a Bourgeois Dog),
10, 144, 163–68, 170–74, 177
sensorium, 210, 213–14, 216
setting, 1, 22–24, 28, 42, 72, 75, 153,
208–9, 213–14, 216
sexuality, 33, 42, 186, 197; as
category, 43, 145, 149, 152
shipwreck, 8, 83, 94
Shipwreck at the Threshold of Europe,
Lesvos, Aegean Sea, 8–9, 83, 85

slapstick, 144, 177
socialism, 16, 19, 162, 164, 175;
socialist cinema, 165, 173
Socialist Patients' Collective (SPK),
9, 103–7, 110, 112, 114–16;
definition of, 102
solidarity, 3, 6, 26, 87, 145, 157, 177
sonority, 199
sound, 10–11, 55, 77, 95, 104–5,
112–13, 115, 193, 198, 209–10,
213–14; acousmatic, 110;
ambient, 95; art, 229; bridge, 223;
harmonious, 233; soundscape, 203,
213; soundtrack, 105, 107, 113,
155, 176–77, 194, 203; stage, 188,
191; technology, 110; textures of,
185; waves, 78
spectatorship, 202; experiential, 216;
respiratory, 206
Speth, Maria, 11, 143n5, 221–22,
232, 234
SPK Komplex, 9, 102–4, 107, 109–11,
113–16
Stalinism, 10, 174
Stöckl, Ula, 148, 152, 158
Straub, Jean-Marie, and Danièle
Huillet, 163–64, 165n12, 172,
175
storytelling, 3, 7, 169; nonlinear, 37;
techniques of, 11, 57
surplus humanity, 25, 34
Syria, 70, 87, 97

Tamás, Gáspár Miklós, 15–17, 22,
26
Taylor, Charles, 219–20
terrorism, 51, 53–54
theory, 121–26, 128, 130–32,
136–37, 164, 169–70; anti-
reproduction (Edelman), 3; critical,
144, 146, 156; cultural, 162–63,
220; dialectics, 15, 23, 87, 124–25,
129, 138; feminist, 157, 233;
feminist film, 143–44, 146, 149,
151; of resistance, 212
Top Girl, 10, 144–45, 148, 152,
157–59
Transit, 7, 15, 19, 25, 27–29

transnational film, 147; definition of, 6–7

Traverso, Enzo, 15, 19, 22, 28–29

Tremblay, Jean-Thomas, 205–6

Treut, Monika, 11, 202–3, 205–7, 212–14

Turanskyj, Tatjana, 144, 145, 148–49, 151–53, 154n30, 157–58

Turkey, 59–60, 77, 83, 86, 91

undocumented migrant, 7, 32–36, 39, 41, 43–45, 168–69

utopia, 4, 9, 29, 124, 137–38, 156, 166, 175, 234; heterotopia, 124, 133, 137; utopian gesture, 28; "utopian impulse" (Pantenburg), 163n8; utopian mode, 22, 64

Vertov, Dziga, 133, 135; Academy, 134–36; Group, 125, 129

violence, 5, 7, 17, 32, 42–43, 54, 70, 73, 76, 87, 198, 205; counter, 53; network of, 57; racist, 50, 53, 61, 74–75; regime of, 51, 62, 64; sexual, 11, 32; state, 25–27, 91; structural, 202

voice-over, 9, 11, 25, 37, 91, 95, 97, 106–8, 125, 194–95; narration, 93, 104, 193; narrator, 7, 94, 165, 171; voice-of-God narration, 104, 110, 112, 115

Volk, 191

Volkssempfänger, 191

Von Mädchen und Pferden (*Of Girls and Horses*), 11, 202–4, 211–17

Waldheim, Kurt, 184, 186, 193–95

Waldheims Walzer (*The Waldheim Waltz*), 10, 182, 184, 186, 193

war, 2, 92, 97, 154, 195, 222; Cold War, 86; postwar, 38, 42, 69, 106, 127, 129, 163, 165, 167–68, 172, 183, 186, 188, 190, 193, 203; Syrian, 97; in Ukraine, 174; World War I, 21; World War II, 26, 35n12, 47, 187, 189, 195, 222

Weimar Republic, 1, 7, 36, 173

worldmaking, 53, 166, 223

You & I, 11, 202–3, 207–8, 210–12, 216–17

Printed and bound by CPI Group (UK) Ltd, Croydon, CR0 4YY
17/12/2024